ANALYSIS IN QUALITATIVE RESEARCH

About the author

Hennie Boeije received her PhD from Erasmus University Rotterdam in Health Care Policy and Management in 1994 and a Master's in Sociology. She is currently an Associate Professor with the Department of Methodology and Statistics of the Faculty of Social and Behavioural Sciences at Utrecht University, the Netherlands. Her primary areas of teaching and researching are qualitative research, mixed methods research, and pretesting surveys. Dr Boeije has written extensively in Dutch and internationally in the area of research methodology including the constant comparative method in data analysis and the presence of third persons in interviews. She has published qualitative research on the areas of refugees, nursing homes, informal caregiving and the chronically ill. She is currently working on a number of projects related to trauma issues.

ANALYSIS IN QUALITATIVE RESEARCH

HENNIE BOEIJE

Los Angeles | London | New Delhi
Singapore | Washington DC

© Hennie Boeije 2010

First published 2010

Apart from any fair dealing for the purposes of research
or private study, or criticism or review, as permitted
under the Copyright, Designs and Patents Act, 1988,
this publication may be reproduced, stored or transmitted
in any form, or by any means, only with the prior
permission in writing of the publishers, or in the case
of reprographic reproduction, in accordance with the
terms of licences issued by the Copyright Licensing
Agency. Enquiries concerning reproduction outside
those terms should be sent to the publishers.

SAGE Publications Ltd
1 Oliver's Yard
55 City Road
London EC1Y 1SP

SAGE Publications Inc.
2455 Teller Road
Thousand Oaks, California 91320

SAGE Publications India Pvt Ltd
B 1/I 1 Mohan Cooperative Industrial Area
Mathura Road
New Delhi 110 044

SAGE Publications Asia-Pacific Pte Ltd
33 Pekin Street #02-01
Far East Square
Singapore 048763

Library of Congress Control Number: 2008943686

British Library Cataloguing in Publication data

A catalogue record for this book is available from the British Library

ISBN 978-1-84787-006-3
ISBN 978-1-84787-007-0 (pbk)

Typeset by C&M Digitals (P) Ltd, Chennai, India
Printed in Great Britain by Ashford Colour Press Ltd
Printed on paper from sustainable resources.

To Ton and Grace

CONTENTS

LIST OF FIGURES AND TABLES

FIGURES

TABLES

PREFACE

This book originated in the need felt by social science students and researchers for a practical guideline about qualitative data analysis. However, none of them wanted a recipe with some simple ingredients that prescribed how to go about analysis. They wanted to do justice to the specifics of their individual research projects. What they asked for were tools to help them think about their data and to analyse the complexities present in their data. That is exactly what this book attempts to do: it sets out a step-by-step procedure to start and finish an analysis, thereby focusing on thinking and doing.

Students embarking on their first research projects often feel overwhelmed by the mass of qualitative data produced during their field work. Questions about 'where to start' and doubts about 'selective observation' and 'bias' occasionally temper their enthusiasm. Master's students and postgraduates, ambitious to analyse modest-complex social issues that really matter, at times lack confidence in their abilities to discover the core issue and to correctly interpret the data. Many experienced researchers have been educated in quantitative research; during their work they may feel inclined to incorporate qualitative research methods in their work but then struggle with the legitimacy of their analytical activities that 'involve so much of the researcher' and the credibility (and acceptability) of their findings.

Many of these questions and problems arise from a felt vagueness of qualitative research and in particular the perceived hidden nature of qualitative analysis. What it is that analysts do inbetween data collection and writing the report is to a certain extent a black box. In turn this raises suspicion about the credibility of the conclusions of a particular research endeavour. Formerly, vagueness could be explained by the lack of example studies that reported how the analysis had been conducted. Researchers talked in great length about their experiences during field work, but skipped the analysis because they thought it was much less interesting. As a consequence their work could not be verified by others and unfortunately not much could be learned from the analysis. This book addresses the essential issue of how to present both research findings and the analysis process so that readers may make their own judgement.

Many techniques and procedures for qualitative analysis have been developed, yet it still seems unfathomable to some. I suggest this has to do with the involvement of the researcher in the analytical process. The influence of the analyst's experience, knowledge, and sensitivity to the field is beyond dispute. It is difficult for analysts to discern and to account for theoretical insights and to recall how salient interpretations came to exist. An analysis for some part consists of doing, applying methods and techniques, and for the other part of thinking, of interrogating the data and looking at them from different angles in order to make sense of them.

This book attempts to decrease the vague nature of qualitative data analysis in three ways. First, it addresses what analysis is supposed to be, i.e. segmenting and reassembling the data. Then it explains three procedures that have been developed to carry out a qualitative analysis, namely constant comparison, analytical induction and theoretical sensitivity. The outcomes are joined in a model for analysis: the spiral of analysis. This exercise will bring across a general idea of what qualitative analysts are involved with.

Second, the spiral of analysis is used to set out the methods and techniques for handling the data. The focus is on the 'how to' of data analysis as well as on the thinking part. An analysis, in particular the reassembling stage, makes an appeal to interrogating the data, to visualising them, trying to organize them in different ways, testing different combinations and reasoning about them. This aspect of analysis has been underexposed in the literature in my view and therefore this book sets out a number of heuristic aids to integrate the data again after having been segmented.

Third, the book will deal with the findings that can be expected from a qualitative data analysis. In my experience it is not only puzzling to students and researchers what qualitative analysis entails, but it is also unclear to them what is to be expected of it in terms of findings. Qualitative data analysis is depicted as 'the making of' the findings. In order to gear your methods of analysis with your aim, the aim must be defined from the outset. Therefore the book explores the different types of findings of qualitative research as well as on their use in meta-syntheses and mixed methods.

How are we going to realize this? All chapters finish with a section called 'Doing your own qualitative research project'. Qualitative analysis is positioned as an ongoing process occurring over the life cycle of a project. The indications and guidelines will guide you through all the steps needed from writing the research proposal to starting and finishing the research in the real world. At times this section is in the format of assignments and 'things to do', and at others it is more of a checklist and 'things to think of'. The stepwise procedure envisages you doing a small-to-moderate-scale qualitative research, such as in the context of a methods course into qualitative research. The steps have been adjusted somewhat for this purpose, although they can be easily used for larger and more advanced projects as well.

The book also contains numerous pedagogical features. Tips are given in most chapters, and some chapters feature some useful 'frequently asked questions' (FAQs). All chapters provide learning objectives and plenty of references. The numerous boxes sometimes contain examples, some drawn from classical studies and others from contemporary publications. Sometimes examples are used to elaborate specific points or highlight certain aspects of the text.

I am of opinion that while you can read a lot of books, so much more can be learned from practical experience in problem solving and on-the-spot creativity. You can review many examples, but insight is best gained by actually applying knowledge. You can discuss a matter, but will only see the point during field work. For this reason I have integrated many engaging 'real-life' examples into the text.

ACKNOWLEDGEMENTS

The Dutch version of the book came into existence with the help of many colleagues and students who shared their questions, struggles, insecurities, solutions and insights. Their experiences are the basis for this book as well, and therefore I want to thank them. Evert-Jan van Doorn instigated the translation and suggested the introduction of the assignments. Eva Alisic gave valuable comments on several chapters. Carola Hageman from Boom Educational Publishers encouraged me to rework the Dutch book and to write for an international audience.

The department of Methodology and Statistics of the Faculty of Social Sciences of Utrecht University as well as the research institute for Psychology and Health were supportive of the project to write a book about qualitative research. Together we considered the book as a bridge to get more understanding and cooperation between quantitative and qualitative researchers. I want to thank my colleagues, especially Nijs Lagerweij, Irene Klugkist and Kirsten Namesnik who were always helpful and were there when I wanted to talk about the progress of the book. Kirsten also helped me phrase what I really wanted to say in English.

Some people kept me on track. In my professional context, Maureen Postma, Denise Hulst and Annette Veldhuizen urged me to focus activities and follow my passion. In my private context many people were instrumental in persuading me to finish the book, but five in particular. My father and mother, who always understand me despite the fact that the world was different when they were young. My friend Marieke van der Waal, who provided me with meals, rest and a listening ear. My husband Henk van der Velden, who cares about me, supports me and believes in my abilities. And my daughter Roos, who demonstrated how play and fun can lead to fabulous learning experiences.

Hennie Boeije
Utrecht, The Netherlands
April, 2009

1
INTRODUCTION TO QUALITATIVE RESEARCH

Research is concerned with asking and answering relevant and researchable questions. To be referred to as social scientific research, the investigation should stick to the rules of the game called science. This book addresses the rules of the game for qualitative researchers and in particular how they are to shape their analytical activities. To begin the chapter, we draw the contours of qualitative research by briefly comparing it with quantitative research within the social sciences. Then we focus on the diversity within qualitative research and elaborate on the grounded theory approach that has mainly inspired the representation of qualitative research in this book and in particular how we look at qualitative data analysis. Considering the multiplicity of research types, why do scientists often pose the same sort of research questions and choose to work with more or less the same tools in their projects? At the end of the chapter we will outline the qualitative research process, position qualitative data analysis and give a summary of the contents of the book.

LEARNING AIMS

By the end of this chapter, you will be able to:

- Mention the necessary preparations when initiating scientific research
- Distinguish between quantitative and qualitative research
- Explain the role of theory in deductive and inductive approaches to research
- Define what is commonly referred to as a paradigm
- Know what paradigmatic issues qualitative researchers mostly agree on
- Outline the origins and purposes of the grounded theory approach
- Define qualitative research and elaborate on its three key elements
- Reproduce the steps of the qualitative research process and place data analysis within this process

Preparatory thoughts

If there is one activity in which thinking needs to precede doing, it is in a social science research enterprise. Science is only recognized and accepted as such when researchers stick to the rules that apply to conducting scientific research, the most important of these being that the study is theoretically informed, that it uses a systematic procedure, that approved methods and techniques are used, and that the study is documented in a way that allows others to assess the findings. This means that there is a lot to decide upon when thinking of starting a qualitative research project, such as: How will we deal with theory? What theories can be keys to our research? What steps are we going to take in the research as a whole? What steps will we use for analysis? How will we collect the data? What are common instruments for ensuring quality? Exactly what needs to be reported to convince our readers? Before exploring these issues, we will briefly look at some aspects which are probably already common knowledge to you.

It is evident that you have to come up with a research topic that is of interest to you and will engage you. Just as important, the topic needs to be viable to turn it into a small- or moderate-scale scientific research project. Studying the literature and talking to experts can lead you to research questions that lend themselves to scientific methods. And although all scientific research is about posing and answering questions, this cannot be reversed: not all endeavours to find answers are worth the label 'research' let alone earn the label 'scientific'. For scientific research the questions asked need to be related to theory in some way, and the answers need to be found by the use of systematic methods that must be adequately documented.

You will have to find out what type of research is needed to answer your questions as well. The choice to use qualitative research methods has implications for your way of working, for the research design, the use of theory, the sample, the data collection methods, the data analysis, and the final publication. You may be in doubt about what research type matches best with your questions, or you may consider using a combination of both qualitative and quantitative research. In the next section, a comparison is made between qualitative and quantitative research to sharpen our insight in what it means to work within the qualitative approach. Whatever you choose, you have to convincingly legitimize the choice.

Answering the research questions in social scientific research is always done with a specific purpose. In other words, there is a reason why you want to answer these particular research questions. Whatever it is that you want to know, you must consider why you need this particular knowledge and what you need it for. If it is something you want to do, you must consider what problem you are trying to solve and who will benefit from the results. If your aim is predominantly to gain knowledge, it is referred to as fundamental research. If it is predominantly aimed at the use of knowledge to change or improve situations, then it is referred to as applied research. A qualitative research can be a fundamental one as well as an applied one.

Now that some preparatory thoughts have been put into your mind, we will elaborate on them with the aim to sharpen the contours of qualitative research and to delineate the focus of this book. We will start with a comparison between quantitative and qualitative research, because by concentrating on the commonalities and differences we will better understand what is meant by qualitative research. This might suggest that qualitative research is one clearly defined research approach. However, this is not the case. We will briefly look at different traditions and types of research and then we will specify the area of qualitative research that is covered in the book. Next we will formulate a definition and touch upon the distinguishable features of qualitative research. Finally, we will present an overview of the qualitative research process including the analytic stage, which is the focus of this book, and have a look at where the different aspects of the research process will be dealt with in the rest of the book.

Considering quantitative or qualitative research

To get a better grasp on qualitative research we will look at two example studies that initially start with an interest in the same research topic but use different research methods (Boxes 1.1 and 1.2). Both cases are concerned with partners who care for their spouses who have a severe illness. The outcome of each study is very different because the researchers use different approaches. The first study is an example of a quantitative research, whereas the second study applies qualitative research methods.

BOX 1.1   A QUANTITATIVE RESEARCH ON PARTNER RELATIONS

Kuijer, Buunk and Ybema (2001) studied the partner relationship from an equity theory viewpoint. This theory poses that a situation of inequity arises when the ratio between the outcomes and investments of one partner are different from those of the other partner. When someone is struck by a severe illness, such as cancer, the balance between giving and taking in a relationship may shift. It is assumed that on the one hand the patient is less able to contribute, and on the other hand receives more help and support from the partner. On the basis of this theory two hypotheses were formed, to be tested in the investigation. The first hypothesis was that people who, in terms of outcomes, comparatively receive a lot (patients) or a little (partners), will feel respectively either advantaged or disadvantaged in their relationship. The second hypothesis was that experienced inequity is correlated with dissatisfaction with the relationship.

The researchers decided to use questionnaire research, as well as other strategies of investigation such as the experiment. There are existing questionnaires which validly measure the variables that the researchers are interested in. For example, there is a nine-item questionnaire which measures relationship satisfaction. Additionally, there is a measure devised to assess physical fitness. In order to measure equity, participants were asked to rate giving and taking in the relationship

(Continued)

(Continued)

on a five-point scale ranging from 'My partner does a lot more for me than I do for him/her' through 'My partner does the same for me as I do for him/her' to 'My partner does a lot less for me than I do for him/her'. The research involved the participation of 106 cancer patients and their partners, as well as a control group of 80 healthy couples.

One of the outcomes of this study was that patients generally feel advantaged in the relationship. The hypothesis that partners feel disadvantaged was not confirmed. Various explanations were provided for these findings. It is possible that partners take into account the limitations which are imposed upon the patient by the disease, and that they are grateful for any support the patient is able to offer. In accordance with equity theory, patients reported the most anger when they were feeling disadvantaged. They reported the most guilt when they were in an advantaged situation. When the patient was in bad physical shape, partners reported being satisfied with the relationship, regardless of whether they feel advantaged, disadvantaged or equally treated. Partners seem to think it is only fair that they are doing more for the patient than the patient is doing for them. In such situations, the patient's need is more important than equity in the relationship.

BOX 1.2   A QUALITATIVE RESEARCH ON PARTNER RELATIONS

Boeije, Duijnstee and Grypdonck (2003) investigated the relationship between individuals who suffer from multiple sclerosis, a severe neurological disease, and their partners who provide care. Previous research has shown that partners of people with multiple sclerosis often feel heavily burdened as a consequence of the debilitating character of the illness. Although a lot has been written about the burden of caring, a number of studies were also found which focus on the benefits of caring. These latter studies suggest a balance between giving and taking. Additionally, the perspective of the receivers of care often does not seem to be accounted for. Based on the findings of the literature study, the researchers examined what it is that binds both partners to the relationship, and in particular, what both partners do to continue the caring within the relationship.

Seventeen couples participated in this study. The partners were interviewed separately. The interviews were recorded on tape and transcribed. The interview questions dealt with issues which had predominantly been taken from the literature. The carers were asked how they fulfil their role, what changes have been made in their lives, how their partners handle the situation, what motivation they have to go on, and what doubts they may have. The patients were asked what it is like to receive care from their partners, how their spouse deals with the situation, and what their role is in the relationship.

Analysis of the collected data yielded three elements that link partners to one another. First, both the afflicted and the carer viewed the situation as inevitable; the reason being that they either have the disease or promised to care for their partner upon marriage. Second, both partners felt that they are in it together, and realized that the reverse could have been the case as well. In terms of exchange theory, this is known as 'hypothetical trade' or 'hypothetical reciprocity'. Third, both partners expressed the desire to postpone institutionalizing the ill partner to a nursing home for as long as possible.

The examples demonstrate that different approaches and methods can be used to study the same subject. In the first example a quantitative research is carried out. Literature and previously selected theory are used to deduce hypotheses. These hypotheses, or propositions, are tested by means of the research. The building blocks of hypotheses and the relationships between them are interesting attributes, commonly referred to as 'variables'. In Box 1.1 these are, among others, the severity of the illness, relationship satisfaction, experienced equity and feelings of anger and guilt. Observations are made on a sizable number of cases, in this case couples, mainly by means of standardized measures. Results are reached by working with numbers, and statistical criteria are used to determine whether the results offer support for the hypotheses or not. Subsequently, the findings are fed back into the theory in an attempt to explain the results and reflect on the implications.

Box 1.2 is an example of qualitative research. Here, literature including theory is used mainly to understand what is going on in the field and to discover theoretical perspectives, including proper concepts to look at the social phenomenon of interest. Data collection takes place by means of semi-structured measuring instruments that are tailored to the research subject and refined as the research progresses. In general, the research sample should accurately represent the research subject and must be studied intensively. During data analysis, the textual accounts of interviews or observations are searched for common themes and regularities. The findings consist of descriptions of the field using the various relevant, theoretical concepts necessary to interpret the participants' view of their social world and their behaviour.

It is worth drawing our attention to the use of theory in both types of research. Theory here is viewed as an attempt to describe, understand and explain a certain social phenomenon. The use of social theory is often seen as the main difference between quantitative and qualitative research (Bryman, 2008). In quantitative research a deductive process is employed, which means that theory is the starting point for formulating hypotheses that will be tested in research. The outcome of this process, of course, says something about the theory that was tested. In qualitative research inductive thinking is paramount, which means that a social phenomenon is explored in order to find empirical patterns that can function as the beginning of a theory. The choice of whether you test a theory or build one naturally influences how the research is carried out. In practice, however, it is never this black and white. Quantitative research can be used to explore scientific domains and make use of an inductive approach as well, while in qualitative research existing theory can be used more deductively as a background to see whether it applies to other settings or contexts (see Chapter 6).

The choice of research method, either quantitative or qualitative, tells us something about what we think research in the social sciences should look like. In fact, there are systems of beliefs and practices that guide a field of study regarding social science research methodology. Such a framework for thinking about research design, measurement, analysis and personal involvement that is shared by members of a speciality area is called a paradigm (Morgan, 2007). Paradigms reflect issues related to the nature of social reality and to the nature of knowledge. The nature of social reality, referred to as ontology, attempts to answer the question whether the social world is regarded as something external to social actors or as something that people are in the process of fashioning (Bryman, 2008). The nature of knowledge, referred to as epistemology, is concerned with whether there is one single route to truth or that diverse methods are needed to grasp the meaning of social experience.

Qualitative research generally starts with the assumptions that individuals have an active role in the construction of social reality and that research methods that can capture this process of social construction are required. The ontological stance of constructivism asserts that social entities are not pre-given but that human beings attach meaning to their social reality and that as a result human action should be considered meaningful. Some researchers study how people construct reality with the use of language, such as specific arguments, rhetoric devices and words, and others study how people construct reality while interpreting the acts of others and the world around them and grafting their own behaviour on these interpretations. This epistemological stance can be termed interpretivism.

Groups of researchers working within a current system of beliefs, i.e. a paradigm, do not often cross the borders of that system. They are used to working within the practices that the system prescribes, allows and rewards. A research group that is used to employ quantitative methods will usually ask research questions that can better be answered with the use of quantitative methods. The same holds for a group of qualitative researchers that will usually ask research questions for which qualitative methods are best suited. A research group would normally pose and frame research questions that fit their usual way of working. If, however, they come across questions that cannot be answered with the methods they usually employ, they can either decide not to pose these questions at all or they can employ alternative methods. This could lead to combined quantitative and qualitative research in one single research project, which is described in more detail in Chapter 8.

In Box 1.3 some history is provided about the relationship between quantitative and qualitative research and the position of qualitative research in contemporary social science.

BOX 1.3   THE POSITION OF QUALITATIVE RESEARCH IN
THE SCIENTIFIC WORLD

Quantitative and qualitative researchers have not always worked peacefully alongside one another. A paradigm war existed between quantitative and qualitative researchers, in which the stakes were the acknowledgement of qualitative research as a scientific endeavour and the superiority of certain methods of enquiry over others (Hutchinson, 2001). In many countries quantitative research still holds a dominant position in the field of academic research. History shows that scientific research develops in movements and is subject to trends as well. Some perspectives and methods become obsolete or are used less, whereas others increase in popularity and come to be regarded as state of the art. It seems that the separation between quantitative and qualitative research is fading and that the combined use of the two methods in a single project is gaining popularity (see Chapter 8) (Morgan, 2007).

Qualitative research is blossoming at many universities and institutions. In a special issue of the on-line journal *Forum: Qualitative Social Research*, Knoblauch, Flick and Maeder (2005) describe the state of the art of qualitative methods in different countries in Europe, and in the same issue its use in Europe is compared with that of the United States. Next to potentially different developments between countries, the various disciplines such as sociology, psychology, anthropology, educational science, social geography, political studies and linguistics have developed their own uses of qualitative methods. Furthermore, applied studies have embraced them and established focal points in the fields of, for instance, health sciences, criminology, business studies, management, women's studies, communication science and nursing science.

The qualitative approach has proven to be useful for research questions in a wide range of areas. As qualitative research becomes more accepted and established, it is increasingly being conducted by formally funded research groups (Barry, Britten, Barber, Bradley & Stevenson 1999). Qualitative research programmes consisting of collaborative and multidisciplinary research projects are strived for (Hutchinson, 2001). With the development of more extensive programmes it is likely that researchers will work in teams rather than alone, which should lead to improved morale and job satisfaction, productivity and quality of research (Barry et al., 1999).

Many qualitative research resources are at our disposal. There are many institutions worldwide organizing conferences, workshops, training courses and so on. Numerous textbooks, handbooks and software packages for qualitative data analysis are readily available. Additionally, there are many electronic sources such as websites, journals, listservs, discussion groups and message boards. (For many such resources see Janesick, 2004 and Hesse-Biber and Leavy, 2006.) A popular new branch is mixed methods research, in which qualitative research is conducted in the context of a combination of quantitative and qualitative research (see Chapter 8). For both beginning and more experienced researchers, there is plenty of gold to be unearthed in various areas of scientific research.

Diversity in qualitative research

Qualitative researchers generally agree upon the assumptions attached to constructivism and interpretivism, but there are many nuances, traditions and specifics which cause the qualitative research practice to be very diverse. As mentioned above, some researchers are particularly interested in the use of language and communicative processes, as in, for example, conversation analysis and discourse analysis. In these types of research the analysis of data is language oriented. Other researchers are interested in understanding how people give meaning to their lives by interpreting their thoughts, experiences, actions and expressions. Some traditions that fall within this category are ethnography, phenomenology, biographical research, grounded theory, narrative analysis, case-studies and participatory research. Their analyses are geared towards the interpretation of human experiences and behaviour. They will use textual data as well, but for them language as such is not their key interest. Language is considered an important vehicle to express meaning.

TIP
_____

Authors of methodological textbooks usually favour a certain approach, whether phenomenology, grounded theory, ethnography or some other tradition. Readers may deduce the preference from the information that the author gives on each, as well as from the terminology that is used in describing the particular type of research. Researchers are well advised to select a book which matches their own perspective and approach.

_____

This book is mostly inspired by and dedicated to the grounded theory approach. The pioneers of grounded theory, Glaser and Strauss, described the origins of this approach in their book *The discovery of grounded theory: Strategies for qualitative research* (Glaser & Strauss, 1967). They aimed to rekindle the vitality in empirical research with this research strategy, and as such their book must be read as a polemic. First, it is a polemic on social science research which, in those times, was dominated by hypothesis testing and, was devoid of any connection to everyday reality according to Glaser and Strauss. Second, they felt that ethnographic research was too preoccupied with description instead of explanation of social phenomena, and wanted to provide researchers with an alternative research strategy (Seale, 1999). With their methodology they made an important contribution to the systematic approach to qualitative research in general, and, more specifically, to the systematic approach of qualitative analysis.

Glaser and Strauss offered a methodology in which the data became centre-stage in reaching a theoretical description of a phenomenon and explaining it. The data are systematically generated and analysed step-by-step in order to develop a theory. In the beginning the research has mainly an explorative nature, but as the research progresses, data generation becomes more aimed at verifying results found earlier on in the research process. Then comparative cases are sought to expand, confirm or deepen the assertions. This is referred to as theoretical sampling, since the choice for new cases depends on the theoretical needs of the researcher (see Chapter 2). The resulting theory will match the situations that are investigated, as it is directly derived from and supported by, and therefore grounded in, the collected data.

Its emphasis on theory development sets grounded theory apart from other branches of qualitative research. Originally, grounded theory was framed in terms of a series of cycles in which the researcher moves back and forth among the data collection and the analysis (see Chapter 7). The data are analysed with a technique called 'coding', in which relevant parts of the data are indicated and labelled. By constant comparison of the newly collected data with the initial results, the process gradually advances from coding parts of the data to conceptual categories, and subsequently to conceptual modelling or theory development (Harry, Sturges & Klingner, 2005).

Many researchers were initially drawn to this novel procedure, which held the promise that theory could be shaped (Seale, 1999). The method enabled researchers to discover the basic psychological processes that the participants were involved in and the strategies they used in dealing with events. Additionally, many methodological principles were outlined, such as constant comparison, theoretical sampling and saturation. However, as it is not immediately clear how to employ for instance constant comparison, more concrete guidelines, and possibly examples, methods and techniques, need to be developed in order to put the grounded theory approach into practice. Glaser and Strauss, their colleagues and others developed the approach over time, and a number of different variants of the approach exist today (Strauss & Corbin, 2007; Charmaz, 2006; Strauss, 1987; Glaser, 1978).

Ideally, the contours of a theoretical model emerge during the process of investigation. In practice, the findings of many grounded theory studies do not represent a social theory. Outcomes of this type of research often can be depicted as a thematic survey, giving descriptions of themes and the variety within themes as presented by participants of a particular population (see Chapter 8). Several discussions have been waged over the expectations and the application of grounded theory in practice (Charmaz, 2006; Walker & Myrick, 2006; Strauss & Corbin, 2005; Dey, 2004; Eaves, 2001). Still, grounded theory is a popular approach and has influenced this book to a high degree. Box 1.4 provides a summary of Glaser and Strauss' classical study with which they demonstrated what their grounded theory approach, as a research strategy, was capable of (Glaser & Strauss, 1965).

BOX 1.4   ORIGINS OF GROUNDED THEORY: AWARENESS OF DYING

In *Awareness of dying*, Glaser and Strauss describe a theory on the method of communication between hospital staff, dying patients and their relatives (Glaser & Strauss, 1965). Some of the questions which arose during their investigation, and which are still relevant today, were: Should patients be told that they are dying, or should they not be made aware of this? Under which circumstances is such an awareness beneficial, and to whom? How much strain does it put on the family? Which feelings arise when one knows one is about to die, and how does one handle these feelings?

The core concept that Glaser and Strauss identified in their theory is 'awareness context'. Awareness context refers to 'who knows what' regarding the

(Continued)

(Continued)

imminent death. This theory acknowledges that the behaviour of all involved individuals is dependent on what each person knows about the situation at a given moment, as well as on the knowledge about what others in the situation know. Therefore, the core concept explains diverse communication events in the hospital. The researchers distinguished between four possible awareness contexts from the patient's perspective:

1. Closed awareness context
2. Awareness context based on suspicion
3. Awareness context based on mutual pretending
4. Open awareness context.

Subsequently, they indicated what the characteristics of each of the contexts were, what consequences were attached to each context, and how each of the participants might change the situation. Structural prerequisites which are a part of an awareness context may change. For instance, the patient's physical condition may deteriorate which may indicate to everyone how serious the situation really is. This may lead to a shift from one awareness context to another. These prerequisites may have to do with the patient, hospital staff members, the family or the organization.

The researchers describe how hospitalized patients often fail to see that their death is imminent, even though hospital staff may know that this is the case. This situation is described as 'closed awareness'. In order to maintain the context of closed awareness, staff members have to maintain a neutral facial expression when they discover something which upsets them. Additionally, they are not permitted to speak loudly about the patient's condition, and they have to convince the patients that they do not believe they are dying. This awareness may shift to an 'awareness based on suspicion' when the patient develops new symptoms, when the doctor decides to tell the patient or when staff members accidentally tell the patient.

With their grounded theory on awareness contexts, the authors offer a theoretical lens which facilitates understanding of the thinking and acting of the parties involved. The authors would rather show the process of dying than death itself, and they preferred describing contexts to the more static attitudes towards dying.

Defining and delineating qualitative research in this book

As the term 'qualitative research' is well-known and widely used, it is also used in this book. With regard to the diversity within qualitative research, a definition and delineation are necessary to make clear what we mean by it.

TIP
_____

Although qualitative research is a commonly used term for the research which is addressed in this book, a large number of other terms are available, such as interpretive research, naturalistic research, constructivistic research, ethnographic or intensive research, fieldwork, and participatory research or participant observation. The difficulty is that these terms are sometimes used as synonyms and on other occasions are used to indicate different philosophical stances, specific research methods or particular methods of data collection. When reading publications, find out which term is used and what is meant by it. When searching for publications of qualitative research you can use some of the above-mentioned terms as alternative keywords. In some cases they will produce different results.

_____

We use a definition of qualitative research that reflects the focus of the book, namely qualitative data analysis, and our view on qualitative data analysis as inextricably connected with all other parts of the research. The following definition is used:

> The purpose of qualitative research is to describe and understand social phenomena in terms of the meaning people bring to them. The research questions are studied through flexible methods enabling contact with the people involved to an extent that is necessary to grasp what is going on in the field. The methods produce rich, descriptive data that need to be interpreted through the identification and coding of themes and categories leading to findings that can contribute to theoretical knowledge and practical use.

The definition has three key elements, namely: 1) looking for meaning, 2) using flexible research methods enabling contact, and 3) providing qualitative findings. Before elaborating on these three elements, an example is presented in Box 1.5. This example will then be used to explain the three elements.

BOX 1.5   TEENAGE MOTHERS

Horowitz (1995) reports in her research on the implementation of a one-year welfare programme for African-American teenage mothers in an American town. Many teenage mothers are still in school and dependent on welfare. When they do not finish high school, their job prospects are limited and it becomes difficult for them to build a financially independent life. This is the first meaning of the subtitle of Horowitz's book: *citizens or dependents?* The programme provides education and training of skills, and is aimed at employment for the participating girls. Horowitz attempts to describe the culture of the teenage mothers and staff members in the programme, in order for the reader to develop an understanding of their world.

(Continued)

(Continued)

The researcher believes that the goal of the programme can be realized through daily contact between the staff members and participants. She investigates how caregivers shape the relationships with the teenage mothers, and on which image of the mothers these relationships are based. She also wants to get a better picture of the world the teenage mothers live in, for instance the way in which they raise their children, how they experience going to school, how they maintain relationships with the child's father and how they spend their free time. To find out 'what was really going on' she uses participant observation and attends staff meetings, follows classes, has conversations with staff members, joins the girls for lunch and talks with them informally.

One of the insights the study yields is that the caregivers who are actively shaping the programme hold different perspectives on their work. There are two distinguishable groups, which Horowitz refers to as 'the arbiters' and 'the mediators'. The arbiters, who stand in a hierarchical relationship with the participants, convey a strict separation between the work and private settings. The private life which the girls lead as friend, mother, daughter and girlfriend, and the fact that they are entitled to social benefits are considered to be 'dirty laundry'. The mediators, on the other hand, attempt to create a basis of trust within the programme, by allowing the mothers to talk about anything that is on their mind. They emphasize that the making of choices and taking into account how others view them is important. Mediators value motherhood and education equally.

The girls experience their relationship to the two groups differently. During the arbiters' classes, they do not expose themselves. In contrast, they show more initiative and tell more about themselves in the mediators' classes. They indicate that the arbiters do not treat them with respect and look down on them, whereas the mediators treat them as equals.

The research demonstrates that the staff members carry a large responsibility for obtaining cooperation of the participants and making the programme succeed. The effectiveness of programmes like this is debated. With her research Horowitz has explicitly tried to become involved in the debate concerning welfare policy, citizenship and social facilities. She intended to demonstrate how social policy functions in practice: on paper, a programme can often be interpreted in various different ways. Because the implementation of the programme is usually left up to the discretion of the involved participants, this can lead to difficulties in reaching the programme's goals.

Looking for meaning

The starting point for a qualitative inquiry, and thus for a qualitative analysis, is to discover the meaning that people award to their social worlds and to understand the meaning of their social behaviour. The focus of qualitative methods on 'what it all means for the people involved' is often a main attraction for qualitative researchers (see Chapter 2). In order to find out about the participants' point of view, qualitative social scientists have to collect data that capture this view, and when analysing the data they will have to be sensitive to extract only what is relevant. People talk about their social reality, they express their opinions on what they think is happening, they share experiences, show what they feel, demonstrate what they do. So there is an already interpreted reality from which researchers must then make their interpretation of how participants understand their daily life.

But meaning-giving processes do not yield everything required for analysis. There are also socially 'hardened' ways of thinking, feeling and acting. For instance, debates about teenage pregnancies in westernized societies revolve around the mother's childhood, the mother's education, the quality of the child's upbringing and the stability of family life. This has led to the creation of systems that help teenagers deal with parenthood and provide support for them to finish school. In addition, there are talk shows and websites for teenage mothers and fathers that allow them to exchange their experiences. This fits in beautifully with William Isaac Thomas's famous formulation, taken from his 1928 study (cf. Jorgensen, 1989: 14): 'If people define a situation as real, it is real in its consequences'. In other words, institutions, welfare programmes and websites reflect how teenage pregnancies are conceptualized, i.e. that the mother and her baby are a problem to society. This is the broader context that qualitative researchers have to consider.

Using flexible methods that enable contact with participants

It is characteristic for a qualitative undertaking that the participant's perspective is not (entirely) known before the inquiry. Field work, as a consequence, requires a constant redefinition of what is problematic and needs a logic and process of inquiry that is flexible and open-ended (Jorgensen, 1989). As opposed to, for instance, laboratory research, the qualitative research design has an emerging nature, and methods of data collection are used that enable close contact with the field of research (see Chapters 2 and 4). Horowitz (1995) achieved immersion in the field by extensive participant observation of different layers of the social programme. Glaser and Strauss (1965) were able to collect crucial information in communication about dying due to their prolonged participant observation on different hospital wards.

This flexible approach holds true for the analysis as well (see Chapters 5 to 7). As far as an inductive approach is concerned, it is generally unknown beforehand what data will be generated and what the frame of analysis will look like. Therefore improvisation, creativity and flexibility must be allowed for in the analysis stage as well. The results and the focus of the analysis will slowly develop or emerge during the research process. Analysis of qualitative data is interlinked with data collection and sampling in several small cycles. Each cycle fuels the next one in order to build knowledge. However, openness is counterbalanced by a thorough preparation consisting of an appropriate literature search, well-formulated research questions, adequately developed instruments and a well-structured analysis plan (see Chapter 2).

Providing qualitative findings

When researchers guide readers through a different cultural world, they have to provide the readers with a description of daily life. Not just a description, but a detailed account of what the setting looks like, what keeps people busy and what they take for granted. Qualitative researchers have different means with which to do this, for instance paraphrasing what they heard, presenting excerpts of their field notes, offering fragments from interviews or showing photographs (see Chapter 10). However, researchers cannot present 'raw data' alone, such as a transcribed interview; instead they are required to re-interpret the information while preserving the participant's meaning. It is while analysing the data that they reduce, select, interpret and decide what they will use to convey their message to the reader.

Sometimes researchers not only aim to describe what is happening, but also want to explain how it works and why it is that things work that way. In Horowitz's research, the explanations are given in various layers. First, she explains the chance of success of the programme in terms of the message that staff members convey to the participating mothers. Staff members who work with the citizen-orientation of the girls, as the mediators do, have a bigger chance of success than the staff members who operate as arbiters. Horowitz suggests the reasons that some staff members act as mediators whereas others act as arbiters, lies in the way that each caregiver interprets the formal goal set by the programme to be congruent with his or her experiences as a middle-class African-American.

Second, microscopic insights can be placed against theoretical and societal backgrounds or macroscopic conditions to explain the research findings (Strauss, 1987). The programme for teenage mothers was formulated following demonstration projects. However, decisions made at policy level may translate into practice very differently than was first expected. The interactions at the micro-level are crucial in determining the success of the programme. Reflection may also be related to the circumstances of African-American residents in American society, an ethnic group of which both the staff members as well as the participants are comprised. It is in the analysis stage that the researcher can connect macroscopic and microscopic data. In doing so the qualitative methodology can generate practical and theoretical truths about human life grounded in the realities of daily existence (Jorgensen, 1989).

Overview of the qualitative research process

Qualitative data analysis is considered as an ongoing process occurring over the life cycle of a research project. The research process is the backbone of the book and schematically depicted in Figure 1.1; the diagram runs from the bottom upward.

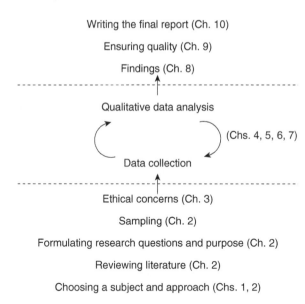

Writing the final report (Ch. 10)

Ensuring quality (Ch. 9)

Findings (Ch. 8)

Qualitative data analysis

(Chs. 4, 5, 6, 7)

Data collection

Ethical concerns (Ch. 3)

Sampling (Ch. 2)

Formulating research questions and purpose (Ch. 2)

Reviewing literature (Ch. 2)

Choosing a subject and approach (Chs. 1, 2)

FIGURE 1.1   OVERVIEW OF THE QUALITATIVE RESEARCH PROCESS

The choice of a topic, the research design, ethical issues and data collection are things to be considered at the beginning of each research project. They are dealt with in Chapters 1 to 4, which detail the initial start-up. The heart of the matter of qualitative data analysis is described in Chapters 5 to 7. Chapters 8 to 10 outline the final stages, where the analysis is concluded by a reflection on the findings and their uses, the application of quality procedures and reporting the findings. The core of analysis is depicted between the two horizontal lines and is fully explained starting in Chapter 5. A more detailed summary of each chapter follows.

Chapter 2 deals with the planning of the research, often written down in a research proposal. It describes the kinds of research questions that can be answered with qualitative research and various types of research goals of qualitative researchers. The writing of the provisional literature review is addressed in particular with concern to the generation of a 'skeletal framework' that plays an important part in qualitative data analysis. Sampling is addressed, including widely used strategies like purposive sampling and theoretical selection. The chapter ends with participant recruitment and strategies of gaining access to the field.

In Chapter 3 ethical issues and guidelines are elaborated on. The existing guidelines have predominantly been developed with an eye on survey and experimental research. Qualitative research has its own challenges with respect to ethical issues regarding the sensitivity of the subjects to be studied as well as the methods to be used. The basic rules for researchers and their professional codes should make all researchers aware of ethical issues and how to make the right decisions in balancing harm and benefits. Emphasis is given to ethical issues in qualitative research for participants as well as issues for researchers, such as uncertainty and stress. The benefits of participating are also examined. Ethical issues surrounding data analysis are described here too.

Data collection is the subject of Chapter 4. After defining the meaning of data in social science research, this chapter describes some commonly used methods in qualitative research, namely participant observation, interviewing, focus groups and collecting visual data. It highlights the skills required to gather the right kind of data to enable an interpretive reading of the data, such as the level of detail and use of the participant's words and activities. The interchange between data collection and data analysis is discussed along with methods for writing memos and recording ideas throughout the research process. Finally, a description is given of data management (both preparation and storage).

Chapter 5 sets the stage for qualitative data analysis by defining it and looking closely at its basics, namely segmenting and reassembling the data. This chapter elaborates on the mental activities that a researcher is engaged in when analysing qualitative data. A definition of analysis is given, thinking and doing are emphasized, and three important principles are explained: constant comparison, analytic induction and theoretical sensitivity. These principles form the basis of the analysis process. At the end of the chapter this cumulates into the presentation of the spiral of analysis, a step-by-step model for qualitative analysis that will be integrated into Figure 1.1. The basic ideas of the model are explained and it shows that data collection, sampling and analysis are intertwined.

Chapter 6 is the practical sequel to the theoretical overview given in Chapter 5. The spiral of analysis is the backbone of this chapter that deals with open coding, axial coding and selective coding. All steps in the spiral of analysis are translated to practical and 'how to' methods and techniques. Here we learn how to build on the bedrock of the previous chapter. The main activities are coding, reading, interpreting, comparing, verifying, selecting and writing. In the text useful 'frequently asked questions' (FAQs) are included. Where relevant, the use of software tools is mentioned. The chapter finishes with a reflection on what is achieved by coding the raw data and how it transforms them into findings.

Chapter 7 is invaluable since it describes a number of aids for the most difficult part of the analysis process: reassembling the data in order to answer the research questions. Ten heuristic devices, including matrices, coding families, visual diagrams, searching and counting, and typologies are reviewed. A comprehensive example of an analysis in the shape of a 'think aloud' report follows. Attention is given to two special types of data: focus group data and visual data. Next, a description follows of the current software tools for code-and-retrieve and theory-building.

Chapter 8 clarifies what results can be expected at the end of qualitative research. These results can consist of descriptions, conceptual clarifications or theory. The chapter touches on mistakes in qualitative research as well as on opinions that claim that sound results cannot be produced by blurred traditions. Then attention is paid to the use of qualitative research in mixed methods designs. This is a rapidly growing field of interest that can lead to fruitful cooperation between quantitative and qualitative researchers in the future. Finally, some words are dedicated to the use of qualitative research and what its results can add to science and society.

Chapter 9 describes how the problem with quality in qualitative research is related to its flexible nature, the difficulty with repeating the research and the role of the researcher. Further on, three opinions on quality are addressed and one is supported. Then the chapter continues with quality procedures, like triangulation, member validation, methodological accountability, reflection on the researcher's role and multiple researchers. Checklists and review criteria for publication are given, relating specifically to the analysis, and external validity or generalization is addressed. The chapter ends with challenges for qualitative research in relation to journalism and the use of scientific rhetoric.

In Chapter 10, the writing of the research report is addressed. Alternative ways of writing are reviewed, including images as 'writing', but emphasis is placed on traditional writing and its structure. The chapter demonstrates the entire course of action, starting with raw material, through transcription, analysis and editing, to the final report. The position of the researcher as a writer is considered, as well as the position of the researcher with respect to the participants. Writing the common parts of a research report is given attention: the introduction, method section, results and discussion. If we consider the results section 'the movie', the method section can be considered as 'the making of' part of the movie. The book comes to an end with details of the procedure of publishing the report.

Readings I learnt much from

Bryman, A. (2008). *Social research methods* (3rd ed.). Oxford: Oxford University Press.
Creswell, J.W. (2006). *Qualitative inquiry and research design: choosing among five traditions* (2nd ed.). Thousand Oaks, CA: Sage.
Denzin, N.K. & Lincoln, Y.S. (2005). Introduction. Entering the field of qualitative research. In: N.K. Denzin & Y.S. Lincoln (Eds.), *Handbook of qualitative research* (3rd ed.) (pp. 1–17). Thousand Oaks, CA: Sage.

Doing your own qualitative research project

Step 1: Thinking about your research

1. Write two pages of text about a subject that is really of interest to you and that you would like to examine. Write down why it fascinates you. To come up with a topic think about:

    - Your interest or fascination. What news items grab your interest? What's on your book shelves? What do you talk about with friends and parents? Which (college) courses really inspired you? What do you fancy as the perfect job for you? In short, what keeps you going?
    - Projects faculty in your department are currently involved in.
    - Sponsored research programmes. You do not need to apply for these grants, but the subjects might inspire you.
    - The literature, in particular interesting scientific books and articles.

2. Familiarize yourself with the topic. Is a scientific inquiry appropriate for this topic? Does the topic lead to research questions that can best be answered with qualitative methods (see also Chapter 2)?
3. Search for some research reports about the topic to acquaint yourself with that field of study. What exactly has been examined? What type of research was used, i.e. dominantly quantitative or qualitative research? Are specific qualitative traditions of research mentioned? Are there any suggestions for further research?
4. What attracts you most in the qualitative research reports that you found, and do you think you are able to learn and use the necessary research skills? If not, what steps are necessary to prepare yourself for this task?
5. Try to detect a convergence between your topic of interest and your favourite approach. Remember: a research project is more fun when the topic interests you and the approach suits you.

2
RESEARCH DESIGN

The flexible research procedure of qualitative research that was touched upon in Chapter 1, might suggest that this type of research requires little or no planning and that researchers can work with whatever they encounter. Nothing is further from the truth. Researchers face the difficult task of finding a balance between their preparations, resulting in a research plan and conducting the research in practice. The research plan contains the research questions, the research purpose, an ethical paragraph, a plan for disseminating the findings and an outline of the overall research strategy as well as the specific methods, techniques and instruments to be used. A plan provides structure, but it should not interfere with flexibility. A plan provides certainty, but should not block other promising options. This chapter provides pointers for handling this ambivalence in the design of a qualitative research project.

LEARNING AIMS

By the end of this chapter, you will be able to:

- Name and reflect on all elements of a research plan
- Reflect on the use of literature in a qualitative study
- Recognize a research question that is framed in a way that demands qualitative methods
- Formulate a qualitative research question when a research topic is given
- See how descriptive and explanatory purposes of research are related
- Distinguish between the purposes of fundamental and applied research
- Account for the choice of qualitative research methods in a study
- Work out the composition of a sample when starting with an a priori theory
- Employ theoretical selection in a qualitative project
- Identify some commonly used strategies for getting access to and recruiting participants

Planning a research project

The planning of a qualitative research project seems to run counter to the open procedure described in Chapter 1. The open and flexible approach should not lead to a non-committal attitude in which anything goes. Thorough preparation, resulting in a research plan or project proposal, prevents distraction from the actual topic. A research plan also promotes the (continual) fit between the parts of the research. The research problem, research questions, purposes, sample, data collection, analysis and reporting should be tuned to each other.

A research proposal not only has a function for you as a researcher, it is also extremely important for third parties, such as instructors, supervisors, granting organizations, commissioners, ethical committees and so on. Since in modern day research no one can afford to skip writing a research proposal before commencing the actual research, a lot of attention is paid to the quality of research proposals in recent years (Sandelowski & Barroso, 2003a; Connelly & Yoder, 2000).

A proposal needs to demonstrate what the research entails. This means that it has to provide answers to the following questions: What is being researched? Why is this subject examined? How will this be done? Where will the study take place? It is important that these questions are answered in a logical and convincing manner. Maxwell (2004) describes the research proposal as an argument which should convincingly demonstrate why this research should be done, what activities it will consist of, and to which results it will lead. This last point refers to the researchers being able to assess what they think they will know, and potentially what they will be able to do, once the research has been conducted.

Planning the analysis stage already in the research plan is probably the most difficult part. Of course, the chosen research approach (see Chapter 1) will determine what needs to be done during analysis. When, for example, one is aiming for an ethnographic study, a study using conversation analysis or a case-study, the relevant methodologies prescribe certain procedures. When the purpose is to generate a grounded theory about a basic human psychosocial experience, you might say something about the concepts you are probably going to use in the analysis and how you will approach the analysis, for instance how coding will be employed and which software for qualitative analysis will be used (see Chapters 6 and 7).

An essential part of your analytic plan in the research proposal is to indicate to reviewers that data collection and data analysis alternate in qualitative research. This is a vital part of the qualitative research procedure, and one of the main reasons that not all parts of the research can be planned in advance (Bruce, 2007). In the design stage you need to indicate how you plan for the interchange of data collection and data analysis and in how many cycles you plan to finish. For example, you may plan to observe two school classes, analyse the data and then search for two new classes. You plan to do so in three rounds until you have a minimum of six classes. If that turns out not to be enough, your plan will include the search for more classes (see last section of this chapter).

However, as Patton (1999) acknowledges, research proposals are judged not only on the use of rigorous techniques and methods for gathering data and careful analysis, but also on the credibility of the researcher, which includes training, experience, track record, status and presentation of self (Chapter 9). Moreover, the quality issue is related to the philosophical belief in the value of qualitative inquiry (see Chapters 1 and 8). Judgement is also dependent on the fundamental appreciation of qualitative research methods and it is to be expected that some people will probably never be satisfied with whatever 'quality outcomes' the research proposal promises. All researchers should be aware of this strategic or political dimension involved in judging and funding research proposals.

TIP

Several criteria for the evaluation of qualitative proposals have been developed. These standards are used by reviewers of, for example, funding agencies. If the series of questions can aid the reviewer to evaluate qualitative research, it can also help you to prepare your proposal and argue your choice for qualitative research methods. See, for instance, Morse (2003) about the review committee's guide for evaluating research proposals.

Literature review

Various resources are available for choosing a research topic and arriving at a proper problem formulation. A very important resource is literature, next to, for example, talking to field experts. Reviewing literature means that the researcher has taken notice of the accumulated knowledge gleaned from books and articles on a certain topic. Sometimes this background literature provides current social science theory. Theory is not the same as literature, and although both terms are sometimes used to depict what has been written about a certain area, theory refers to coherent frameworks that try to describe, understand and explain aspects of social life.

At one time it was considered inappropriate to read about a research topic before embarking on a qualitative undertaking. As an extension of this rule, no clear research question was formulated. Why was this so? Qualitative researchers wanted to do justice to the research subject and be open-minded about what they would encounter in the field of research. Their argument was that if they were to read in advance, they would have an opinion by the time they reached the field. Reviewing previous research, and especially getting acquainted with prevailing social theories, would distort their receptiveness to new ideas and discoveries. It would block their inductive reasoning necessary to generate new theories.

This idea was challenged. An argument for reading other people's research is that scientific knowledge has to accumulate. If no one takes notice of previous work the wheel keeps on getting re-invented. This is time-consuming, unethical, costly and not in the spirit of scientific work. At about the same time that this argument was issued, the research climate formalized. A research proposal without a description of the problem area and without a research question all of a sudden did not stand a chance with supervisors, granting organizations, commissioners and hosts.

The problem statement then came to be seen as a preliminary guideline for the research instead of a fixed starting point that determined the entire research procedure. It was acknowledged that the research problem and the research questions are generated at the start of the study and based on available but limited knowledge. Therefore it is permitted to adjust the research questions during the research if there are good arguments to do so (see the next section). This reasoning takes into account that it is very difficult to formulate a proper research question before a connection has been established with the field of research. Researchers sometimes use a pilot study to get familiar with the field.

Taking notice of the literature does not automatically imply that the whole idea of openness to the field has been abandoned altogether. Researchers try to put the knowledge they extracted from the literature aside in order to approach their field work with an open mind. 'Bracketing' is the common term for this process, although it has some deeper thoughts connected to it in phenomenology. It is only in the analytic phase that the knowledge is brought forth and used again.

Is a blind or naive undertaking of research possible anyway? And are you capable of temporarily disregarding knowledge that you obtained from reading at all? If you thought that you could design a research project without theoretical notions, then just think for a moment about your topic choice and problem formulation. The choice to study a particular topic and the way it is phrased already show a way of thinking about the issue and your theoretical stance. And it should, because by embedding yourself in a theoretical context you also find out what is of significance for you and what you consider worth putting energy into. It is part of ethical awareness in research to subscribe to research which is congruent with your values (Miles & Huberman, 1994).

TIP _____

Novice researchers are often daunted by doing a literature search. The amount of publications is overwhelming. Every single publication found leads to new literature references. Some of these detail only one aspect of your research problem, but since you are not sure yet what you are going to study you cannot find out how much detail you will need for a certain topic. This is a chicken and egg scenario. There are good books available to help you through this phase, such as Fink (2004).

_____

Gradually researchers realized that a literature search had an important function in the planning and execution of research. First of all, literature helps you to come up with a research topic. Not only does previous research provide numerous topics in your area of interest, it also shows which answers have already been given to certain questions. Consequently, it allows you to identify a gap in the existing knowledge and to delineate your own research. The connection of your research to recent theoretical ideas and debates makes it easier to identify the scientific area that you want to contribute to. The literature might make you aware of different angles of study, as you may have a one-sided view of your subject.

TIP _____

Most publications mention keywords that indicate what the study is about. With the use of keywords the study is embedded into a certain discipline, such as psychology or sociology, and the smaller areas within these disciplines, like counselling psychology organisational sociology. At the same time they make clear to which speciality the study contributes. Readers may use the keywords to search for additional, related literature.

_____

A literature study can make you streetwise with regards to certain limitations and/or opportunities in the field, for instance with gaining access to the field (see last section of this Chapter). You absolutely need literature to help you generate your measuring instruments, whether this is a topic list for interviews or an observation scheme. Sometimes you can 'copy' the questions posed by others and replicate some of their work, and the previously used instruments can also inspire you to generate your own.

A literature review facilitates the analysis. A theoretical framework derived from literature indicates how you will approach the research analytically. This is not to say that the framework will dictate which variables will be examined. It is not in the nature of qualitative research to use a fixed coding scheme that constricts data collection and pre-sorts data. Instead, the literature could provide a 'skeletal framework' (Morse, 2003). The skeletal framework is taken quite seriously in that some researchers limit the findings of their literature search to some global notions and ideas, while working with only a few concepts. These concepts have not yet been formalized and are therefore known as 'sensitizing concepts' or 'guiding concepts'. The term 'sensitizing concepts' was coined by Blumer (cf. Bryman, 2008), who contrasted them with 'definitive concepts'.

Definitive concepts have a fixed content that is reflected by its measure, i.e. the indicators that stand for the concept. For instance, equity in caregiving relationships is thought to be measured by the items on a survey (Box 1.1). In contrast, sensitizing concepts start out with a broad and general description and as such they can function as the researcher's lens through which to view the field of research. The principal role of the concept is in ordering the collected data, while the specification of the concept and its clarification take place in the analytical stage. This concept clarification contributes to theory development. Examples of sensitizing concepts from a study on alcohol use by adolescents are social identity, escapism and risk behaviour (Engineer, Phillips, Thompson & Nicholls, 2003) (see next section). The use of sensitizing concepts in the analysis process will be treated in more detail in Chapter 6.

Be aware that you can consult the relevant literature whenever you need to. You do not need to finish the reading stage before you can start your research. When you feel confident that you are on the right track and have read the key publications on your topic, start your research project. The research questions may need adjustment at various points throughout the research project. As the problem changes and is refined, it is generally necessary to refer repeatedly to relevant literature and read things that are deemed important at that moment.

TIP _____

Examples of reviews of qualitative research can help you to find a useful way of cataloguing the findings of a literature search. You could benefit from a rather simple table listing all relevant studies, like the one presented by Chapple and Rogers (1999). They headed the columns 'Author', 'Aim of the study', 'Method', 'Main findings' and 'Examples of why a qualitative method is illuminating', and in the rows they placed the different publications in alphabetical order. Such an aid forces you to summarize what is useful for you in each particular publication. It will also encourage you to formulate why a qualitative design is appropriate.

_____

Research question and purpose

A research proposal starts with a research problem. Based on the research problem is the formulation of the problem statement that can be thought of as consisting of a research question and a research purpose. A clear research question and purpose direct the entire research project, including the data analysis. Asking relevant research questions is essential for gathering the right data and consequently to provide the analysis with the necessary input to ultimately answer the research questions. The answer to a research question is knowledge. The research goal indicates what the knowledge obtained will be used for. In other words, why is it worthwhile to answer the research question? What is the use of the whole endeavour? It is important that the research question and research purpose match. Both are discussed in more detail below.

Research question

The research question is the central question which the researcher wants to answer by doing the research project. The research problem must be sufficiently focussed and defined in order to formulate clear research questions. Qualitative inquiry allows one to answer questions about the nature of social phenomena under study rather than the prevalence of phenomena. This means that all aspects of a phenomenon will be dissected and described, and possibly an attempt will be made to understand how the phenomenon is built-up, what the relationships are between the different parts, and what influences the absence or presence of certain parts.

From the above-mentioned it follows that qualitative research can deal with so-called descriptive questions as well as with explanatory questions. For instance, in a study into binge drinking (Engineer et al., 2003) a descriptive question is 'What experiences do adolescents have with criminal behaviour, misbehaviour and risky behaviour during night life?' An explanatory question in the same study is 'How do criminal experiences of these adolescents relate to their use of alcohol and the effects of excessive alcohol use?' Descriptive questions deal with the 'what' of social phenomena, while explanatory questions deal with the 'why' of these phenomena.

Research questions in qualitative research often start with words such as 'how', 'which' or 'what'. Box 2.1 provides a number of examples of research questions from qualitative studies.

BOX 2.1 EXAMPLES OF RESEARCH QUESTIONS FROM
QUALITATIVE STUDIES

- How can we explain the extent and nature of football hooliganism at different football clubs and in different countries, and variations therein over time? (Spaaij, 2006)
- Do psychiatric/mental health nurses provide meaningful caring response to suicidal people, and if so, how? (Cutcliffe, Stevenson, Jackson & Smith, 2006)
- What perceptions about information systems/information technology (IS/IT) are held by government authorities and how are they reacting to problems they have in IS/IT initiatives in government? (Lee & Kim, 2007)
- What are undergraduate medical students' perceptions and experiences of teaching in relation to gender and ethnicity? (Lempp & Seale, 2006)
- What are young people's experiences of crime, disorder and risk-taking in the night-time economy and in what ways are drinking patterns, attitudes to drinking alcohol and the effects of binge drinking related to these experiences? (Engineer et al., 2003)
- How do unaccompanied minor refugee youths, who grew up amidst violence and loss, cope with trauma and hardships in their lives? (Goodman, 2004)
- How has the meaning which women attribute to sedatives and their use been influenced by information which they have gathered from their daughters, people in their social networks or other sources? (Haafkens, 1997)

The research question is often broad and encompassing, and is usually divided into multiple sub-questions that further structure the research. Formulating sub-questions is difficult for a number of reasons:

- They must use the terminology that fits the chosen approach or tradition (see Chapter 1).
- They need to fall under the umbrella of the overall research question, confining the research to topics described in the overall question and allowing you to make a contribution to the knowledge in a particular scientific area.

- Research questions must match one another and follow logically one after the other. By answering the related research questions you build an argument in the research report.
- The questions need to be answerable by means of the proposed research. This implies that abstract concepts may only be used when they can be defined and translated into operational terms. Only then will they become researchable, which means that empirical data can be collected in relation to the operational terms in order to observe the concepts.

In Chapter 1 the emergent design of qualitative research was discussed. In proceeding from a problem to more specific issues and questions defined by information collected in the field, the researcher may realize that the initial question is somehow inappropriate; that it just does not make sense in terms of the realities of everyday life. Or the researcher may discover that many important issues in need of study were not anticipated at the onset of the project. If the research project were to continue as planned, it would yield less interesting results than if adjustments were made now. Researchers may also discover that they do not get access to their preferred field of research, forcing them to reformulate the research question in such a way that they are able to get access. Although there can be good reasons for tightening the research question(s) during the research process, it still needs to be motivated. However, researchers rarely include these changes in the original questions in their report. One exception is the example in Box 2.2, taken from a study on caregivers to people with dementia in nursing homes (Bosch, 1996).

BOX 2.2   ADJUSTING RESEARCH QUESTIONS TO THE FIELD

Bosch (1996) started her research with the global question: How do elderly with dementia experience reality? This was divided in the following sub-questions:

- What is 'reality' for elderly suffering from dementia?
- How do caregivers define this reality?
- Are there differences and similarities between these definitions of reality?
- What are the consequences of these differences in perceived reality for nursing home care?

Bosch writes that during participant observation in nursing homes, these questions became increasingly focussed on differences in life course between female residents who had been housewives, males who had been in paid employment or religious females who had lived in a monastery. Also the level of trust the nursing home residents experienced was highlighted. The extent to which staff attempted to create trust became an important subject of study. The questions Bosch formulated during the research process were:

- How does the social biography influence the resident's behaviour when living in a nursing home?
- Are there differences in behaviour between former housewives, males with paid employment and nuns?

- Can these differences be explained by the social biographies?
- To what extent does social biography play a role in the longing for and experience of trust on psychogeriatric wards in nursing homes?
- Which problems do staff members face when creating trust?

Knowing that you can adjust the research question during the research process does not mean that you can relax at the start of the process and expect the research question to take shape later on. Researchers who use an emerging approach know that a well-prepared research plan will serve to keep the process on track rather than going off at a tangent. Jorgensen (1989) recommends that the problem statement, including the research question and purpose, should be sufficiently broad to permit inclusion of the central issues and concerns, yet narrow enough in scope to serve as a guide to data collection. A proper literature search enables formulation of related questions and highlights the difficulties that can be expected when working in the field.

TIP

Researchers should not be discouraged by the quality of the research questions that are reported in publications. Those reported questions are the final, definitive questions formulated by researchers at the end of their research process. They make it seem as if the researchers knew exactly what they were looking for from the beginning. Usually this is not the case; it is considered quite normal that the formulation of a proper research question is fraught with joys and perils.

Research purpose

Two distinctions can be made with regard to the research purpose. The first distinction is between research mainly aimed at description and research mainly aimed at understanding or explanation. The second distinction is between fundamental and applied research. We will look at each of these in turn.

Describing what people think and don't think, believe and don't believe, and do or do not do is a contribution to scientific knowledge in itself. On completion of the research we will know more than we knew before about the way some people think about certain things, what certain places look like, or what activities take place somewhere. When describing certain phenomena while examining a particular scene, the researcher must judge these phenomena as relevant. In qualitative research, the phenomena are commonly referred to as 'categories'. A description of what takes place adds to the empirical knowledge of a certain field of study.

Box 2.3 gives an example of a research project into football hooliganism from an international perspective. Football hooliganism is defined by the author as 'the competitive violence of socially organized fan groups in football, principally directed against opposing fan groups' (Spaaij, 2006: 6). It is clearly descriptive knowledge derived from the literature that demonstrated similarities and differences between various countries and football clubs as well as changes over time concerning hooliganism.

BOX 2.3   DESCRIBING FOOTBALL HOOLIGANISM

For hooligan rivalries to develop and persist, the existence of at least one similar, oppositional fan group is a necessary condition (Spaaij, 2006). However, hooligan behaviour is not restricted to intergroup fighting but may also include missile throwing, vandalism, racial abuse, or attacks on police or non-aggressive supporters. The violent behaviour takes place not only at or in the immediate vicinity of football stadiums or fields, but also in other places, such as city centres, pubs, nightclubs or railway stations.

Previous descriptive studies show the 'what' of the social phenomenon of football hooliganism. Research clearly shows that football hooliganism is not a universal phenomenon, but a European, Latin American and, to a far lesser extent, Australian phenomenon. However, there are differences depending on the particular countries or football clubs involved, for instance with regard to scale, nature and time of origin. In North America there is no equivalent of football hooliganism, although individuals or small groups do participate in common assault, drunken and disorderly behaviour and confrontations with the police during sports matches. The same applies to Asia.

All cases of hooliganism that take place at different football clubs within a country seem to be similar at first glance. For example, British research demonstrates that the typical hooligan is a mainly male, white, working-class young adult. But when Western European countries are compared, there appear to be local and regional variations in the social backgrounds of football hooligans. In some countries the middle- and upper-classes have also been involved, as well as women and middle-aged individuals.

Scientists, however, are a special breed. They not only like to see what is there, they also like to know why it is there. Spaaij wonders 'why' the extent of football hooliganism is not evenly or randomly distributed and 'why' not every country or football club is equally affected. His aim is to add to sociological theory regarding football hooliganism and for this to serve as a basis for more effective and more proportionate policies at international, national, regional and local levels. Researchers often prefer to contribute to explanations in order to further develop the current theory on their field of interest. Description is considered more limited than explanation: it is possible to describe without explaining, however it is not really possible to explain without describing.

In the literature Spaaij (2006) already found several theories that applied to football hooliganism, such as the 'cleavages theory'. This theory states that the fault lines that exist in every society, whether with a religious, linguistic or class orientation, shape the nature of the hooligan groups. Another valid theory is the social identity theory that assumes that hooliganism offers young, male adults a possibility to demonstrate their masculinity and superiority towards significant others and establish their social identities. According to Spaaij, these explanations are insufficient and need to be complemented with the local context, such as the origin and history of a football club and the interpretation and priorities of the parties involved regarding official and informal policies. In his study he compares six Western European football clubs and adds evidence for already existing and new explanations.

In Box 2.4, two cases are presented based on the research of Spaaij (2006). The first one is a case description of Sparta, one of the six studied football clubs. The second one is a case description of one individual hooligan and composed by me on the basis of Spaaij's information. By presenting these materials it becomes clear that description as well as explanation can take place at different levels.

BOX 2.4 UNDERSTANDING FOOTBALL HOOLIGANISM

The case of Sparta: explanation at club level

Rotterdam in the Netherlands is a multi-club city including, among others, Feyenoord and Sparta. Spectator behaviour at Sparta is commonly perceived by the authorities, the media and the supporters themselves as 'friendly' and unproblematic. Sparta is one of the oldest football clubs in the Netherlands, founded in 1888, and has an elite character. When football gradually spread across all social classes, Sparta dreaded the roughness and lack of civilization of the working-class clubs. Their stadium, Het Kasteel [The Castle], symbolizes Sparta fan culture and their roots in the local area.

A historical rivalry with Feyenoord exists which reflects socio-economic and cultural differences between two parts of Rotterdam separated physically as well as symbolically by the river de Maas. Sparta is the community club of the North-West and Feyenoord represents the working-classes in the South of Rotterdam. Sparta has a gentlemen's reputation, which contrasts sharply with the persistent hooligan stigma of the Feyenoord supporters.

During the rise of intergroup rivalries in the 1970s, the club's officials persistently complained about the misbehaviour of opposing supporters. For a 'friendly' club it was difficult to see that the attendance of the home crowd declined because of spectator violence and that the club sometimes had to pay for damage brought on by other supporters. This spiralled further into financial problems, and consequently Sparta failed to attract substantial numbers of new young supporters. The character of the local area in which the stadium was based gradually changed due to an influx of immigrants who had little or no bond with the area and the community, let alone the football community. Due to these events Sparta found their fan base was aging rapidly.

(Continued)

(Continued)

Recently, a small number of young fans have turned to hooliganism, which compromises the club's 'friendly' image and threatens relations between the club and its supporters. These young fans often have not grown up in the area of Het Kasteel, but live in neighbouring suburbs. They have middle-class backgrounds and sometimes higher education. They are attracted to hooliganism as a way to 'spice up' their otherwise boring lives. One of these supporters is Dennis.

The case of Dennis: explanation at hooligan level

Dennis lives in a suburb of Rotterdam. He saw the violence of other hooligan groups and was eager to become a hooligan too. He is a university student but finds it boring. Dennis is a thrill seeker and always looks forward to the excitement of the football games during the weekends. What he really likes to do is to travel to football stadiums in other cities and fight the rival football fans there. Frightening rival supporters, making them run away in their own city is an exciting experience. The opposition is humiliated and then exacerbated when it is in the papers the next day.

Dennis and his friends have formed a group and call themselves the Sparta Youth Crew (the SYC). They are encouraged by few older supporters experienced in fighting and hooliganism. The SYC members wear right-wing symbols not because they are loyal to their political ideas but rather to provoke and shock others. Dennis yearns to be part of one of the most notorious groups with a real reputation in hooliganism.

He thinks of other fans as boring and real softies, but at the same time he does not view himself as a hard-core criminal like the Feyenoord hooligans. The SYC is more 'civilized' and sophisticated than other groups as they have rules that other hooligans do not, such as not attacking non-hooligan supporters and not inflicting injury to someone lying helplessly on the ground. Sparta nourishes the friendly image, and that is where Dennis and the SYC do not fit in. Because they operate away from their own football grounds, however, and have escaped formal social control, Dennis believes that they will not get caught.

The various accounts described in the literature led Spaaij (2006) to propose that football hooliganism might be shaped by the major 'fault lines' of particular countries, whether social class and regional inequalities, religious diversity, linguistic sub-nationalism or political groups. This indeed partly explains cross-national dissimilarities in football hooliganism, yet it fails to account for more specific spatial and temporal variations, i.e. local fault lines. Spaaij's research also confirms the assumptions of the social identity theory. The hooligan groups studied emphasize the differences between themselves and their opponents mainly in two ways. First, in terms of club and/or city, neighbourhood, regional, ethnic, religious, national or political allegiance (cleavages theory), and second, in terms of (de)masculinization ('real' men versus 'boys'). The sense of being a 'hooligan' is a key part of their social identity.

The second distinction that we mentioned at the beginning of this section is between fundamental and applied research. Roughly speaking, research serves to gain scientific knowledge purely to extend what is known on a certain topic. This type of research adds to the existing, theoretical knowledge in a certain area of interest and is also known as 'fundamental' or 'basic' research. Research can also provide knowledge to facilitate change in problematic situations. When the research question is answered, the knowledge may help to apply changes to, for example, formulate policy initiatives or develop fruitful interventions. This type of research is referred to as 'applied' or 'policy-oriented' research (Clarke, 2008).

Applied research aims to resolve an unwanted situation or improve an already functioning situation. A description of a certain situation can be very valuable in itself, but often explanations are necessary in order to be able to predict and direct behaviour. Once the reasons underlying a certain type of behaviour are clear, one could try to reorganize the policy to deal with this behaviour. For instance, because football hooligans are better understood, one can adequately predict which matches are likely to result in riots and destruction. Measures may then be taken in order to prevent this violence from happening. Spaaij (2006) concluded that violence and damage have increasingly displaced to city streets, pubs and railway stations, mainly as a consequence of the constrictive security measures in and around football stadiums. From the example on hooliganism it might be clear that one research project might serve both fundamental as well as applied purposes.

In order to contribute to the solution of problems by means of research, researchers have to ask 'how-can' questions (Zee, 1983). These questions give centre-stage to solutions and alternative measures. An example of such a question is: How can football hooliganism be diminished? At times, qualitative researchers mistakenly assume that their studies will automatically lead to usable results, because their study reflects the participants' perspective. These researchers pose 'how-come' questions and 'sympathizing' questions. A 'how-come' or explanatory question is: How come that recently a more cohesive fan group has originated that regularly engages in football hooliganism and consists of young males with middle-class backgrounds and high levels of formal education? An example of a sympathizing question or interpretive question is: What does it mean for hooligans to engage in violent behaviour during football games? By answering these questions, researchers describe the likely patterns of an individual or a group. However, they do not self-evidently bridge the gap between the participant's experiences on the one hand and research, policy and practice on the other. We come back to this issue in Chapter 8 when dealing with the use of qualitative findings.

TIP _____

Creswell (2006) has developed a very useful format for formulating the research purpose in diverse traditions within qualitative research. In this format, terms are used that belong to certain traditions in qualitative research. The format inspires the researcher to think about the exact framing of the research question and it is an opportunity to signal the reader the specific tradition that will be used. With some minor adjustments the format looks like:

> The purpose of this .... [tradition, type] study is to .... [understand? describe? explain?] the .... [central focus for the study] for .... [the unit of analysis: a person? processes? groups? sites?]. At this stage in the research, the .... [central focus being studied] will be generally defined as .... [provide a general definition of the central concept].

This template forces the researcher to think about all the essential parts of the research and to formulate them as clearly as possible at that moment.

Legitimizing the choice for qualitative research

After having formulated the central focus of the study, including the research questions and goals, arguments why qualitative methods are the best procedure to choose should follow. The most salient reasons to account for qualitative methods are detailed below.

- *Exploration:* When a study has an explorative nature – for instance, a newly emerging field of interest that has not yet been extensively examined – you need methods with a maximum of explorative power. Qualitative methods do live up to this because of their flexible approach. As we have seen, the research questions can be tailored to the field of study. In addition, data collection and data analysis can be continually adjusted to the emerging findings. That is why both activities are conducted in small cycles instead of one after the other.
- *Description:* Qualitative methods offer the opportunity for participants to describe the subject of study in their own words and to do so largely on their own conditions. They may express views, give words to their experiences and describe events and situations. Likewise, with the use of various observation methods, extended descriptions of cultural behaviour, knowledge and artefacts can be obtained (see Chapter 4). The information gained is not limited to preconceived questions and categories, and as a consequence can provide rich and detailed data that leads to focussed descriptions of a given phenomenon in the social world.
- *Explanation:* Qualitative methods can lead to an interpretive rendering of the studied phenomenon. By cycling between data collection and data analysis, early conjectures can be checked in further cycles of new data collection and subsequent analysis of comparative cases. Through the constant comparison of data with the emerging ideas, a more abstract and conceptual model can be generated that is grounded in the data.
- *Change:* Sometimes, manoeuvrable methods are wished for to follow-up on fast developments in the studied area. Some subjects do change really fast as they gain momentum, for instance, the change in focus of a political publicity campaign after

a drop in the opinion polls, or the change in policy when two companies merge. Since qualitative methods are flexible and cyclical, they can be adjusted to the field and measure possibly important decisions and subtle activities that could have major consequences.

- *Use*: Qualitative methods hold the promise to yield findings that reflect the participants' perspective and that fit the substantive field. As a consequence it is expected that the findings will have relevance for the field and can be easily transformed into interventions for practitioners. Although this is only partly the case, as was mentioned above, results relevant to the target group might encourage the adoption of new policy measures.

- *Sensitivity*: Qualitative researchers often choose to examine other people's experiences and emotions. They have a preference for studying topics that are strange, uncommon or deviate from the 'normal' situation. It is assumed that these topics can be more easily captured in research that leaves much of the control to the participants, although within well-defined limits. Sometimes qualitative researchers go to great lengths to recruit participants from populations that are difficult to reach in order to thoroughly investigate topics that desperately need to be studied (see Chapter 3).

In a qualitative research proposal you have to argue that qualitative methods have the potential to produce the findings that are going to realize your goals. By and large, the characteristics of qualitative research as described in Chapter 1 are the selling points of this type of investigation. The reasons for choosing qualitative research methods are not mutually exclusive. In Box 2.5 an example is given in which all reasons for choosing qualitative methods seem to apply (Cutcliffe et al., 2006).

BOX 2.5   A JUSTIFICATION OF USING QUALITATIVE METHODS

Although there is an abundance of literature on suicide and despite the relevance of suicide to psychiatric/mental health nurses, the authors assert that there is a paucity of research in this specific area. In other words, it needs to be *explored* whether nurses provide meaningful caring response to suicidal people, and if so how.

'Meaningful' care needs to be defined by the suicidal people themselves. As participants, people were chosen who had made a serious attempt on their lives or felt they were on the cusp of so doing and had received 'crisis' care from the psychiatric services. In semi-structured interviews participants talk about the caring experiences that were helpful to them. Their perspective including the interactions in which they felt listened to and understood is *described*.

From the analysis of the data about meaningful caring interactions, the researchers deduce that the participants go through a process that leads them from alienation from the world to a new connection with the world. Nurses can help them go through these stages. They do so through 'reflecting an image of humanity',

(Continued)

(Continued)

via 'guiding the individual back to humanity' to 'learning to live'. This theoretical model demonstrates that suicidal people occupy themselves with getting a grasp on life again and *explains* what is considered meaningful care in the different stages.

The practice of providing care for the suicidal client clearly involves at least two people and also occurs over a period of time. A *change* is observed in the basic psychosocial problems that suicidal clients go through. The situation of their inter-actional partners, the nurses, is subject to change as well. Caring as such is a dynamic social phenomenon and qualitative methods fit this nature.

From the findings *practical implications* can be deduced. Based on the findings, a theory of meaningful caring practice of suicidal people is developed. Each of the three stages indicated in the theory is described by way of particular meaningful performances of the nurses. Distinct practice implications arise from this, such as the competence of nurses to be comfortable with co-presencing, that is, to be able to hold back from being too instrumental, and the need to be comfortable with death and talking about suicide.

The *sensitive* nature of the subject makes the choice of a qualitative methodology perfectly understandable. It deals with existential issues and topics such as mortality, death and suicide, the use of mental health services, insecurity and dependability on others. Suicide itself is emotionally draining and subject to stigma as well (see Chapter 3). A face-to-face conversation between a client and a researcher seems to suit this situation best.

Sampling, recruitment and access

When the research question and purpose have been formulated, the next step is to find a setting – participants, locations, organizations, places – in which to conduct the research. The chosen setting should be the best possible to observe your subject. Usually it is not possible to study all aspects of your chosen subject; therefore you have to take a sample, that is, to select cases. There are several sampling strategies in qualitative research, and the main distinctions are described in this section.

Choosing a setting

In selecting a setting, Morse and Field (1996) use the principle of maximization. This means that a location should be determined where the topic of study manifests itself most strongly. They conducted research on pain and the way in which nurses offered consolation and comfort. They considered investigating this topic in the context of childbirth, but decided not to. They reasoned that pain might be maximally present during labour so that, as a consequence, the need for consolation and comfort would be high as well. At the same time, the study would observe pain for a specific period (labour) with a known goal (birth of the baby). These reasons led them to investigate the phenomenon at emergency units. This environment also maximizes the chance of pain occurring, but in a very different and less predictable form. The message is: choose a location in which you can learn most about your topic.

The more abstract the topic of inquiry is, the more the researcher has to determine where the research is to be conducted. The most logical place to go to investigate football hooligans are the football clubs and the football stadiums. However, the increased use of information systems and information technology could be investigated in governments, businesses, public and private sectors, using different kinds of technology systems and on different levels within these organizations. It is up to the researchers to decide which field offers the best opportunities to learn about their research subjects, which field is most interesting, and which field is most likely to be accessible.

Not every research topic requires the researcher to think about the choice of the location. If a football club decides to commission research into new restrictive policies, the field of research is fixed. The case is already specified and constitutes the focus of the research question. However, this does not relieve researchers of having to think about the relationship between their setting and other settings (Mason, 2002). In order to determine the value of research and assess the extent to which findings may be generalized, it is important to consider what a particular setting may or may not teach us about the phenomenon we are studying (see Chapter 9).

Purposive sampling

Composing the sample in qualitative research is different from the common sampling approach used in quantitative research. There has even been an objection to the use of the term 'sample' since it carries connotations that some find undesirable for qualitative research. These connotations have to do with the following. In quantitative research it is paramount that statistical representation is implemented. The probability that the case falls within the sample is determined by chance, and the sample reflects the proportional distribution of relevant population characteristics. Based on the findings in this randomly selected sample, probabilistic assertions may be made about the entire population, commonly referred to as generalization or statistical inference (see Chapter 9). Statistical rules and procedures are used to make such assessments.

Although both procedures – random sampling and statistical inferences – do not apply to qualitative research, the term 'sample' is widely used in qualitative research terminology. A sample consists of the cases (units or elements) that will be examined and are selected from a defined research population. In qualitative research the sample is intentionally selected according to the needs of the study, commonly referred to as 'purposive sampling' or 'purposeful selection'. The cases are specifically selected because they can teach us a lot about the issues that are of importance to the research (Coyne, 1997).

All samples in qualitative research have some features in common (Curtis, Gesler, Smith & Washburn, 2000). The samples are often small, although that is not a fixed rule. Cases are studied intensively, and each case typically generates a large amount of information. Generally samples are not predetermined, and selection is sequential, interleaved with data collection and analysis. Sampling strategies in qualitative research typically aim to represent a wide range of perspectives and experiences, rather than to replicate their frequency in the wider population (Ziebland & McPherson, 2006).

Two types of purposive sampling can typically be distinguished in qualitative research (Curtis et al., 2000). One form of purposive sampling is suitable for qualitative research, which is informed a priori by an existing body of social theory on which the research questions are based. In this case the sample selection is driven by a theoretical framework which guides the research from the outset. Many different sampling strategies can be found, for instance drawing a unique case, a critical case, an extreme case or a typical case, drawing for maximum variation and homogeneous drawing (Miles & Huberman, 1994).

The other form is theoretical sampling, designed to generate theory which is grounded in the data, rather than established in advance of the fieldwork. Theoretical sampling is based on the grounded theory approach (see Chapter 1). Theoretical sampling is defined as 'the process of data collection for generating theory whereby the analyst jointly collects, codes, and analyses his data and decides which data to collect next and where to find them, in order to develop his theory as it emerges' (Glaser, 1978: 36).

Examples of both types of sampling are given below. The first type, purposive sampling in research that already starts with a theoretical framework, is illustrated by the study of Spaaij (2006) into football hooliganism. He chose to examine this phenomenon in more than one football club (multiple case study design). In order to make a proper selection of cases, he reviewed the literature and consulted experts on the subject. Because Spaaij had a rather strong theoretical impetus in his research, his sample was chosen beforehand. Box 2.6 describes how and why Spaaij selected football clubs according to the principle of maximum variation.

BOX 2.6   CHOOSING CASES INFORMED A PRIORI BY THEORY

It is logical that Spaaij (2006) would conduct an international comparative study to describe and explain the extent and nature of football hooliganism in different countries. Spaaij wants to describe spatial, cross-case variations: he wants to explain the differences between football clubs in the same country. However, he also wishes to describe within-case variations, that is, variations in hooliganism over time within the same club. Spaaij must therefore study a variety of clubs.

First of all Spaaij chooses three democratic societies in Western Europe – England, the Netherlands and Spain – to study how the fault lines of particular societies shape the manifestation of football hooliganism. Despite significant variations, the socio-economic structures and cultural traditions are comparatively similar in these countries, and historically football has been a popular spectator sport in all three countries. The fault lines in contemporary English society are social class and regional inequalities. In contemporary Dutch society no single dominant cleavage seems to exist, although some socio-cultural differences between the West and other parts of the country remain and local and regional identities prove remarkably strong. The major fault lines in Spanish society are the centre-periphery divide – regional and (sub-)nationalist identities – and the class divide.

Because the fault lines are supposed to operate on a high level of generality, factors that co-shape the nature and development of football hooliganism on a local level need to be examined as well. With this purpose in mind, one multi-club city is chosen in each of the three countries. Here Spaaij employs sampling for maximum variation. In England, London is appointed, with West Ham United that has a violent image and Fulham FC with a friendly image. In the Netherlands, Rotterdam was chosen, hosting Feyenoord which has the hard nature of an urban working-class football club and Sparta which is referred to as a gentlemen's club. In Spain, Barcelona is selected, with RCD Espanyol as a club with a hostile image and FC Barcelona as a friendly club.

Spaaij decided beforehand where his research would take place, and in doing so he seemed not to live up to the tenet of qualitative research to interchange data collection, sampling and data analysis. This is only true to a certain extent. He did analyse one case at a time and studied each case for its unique characteristics (within-case analysis). At the same time, he let the analysis of the next cases be influenced by what he learnt from the previous ones. So although he chose his cases beforehand, he acted upon the emerging knowledge in his analysis.

Box 2.7 gives an example of the second sampling type, theoretical selection, which involves a study into nursing care for suicidal people (Cutcliffe et al., 2006). Theoretical selection means that the ideas and conjectures that result from the foregoing analysis are checked with newly collected data in comparative cases. With the aim to fill gaps in the findings, specific cases – events, participants, organizations, or groups – are chosen to find this missing information.

BOX 2.7   CHOOSING CASES INFORMED BY DEVELOPING THEORY

The sample of 20 participants selected for the study was obtained using the principles of theoretical sampling. Initial sampling started with former clients who had received care for a 'suicide crisis' as 'community clients'. The authors write:

Following this, the emerging theory indicated that there might be merit in increasing the differences in the sample. Namely, the emerging theory indicated

(Continued)

(Continued)

that the particular physical and social environment might have an influence on the person and that adjusting the environment to make it as stress free as possible could be a therapeutic intervention. As a result, the research team accessed former clients who had received care for their suicidal crisis as in-patients.

Following this, the emerging theory indicated that the research team needed to sample formerly suicidal clients who had received care in a 'Day Hospital' or 'Day Unit' setting, because there may have been particular therapeutic value for suicidal people in some of the activities that occurred on Day Units. The emerging theory did not indicate any theoretically relevant differences according to the person's gender; neither did it indicate any theoretically relevant differences according to theological backgrounds or beliefs. Neither did the emerging theory indicate any theoretically relevant differences according to race or culture. Thus, no such variations in the sample were pursued. The research team sampled individuals from several geographical locations. (Cutcliffe et al., 2006: 794)

When research seeks to provide explanations, an active search is needed for so-called negative cases. This means that researchers purposefully look for cases which could disprove the provisional findings so far. Searching for negative evidence in this way may ultimately strengthen the outcomes. When a case is found that does not match the findings in the cases studied up to that point, a so-called rivalling or supplementing explanation may be sought; for example, 'This case does not confirm what I thought to hold true so far because ...'. Specifically this strategy plays a role in checking conjectures by further data collection, referred to as 'analytic induction' (Chapter 5).

One could easily get the idea that the field of research is so large that a researcher's work may never be done. When can you cease data collection and stop sampling new units? This happens when a point of saturation has been reached. Once again, this procedure is shaped in grounded theory, and it means that researchers may stop collecting data when analysis of the newly selected cases yields no further information with regard to the selected research topics. This is slightly too simplistic, hence Chapter 6 will specify the meaning of saturation further, as it plays an important role in several phases of the analysis process.

TIP _____

Once the threat exists that a subject may become too sizeable and complex, the target population can be more homogenously defined in order to decrease the number of cases that need to be involved in the research. In the study on carers of people with multiple sclerosis (Box 1.2), a variety of family members, such as children, parents, partners and brothers and sisters were set to be included. The literature implied that the group of partners was largest, and that this group was generally the most heavily burdened (Duijnstee & Boeije, 1998). In the light of this information, the decision was made to only study the partners, thereby limiting the population, while at the same time increasing attainability.

Even though novice researchers have a hard time believing that saturation is possible, i.e. that cases can be so insignificant that nothing new will be discovered when including them, experienced researchers know that repetition will occur. Once researchers reach the point at which their categories are saturated (see Chapter 6) and they feel like nothing new can be learned from analysing more data, they can cease the data collection. It is not really possible to predict when this will occur, as it depends on the size, variation and complexity of the topic and, again, on the available time and resources.

TIP _____

It is clear that it is difficult to write about the sample in advance in the research proposal. When planning, only approximations of sample size can be given because one cannot predict how much data will be required to identify themes or categories and to begin developing theory (Morse, 2003). It is therefore important to elaborate carefully on the target population, to explain what principle of sampling will be used, why it was chosen and what is meant by saturation. Additionally, a reasonable estimate of the possible size of the sample may be given. In this estimate, attainability will likely play a role. In the final report it should, of course, be clear for readers what the ultimate sample looked like and how the sample came about. We will deal with this subject in Chapter 4 about writing the research report.

From the examples in Box 2.6 and 2.7 it becomes clear that the initial cases are sampled specifically because the phenomena are known to exist in these samples. If possible these should be information-rich cases, that is, cases that fit the purpose of the study (Coyne, 1997). Then as sampling progresses, data collection and analysis are adjusted. The ultimate sampling will consist of balancing a range of sometimes conflicting criteria, for instance, between the maximum informative setting and ethical objections or the possibilities of certain data collection methods and accessibility (Curtis et al., 2000).

Recruitment and access

There is one other important question left with regard to sampling: How do researchers gain access to the field that they would like to investigate and how do they locate participants? Methods of recruitment are very diverse. The same kinds of resources used in other types of research may be used here (Lee, 1993), for instance, placing advertisements in magazines, on billboards or on the Internet. Researchers may also go to places where they would expect to find potential participants; for example, by going to the beach to meet people who are frequent sun bathers. Researchers may attempt to perform tasks in exchange for cooperation; for example, by tending the bar at a local cultural centre or filling out forms. They could write to organizations or groups asking them to approach people for possible participation in the study. On some occasions, it may be possible for researchers to connect with already running, large-scale research programmes of national research organizations.

Another strategy is the 'snowball' or networking method, which means that an initial number of participants are asked for the names of others, who are subsequently approached. This method is useful when studying sensitive or taboo topics or when target groups are difficult to reach. Examples include women who have had an abortion, family members of a person who committed suicide, or sexual behaviour of gay men. Although snowball sampling seems a convenient and easy way to sample participants, there is much more to an adequate snowball sample than is often believed, as Coxon (1993) found when sampling a community of gay men.

For research in organizations it is recommended that the formal path be followed; for example, sending a letter to the board of directors. When the organization appears interested, subsequent agreements can be made on the exact topic under investigation, the time when the research will take place, the provision of a room for the researcher, executive power with regards to the publication and so on. It is quite common for organizations to 'use' research to look into issues which are important to the company. Many qualitative researchers in the field have discovered that access to organizations has to be renegotiated at every level. Participatory approval from the highest authority does not open every door, and therefore every employee whom the researcher contacts will have to be asked for cooperation individually (Lofland & Lofland, 1995; Schatzman & Strauss, 1973).

The ways in which this can be done are many, but researchers will often have to go through a lot of trouble to find participants and to get access to them. Difficulty in finding participants who are willing to cooperate can cause a delay in the time-line of the project. Whether or not a research project is ethically sound is sometimes scrutinized by ethical research committees, whose task it is to weigh the costs of the research against the benefits. This procedure will also take time and must be accounted for. We will deal with this subject in the next chapter on ethics.

Readings I learnt much from

Lee, R.M. (1993). *Doing research on sensitive topics*. London: Sage.
Mason, J. (2002). *Qualitative researching* (2nd ed.). London: Sage.
Maxwell, J.A. (2004). *Qualitative research design. An interactive approach* (2nd ed.). Thousand Oaks, CA: Sage.
Punch, K.F. (2005). *Introduction to social research. Quantitative and qualitative approaches* (2nd ed.). London: Sage.

Doing your own qualitative research project

Step 2: Writing the research proposal

1. Writing the research proposal is the formal beginning of your research. It can consume around a quarter of the available research project's time. Remember to work cyclically: if you have gained new insights, add them to the proposal and adjust the parts that are affected by the change. New ideas about the research questions might, for instance, change the data collection plan. It is of paramount importance that the parts of your project stay connected.
2. Make a preliminary outline of the proposal containing:

   - Working title
   - Introduction
   - Literature review
   - Research questions and research purposes
   - Research methods
   - Approach chosen
   - Ethics
   - Data collection methods
   - Gaining access and selection of participants
   - Data analysis
   - Schedule
   - Estimated costs
   - References
   - Appendices (for instance, experts consulted in the pilot study, topic list, dissemination of results)

3. Formulate a preliminary research question and sub-questions on the basis of the pages written about your interest in step 1. Think about the purpose of your research: why is it useful to answer the research questions? Reflect on the question 'Who would find my findings useful?' Try to think of what benefits society will gain from this research project. Write it down in your concept research proposal. After a few attempts, let the subject rest for a while and go on to the next question.
4. Start reading the literature and try to connect your subject to what has previously been written about the subject. Reviews, meta-analyses and meta-syntheses are fast ways to orient yourself to the well-known authors and the theoretical perspectives used. Be especially on the look-out for social theory that is used and study keywords and key questions from previous work. Be confident to assess the work of others and select the publications that appeal to you, whether because of the subject, the approach, the methods used or the findings. Adjust the size and depth of your literature study to the time available. Remember that you can read as you go.
5. Return to the research questions and purposes. Consider whether the literature search gives rise to adjustments of both elements, in particular the use of concepts and prior knowledge to specify them and eventually delineate the

research any further. Take care that the research questions follow logically from the literature review, and be sure that your argument is clear. Try to use the format that was recommended (Creswell, 1998) if you have difficulty with this part of the proposal.

6. Legitimize the choice for a qualitative methodology and write it down in your preliminary proposal. Most of the time your reasons for choosing qualitative research methods are a combination of two or more reasons, as indicated in Box 2.5. Apply the reasons to your research.

7. Some ethical issues that will reveal themselves in your research will benefit from advanced thinking. While writing the research plan try to anticipate what problems you could encounter during your research and, if possible, try to take preventive measures.

8. Think about getting access to your field of study. Do you already have contacts in the field who can help you enter it? Can they be of help in other ways in your project? How large will your sample be and what kind of sampling scheme are you planning to use: purposive sampling based on theory known beforehand, or theoretical selection? Write your arguments in the research proposal.

9. Reflect on whether the literature has fully worked for you (see 'Literature review' in this Chapter). Have you connected your plan with a scientific area? Can you describe what your research will contribute? Have you become streetwise? Are you still enthusiastic about the endeavour or, better yet, has your enthusiasm grown?

10. Eventually, use a checklist for assessing a research proposal. It will sensitize you for the criteria that are used and what is expected of a proposal. Have you touched upon all relevant topics up to now, and is your first draft convincing to yourself and others?

3
ETHICS IN QUALITATIVE RESEARCH

Theoretically any means can be used to gain the knowledge to answer our research questions, such as eavesdropping at private conversations, undercover participation, photographing intimate scenes, tapping telephones and reading personal letters and diaries. But it does not work that way. Social scientists follow ethical rules of behaviour to prevent them from doing harm to others and to protect themselves. The report of findings based on data that are unethically gathered can lead to harm, enormous dilemmas and possible conflicts. This chapter aims to raise awareness about the effects of social science inquiries for the different parties involved, such as the researched participants and communities, the audience, guest organizations, gatekeepers, subsidisers and society at large. Ethics are concerned with finding a balance between benefits and risks for harm.

LEARNING AIMS

By the end of this chapter, you will be able to:

- Understand the all-encompassing nature of ethics in research
- Think about the ethical principles governing social research in your project
- Identify the need for research ethical committees to judge research proposals
- Acknowledge that covert data collection violates several ethical principles
- Regard ethical planning as an essential part of planning the entire research process
- Detect stakeholders in a specific research project and their sensitivity issues
- Judge the risks and benefits of participation in a particular study
- Ensure that you have adequate support and resources for yourself as a researcher
- Discern the influence of ethics in qualitative data analysis

Ethics in social research

Researchers have to consider the moral accuracy of their research activities in relation to the people they meet along the way, such as participants, hosts, funders, colleagues and parties who are likely to encounter the implications of the research. Research in general is a human practice in which social values and ethical principles apply and moral dilemmas occur. Questions researchers may ask are: Am I exploiting participants and am I in some way deceiving them? When the people in the host organization can recognize each other despite measures to protect their identities, might it hurt or damage them? Is my project really worth doing and is it value for money? Who owns the data and who is entitled to publish the research? Who will benefit and who will lose as a result of the findings becoming public? As Miles and Huberman (1994) conclude, the entire research enterprise is full of ethical pitfalls.

A basic concept in qualitative research is trust. Field workers know that it is often one particular event that develops trust in participants and opens new doors: that specific moment when the researcher's reaction is observed by the participants. My own anecdote while doing field work in a nursing home is that I was invited to be present while enrolled nurses laid out a resident who had died a few moments before. When I showed that I wanted to observe how they dealt with death, they seemed to be aware that I was taking my work very seriously. From that moment on, they were more open about their work, about their worries and about what kept them going.

When the researcher manages to win and does not belie the trust of the participants, they may be willing to say or show more than they had planned to. In particular, interviewees get into a 'telling' mode in which they find it embarrassing or inappropriate to refuse to answer certain questions or elaborate on certain matters. That is how interviewees are socialized and it is after all what researchers try to accomplish by creating a pleasurable atmosphere while generating data. Although trust can increase openness in participants, there can be danger in it as well. Although openness can be fortuitous for researchers, they have a moral obligation to protect individuals from saying more than they want. A colleague researcher took this very literally by offering the children in her interview study a stop sign that they could raise when they did not want to talk any further. None of the children actually used the sign, but it gave them control over what they wanted to reveal.

Ethics in social science research is a broad topic. In this section we first look at the common ethical principles associated with ethical research. We address the professional codes and institutions that have been established with regard to ethical issues. Next, we turn to the relationship between ethical issues and studying sensitive topics, as research subjects in qualitative research are often sensitive. Further on, we discuss balancing harm and benefits for the people taking part in qualitative research, as well as possible stress for the researchers themselves. We finish with narrowing down the subject to the ethical aspects of data analysis.

Ethical principles

Despite different accents in the available valid frameworks that guide ethical choices, there are common principles as well (Miles & Huberman, 1994). Beneficence is considered an umbrella principle that refers to maximizing good outcomes for science, humanity, and the individual research participants while avoiding or minimizing unnecessary harm, risk or wrong (Sieber, 1992). This general principle needs translation to be of practical relevance, which is usually addressed in three dimensions, namely informed consent, privacy and confidentiality and anonymity.

Informed consent

One important general ethical requirement for the researcher's introduction to the field is informed consent. This is the obligation to outline fully the nature of the data collection and the purpose for which the data will be used to the people or community being studied in a style and language that they can understand. Informed consent is intended to ensure that the participants are placed in a situation where they can decide, in full knowledge of the risks and benefits of the study, whether and how to participate (Endacott, 2004). In other words, those who are researched have the right to know that they are being researched, and they should actively give their consent (Bulmer, 2008). When an ethical review committee (see next section) is involved, and in some countries any research study requires approval of an ethical review committee, its members will have to approve of the research proposal including the informed consent before any recruitment of participants or data collection can start.

Additionally, to some, voluntary informed consent is seen as an ongoing, two-way communication process between research participants and the investigator (Sieber, 2008; Cutcliffe & Ramcharan, 2002). The reasons for this view are twofold. First, the practicalities of 'doing research' daily can give rise to a change in design, due to the fluid and open design of qualitative research (see Chapter 2). Such a change of plans needs to be renegotiated with the participants, although a drastic change also needs renewed approval of the ethical review committee, which often keeps researchers from proposing such a change. Second, questions and concerns often occur to the participants only after the qualitative research is well under way. Sometimes it is only then that meaningful communication and informed consent can occur ('If only I had known that ...'). Therefore, it must be made clear to participants that they have the right to refuse or to withdraw from the project at any time without it affecting their/their relative's care, lessons, treatment, professional development or anything else.

The principle of informed consent cannot be reconciled with the use of covert methods. By definition, the subjects of covert research are kept in ignorance of the true identity of the researcher and they have no opportunity to decide whether or not to participate (Bulmer, 2008). However, in overt participation the participants sometimes forget that they are being studied when the researcher becomes a known person who is always around. Participants do not always realize that a friendly conversation might be information ending up in a report. With qualitative methods, it is considered good practice to seek verbal assurance from participants immediately following data collection that the information obtained can be included in the study. This safeguards against use of information which may have been accidentally disclosed (Endacott, 2004).

Privacy

Privacy refers to the interest of individuals to control the access that others have to them (Sieber, 2008). Simply stated, this means that individuals decide to whom they give information about themselves and that researchers may not disclose such information to others. Privacy often plays a part in the public perception of social science since social scientists are perceived to intrude into areas which are considered private. Why such areas are deemed private may vary, as we will see in the next paragraph on sensitive topics. Again, secret participant observation is often an invasion of privacy. To make observations or enquiries under false pretences in order to gather material for research violates the right to privacy of the individual (Bulmer, 2008).

In social research, there are complications stemming from the institutionalized nature of social life. Entry to research settings may be controlled by gatekeepers who are professionals or administrators in charge. Yet they may grant permission on behalf of clients or customers or patients frequenting the milieu – or may deny entry even if members of those groups are willing to grant it and cooperate in the research.

Confidentiality and anonymity

Confidentiality concerns data (records, field notes, digital recordings of interviews, transcripts and the like) and agreement as to how the data are to be handled in the research in order to ensure privacy. Often this is dealt with in the informed consent statement, which clarifies what may be done with information the participant conveys to the researcher (Sieber, 2008). Confidentiality is connected to anonymity, which means that participants' names and other unique identifiers (addresses, places, professions and so on) are not attached to the data (Sieber, 2008). Only the research team that conducts the investigation will be able to identify the researched participants by use of a code book. The code book and all material will be maintained in a locked filing cabinet or will be digitally protected when stored on the computer.

Researchers' interest in the personal beliefs and experiences of participants and the often-used practice to illuminate insights with quotes and observations can cause challenges with respect to ethical conduct. For instance, it can be difficult to disguise the participants' identities when using quotes, constituting a potential violation of confidentiality (Haverkamp, 2005). Assuring that participating institutions, such as associations, hospitals, schools and communities, are not identifiable is challenging, especially when members of an organization are carrying out research in their own environment, such as medical doctors doing research in the hospital where they are employed (Endacott, 2004). On the other hand, there are certain individuals and organizations that may require acknowledgement of their role in the study.

Professional standards

Several professional associations of, for instance, sociologists, anthropologists and psychologists, have defined codes of ethics on many of the above-mentioned ethical issues and dilemmas. They offer professional standards to be found on the websites of the associations in the various countries. Of course, the difficulty lies in applying these guidelines to the decisions to be taken in one's own research. Additionally, there are numerous international guidelines on the ethics of research using human participants. Drawing on features common to these standards, a framework has been developed consisting of seven requirements: social or scientific value, scientific validity, fair subject/participant selection, favourable risk–benefit ratio, independent review, informed consent, and respect for potential and enrolled participants (Emanuel, Wendler & Grady, 2000). Although the framework was originally developed for clinical research, there is common ground with the basic philosophy that is also applicable to the social sciences (Khanlou & Peter, 2005).

Ethical review committees, referred to as Research Ethics Committees or Institutional Review Boards, review research proposals that include humans from an ethical point of view. These committees do a precautionary check of the research proposal to protect the population under study. This responsibility extends to approval of, among other things, the purpose of the study, the design, the main interview questions, measures for confidentiality and the possibility to request follow-up help if participation proves to be distressful. Although in some countries, among them the USA, ethical review committees assess all research, the committees are often connected to hospitals. Their key concerns then can be grouped under three headings (Endacott, 2004):

1. *Is this 'good science'?* The committees try to filter out poorly designed research to prevent participants' time being wasted. In their assessment they include the competence of the researchers to undertake the study successfully.
2. *What are the benefits, costs and risks for participants?* The input of participants often does not yield any personal benefit. Sometimes researchers can, however, reciprocate by presenting the findings to the participants at the end of the project. Potential harm, physical or psychological, in the individual participant should be identified, and reported in a timely manner, and possible intervention should be considered.
3. *What are the benefits, costs and risks for the participating organization?* Costs to be considered include the time needed for staff to provide data or to attend briefing sessions regarding the research. Ethical review committees seek to protect staff and clients from being over-researched.

There is debate about the role, composition and conduct of ethical review committees (Hays, Murphy & Sinclair, 2003; Cutcliffe & Ramcharan, 2002). The committees originate in biomedical research and the question whether the criteria used by these committees fit qualitative research is a recurring theme. Sometimes denying access seems contrary to the best interests of the clients, whether students, patients, prisoners or others (Morse, 2005; Sque, 2000). Although no one denies that committees must be cautious in checking the credentials of the researcher and the ethical validity of the proposed research project, they do prevent others the right to decide for themselves whether or not to participate in scientific research. Morse (2005) adds that this often includes vulnerable groups or situations, such as trauma room patients or school children, but that these groups desperately need to be included in well-founded research. Well-designed qualitative research has inherent checks and balances that ensure participant protection (Koenig, Back & Crawley, 2003).

Sensitive topics

The interest in topics that are by nature sensitive heightens the need for ethical consideration in qualitative research. Qualitative researchers often have the desire to discuss topics that are of interest to them and they assume that the participants can talk, are willing to talk and dare to talk about these topics as well. But there are many topics that participants may not want to talk about because of their sensitive nature. What is permissible to ask in social research? And how do we deal with emotions and stress experienced by both participants and researchers? These questions take us back into the ethical domain again.

First, the nature of sensitive topics needs to be examined. According to Lee (1993), sensitive research topics commonly pose a threat. He distinguishes three broad areas in which research can be threatening: 1. Private, stressful or sacred issues, 2. Deviance and social control, and 3. Vested interests of powerful persons. I will explain these three areas with an illustration from the *Harry Potter* books (Rowling, 2008). I will start with a brief description of Lord Voldemort, one of the characters in these books:

> Lord Voldemort killed Harry's parents when he was about one year old and attempted to kill Harry as well. But mysteriously his attack on Harry was foiled, leaving Harry with a lightning-bolt scar on his forehead, and Voldemort lost nearly all of his power. He has been in hiding for the rest of Harry's life, slowly rebuilding his powers to someday return and finally destroy Harry. Nearly everyone in the wizard world is extremely afraid of Lord Voldemort and will not even utter his name for fear that it may give him strength to return. Lord Voldemort's nicknames therefore are: He-who-shall-not-be-named, You-know-who and Dark Lord.

The first sphere in which a research can pose an intrusive threat is by dealing with subjects that are private, stressful or sacred. If we were able to interview Harry Potter, the character of Voldemort would be an example of such a subject. The assassination of Harry's parents is a deeply held private experience. He rarely speaks about it, not even with his best friends, because it induces stress. It hurts him. At the same time the Dark Lord is very powerful, and a certain secrecy surrounds him.

Second, sensitivity relates to the study of deviance and social control and holds the possibility that information may be revealed which is stigmatizing or incriminating in some way. Harry Potter has a visual stigma: the scar on his head. As the only child of famous and powerful wizards he is perceived as special and there are several people who constantly watch over him to protect him. Others doubt his identity or are jealous of his status. Revealing any more personal information about himself, his family or his friends may damage Harry.

And third, research is often problematic when it impinges on political alignments, and refers to the vested interests of powerful persons or institutions, or the exercise of coercion or domination. Harry is seen as the only one who might be able to defeat Voldemort. Talking about the subject is sensitive in this respect as well. Since Harry has engaged the enemy in battle, more or less unintentionally, he has to be careful about sharing with others what he is up to. He does not know who can be trusted and who is against him.

Back to the non-wizard world. We already came across all three meanings of sensitivity when using examples earlier in this book, including teenage mothers, binge drinking and offending youth, and hooliganism at football clubs. Although all three meanings can arise, in this book we will predominantly refer to the emotionally charged element of dealing with private experiences when we talk about sensitive topics.

Balancing risk and benefits for participants

When defining 'sensitive' as posing a threat, we refer to the risk that some harm, loss or damage may occur (Sieber, 1992). But how exactly can harm be inflicted on participants, when no intrusive, physical treatment takes place, neither while observing or interviewing the participants nor while analysing texts? On the other hand, how can participation in research be beneficial? In this section we will first look at risks in qualitative research, and then at the benefits.

Risk in qualitative research

Dragging it all up

Talking about a sensitive life event, like loss, can be painful and emotionally charging. This can lead people to refrain from taking part in a research. They find the thought of a stranger enquiring about a personal event offensive and they do not want to communicate about it and drag it all up again (Sque, 2000). It is often thought that people who cannot tolerate talking about a topic will simply not do so. They will not consent to the interview, sometimes by directly refusing, by not finding a convenient time or just not turning up for an interview. Participants also protect themselves by circumventing or omitting answers to certain questions (Hutchinson, Wilson & Skodol Wilson, 1994). So basically this risk has to do with raking up emotions and possibly causing psychological harm. Who takes care of the interviewee's well-being once an interview is completed and the researcher has withdrawn from the situation?

Exploitation

Exploitation refers to research that will not produce meaningful results and needlessly exposes participants to risk and inconvenience. To avoid exploitation it is required that research will improve the well-being of people or will increase knowledge. In most research designs the researchers have more power than the participants because they have more knowledge. When this power is misused, it can lead to exploitation. In participatory research models participants are given a more equal role, for instance as interviewers or analysts. Power arrangements among participants are then expressly monitored by the investigator so that the research does not become exploitative (Khanlou & Peter, 2005; Maxwell, 2004). However, the high level of engagement usually required in participatory designs involves other risks, like disappointment and intense levels of emotion and disclosure.

With our data collection methods – sometimes literally our cameras – we invade arenas that are intended to offer a haven to people during times of vulnerability. Although we pay less attention in this book to video, photographs and to visual reporting, we do have to be very careful when using visual materials. Kendrick and Costello (2000) warn us against adopting a voyeuristic gaze, which means that the audience is allowed to gaze covertly and anonymously at a 'private spectacle'. They give the example of a documentary about the experiences of student nurses. It showed a student nurse bathing a naked woman with dementia. The observers did not know anything about this woman other than her name, which reinforced her insignificance: the object that was once a human subject now played a minor part in displaying and conveying the experience of a student nurse.

Reflection on the purpose of what we are producing can protect us in making the right decision. In the above-mentioned programme the purpose was to learn from the experience of the nurse, and therefore the patient did not need to be exposed like this. Patients who are part of the experience need not be dehumanized. Not only do we have to be careful to leave voyeuristic examples out of visual materials, but out of written materials as well, such as quotes and examples. Research material is not written to entertain, so we must take care not to exploit sensational scenarios. The use of theory offers protection. Theory guides what is relevant and what needs to be shown. Theory can also turn a series of 'snapshots' into more general categories and draw a veil over the individual exposure.

Coercion

As stated before, informed consent is essential to ensure that participants offer their free and non-coerced willingness to participate. Consent for vulnerable groups brings an extra risk factor. Vulnerability comes in many forms (Sieber, 1992):

- those whose lives are visible or public
- those lacking resources or autonomy
- those who are scapegoats or targets of prejudice
- those who are weakened or institutionalized
- those who cannot speak for themselves
- those engaged in illegal activities, and
- those damaged by the revelations of research participants (e.g., family members).

These groups sometimes may not understand their rights or may not be entirely capable of exercising their right to refuse to participate in research when asked by someone of apparent authority. The researcher can resolve this problem by appointing an advocate for the research subject in addition to obtaining the subject's assent. For example, children cannot legally consent to participate in research without the permission of a parent.

Sanctions

Research participants must be assured through informed consent that their identities will remain confidential. There is a danger that the institution or community in which the study took place may be recognized. And in a small, tight-knit group, others may find out what a particular informant has said. There is a potential threat to participants if personal or stigmatizing information can be ascribed to them and then held against them. This also accounts for dyads, like couples (Forbat & Henderson, 2003). When involved in participatory research, maintaining confidentiality is difficult since researchers are required to report the findings to other participants to decide on any further action that might need to be taken, hence participants might disagree with each other.

When gatekeepers, i.e. professionals, are responsible for referring candidates for the research, other issues come into play. Candidates may feel pressure to accept participating in the study to avoid compromising their personal situation. In addition, candidates may be afraid that negative feedback and critical remarks during the study can lead to retaliations if confidentiality is not safeguarded. Researchers themselves may also feel pressure to report problems to the professionals (Johnson & Macleod Clarke, 2003).

Benefits of participation

Feeling relieved

Many participants acknowledge feeling better after having participated in a qualitative research project. Talking about one's experiences can be therapeutic and helpful. Talking is seen as a way of letting off steam. In a qualitative interview, participants are allowed to tell the whole story to an attentive listener and this can provide a sense of relief (Hutchinson et al., 1994). Talking makes experiences real and helps in processing them. Interviewees are encouraged to reflect upon events, and talking about them may illuminate issues that help them to make sense of their past and present experiences (Sque, 2000).

Being a worthwhile participant

The overall experience of being a research participant is often evaluated positively (Cook & Bosley, 1995). Realizing that your opinion counts, and that it matters what you think or feel, does people good. Interviews give voice to the participants, which may be particularly meaningful for members of discredited groups, such as substance users, the chronically ill and the imprisoned (Hutchinson et al.,

1994). Feeling that you are heard can contribute to self-empowerment and regained self-worth, especially in persons who have never been allowed to tell their story.

Helping others

Participants can be motivated to join the research if they believe that their experiences may help others. Participation in research gives people the opportunity to contribute to discussions, such as bereaved persons in a discussion of ethics in grief and bereavement research (Cook & Bosley, 1995). The participants' motivation is often to educate and support others going through the same experience, helping professionals, informing the wider public and stimulating open discussion (Cook & Bosley, 1995).

Benefits in institutional research

Institutions participating in research might consider it as a way to improve their services or environment, for example, schools, neighbourhoods, clinics or workplaces. Improvement comes from either 'an actual intervention, staff development, improved morale, insight into problems that need to be solved, collection of data that can be useful for policy-making or political purposes, development of new opportunities and relationships with powerful outsiders, prestige, and new abilities to serve community members' (Sieber, 1992: 102).

Sieber acknowledges that the term 'risk–benefit assessment' is misleading. There is no ratio computed, since most risks and benefits cannot be quantified, are not even known in advance and cannot be weighed against each other. How should we weigh a valuable publication against participants' distress? Or useful information for policy-making against violation of confidentiality agreed upon with informants? Actions that result in benefit for some may occasionally harm others. When writing the research proposal it may be useful to create a list of all who have interests in the research and a list of all possible benefits and threats. Addressing these threats to ensure that potential harm is minimized is of utmost importance. It is entirely the researcher's responsibility to address all these aspects, which can cause quite a bit of mental stress (for further guidelines see: Sieber, 2008; Kavanaugh & Ayres, 1998).

Researcher's stress

Undertaking qualitative research can be stressful to the researcher as well. Five concerns were reported by researchers who were all engaged in sensitive research: inexperience and lack of training, confidentiality, role conflict, impact of the interviews on participants and feelings of isolation (Johnson & Macleod Clarke, 2003). Issues that follow from the effects of research on the participants have been dealt with, therefore we will now focus on the three aspects that directly pertain to the researcher, namely inexperience and lack of training, role conflict and isolation.

Researchers may need a period of preparation to allow them to feel confident in their skills at obtaining information and helping the interviewees in interview situations, should this become necessary. Researchers have reported experiencing anxiety in making the first contact with potential participants and not knowing what to say or to expect (Johnson & Macleod Clarke, 2003). Although it is common for field workers to feel anxiety about dealing with an unknown field, adequate preparation can increase self-confidence and lower the stress somewhat. There are many good books about gaining access to the field, and in anthropological books especially, attention is paid to the many aspects of field work.

Uncertainty often pertains to how researchers need to behave around participants who need help, irrespective of the kind of help. Researchers might feel less nervous when they are well informed about the subject of the research and have prepared themselves to answer questions or give information on where to find adequate support or websites. It is important to follow the procedures below should an informant describe problems requiring intervention. Before beginning the study, investigators should identify a plan that includes referral to an agency or provider that could be available for information should the need arise. This information should be included in informed consent documents, as is sometimes required by ethical committees.

Role conflict mainly deals with choosing the role to play during data collection. For example, will you be a researcher or a caregiver, an interviewer or a friend? Especially professionals – dieticians, counsellors, nurses, teachers, managers – who embark on field work often have conflicting emotions about their two roles: as a researcher they aim to gather information, as a service professional they wish to assist, advise or nurture the participant (Johnson & Macleod Clarke, 2003). At the same time, participants may continue to see them in their role as service professionals, which leads to expectations that are different from the researchers' interests.

Finally, a few words about feeling isolated. Researchers often invest a considerable amount of 'self' into a project, particularly if the research addresses a question about which the researcher has strong feelings. The researcher may encounter feelings of anxiety because of disappointment in the project or in the supervision received. One can even fear the failure of the project. And when working alone, this can be very upsetting. There are some particular considerations that affect the researcher who is involved in studies into sensitive topics. The known sad or upsetting nature of the work requires researchers and interviewers who are qualified to carry out such an investigation and sparring partners to talk to after working in the field (Harris & Huntington, 2001). In Chapter 7 we address how feelings associated with field work can be used in the analysis.

Ethical issues in analysis

Since all parts of research are related to each other, everything that we discussed above about ethics also pertains to the analysis stage of the research. However, it is difficult to disentangle exactly how ethical issues are impinging on the analysis of the data per se. For instance, if informed consent was in fact 'weak consent', then participants will probably be less willing to give detailed insights in their lives or they may even thwart data collection. When they are concerned about inequity of benefits and costs or do not trust your good intentions, this could lead to non-response and is likely to result in less data than planned. Lost responses as a result of distrust or feelings of injustice can never be recovered again. And unclaimed data will not produce results in the analysis stage of the research project. So being clear and specific on your ethical behaviour can increase the quality of your data.

Miles and Huberman (1994) mention competence boundaries. As we will see in the chapters to come, qualitative data analysis is demanding on the researcher's interpretive skills. Researchers should be willing to spend a substantial amount of time on the analysis, and if novice or inexperienced they should be confident knowing where to find help, supervision or training. Unanalysed data or incorrect interpretations that give way to erroneous findings could potentially harm the different stakeholders.

Analyses can lead to information and understandings that may be difficult for the researchers to deal with from ethical and personal standpoints. Therefore, they must be aware that they cannot base their conclusions on selective interpretation and that they must not disregard counterevidence (Haverkamp, 2005). As a researcher into long-term post-abortion experiences, Hess (2006) acknowledged her pro-life position. She could have had a tendency to reflect negatively on long-term effects and interpret the data in a prejudiced way. A research committee was chosen whose members had different opinions on abortion to keep Hess from representing a pro-life argument irrespective of the data.

Using a certain theoretical perspective to interpret your data can evoke a field of tension between the judging interpretations and the rapport developed while in the field (Hoskins & Stoltz, 2005; Snow, 1980). Imagine interviewing overweight people who give you a detailed account of the various desperate attempts they have made to lose weight and how they were unsuccessful each and every time. You may depict them as people who easily give up and who cannot take their lives in their own hands if you have the psychological theory on self-regulation in mind when analysing these stories. This could result in the participants taking your analysis as offensive. The challenge lies in the ability to 'hold an analytic perspective, while remaining empathically attuned to the ways participants make sense of their lives' (Hoskins & Stoltz, 2005: 99).

Another ethical issue stemming from the interpretation of the data is dealing with the different accounts and perspectives on your subject of interest. For example, when interviewing dyads, like employer and employee or teacher and pupil, you come to prioritize one participant's perspective over another. This can originate from your theoretical perspective or purpose of social change. But it can also (unintentionally) flow from personal commitment to a participant or a possible chemistry that exists between the researcher and one of the participants. Forbat and Henderson (2003) reflected on these issues when they felt stuck in the middle, between the accounts of carers and cared-for persons. The potential for taking sides pinpointed the need to ensure that information from one party was not expressed to the other. It is on the basis of this complicated work that the authors concluded that there are no easy or quick-fix solutions for ethical issues and that each research project brings its own potential hazards that the researcher has to deal with.

Readings I learnt much from

Emanuel, E.J., Wendler, D. & Grady, C. (2000). What makes clinical research ethical? *Journal of the American Medical Association*, 283(20): 2701–2711.
Kleinman, S. & Copp, M. (1993). *Emotions and fieldwork*. London: Sage.
Sieber, J.E. (1992). *Planning ethically responsible research. A guide for students and internal review boards*. Newbury Park, CA: Sage.

Other resources

- *Professional guidelines* on ethics can be found in abundance. Some useful websites are American Psychological Association (www.apa.org), the American Sociological Association (www.asanet.org) and the American Anthropological Association (www.aaanet.org) – look for ethical guidelines and the code of ethics. See also the Statement of Ethical Practice on the British Sociological Association website (www.britsoc.co.uk) under the heading of equality. The International Sociological Association website (www.isa-sociology.org) has a Code of Ethics.
- *Guidelines for ethical committees* can also easily be found on the Internet. Searching on 'IRB application' will give several links to IRB forms, the consent process, and guidance stemming from various American universities. You can also visit the National Research Ethics Service in the United Kingdom (www.nres.npsa.nhs.uk) and look for 'Applying for Ethical Review'.

Doing your own qualitative research project

Step 3: Reflecting on ethical research

1. Research can be considered sensitive in at least three ways. Reflect on your topic and determine if it is to be considered a sensitive topic in one or more of these ways. What implications does this have with regard to ethical behaviour, for example, informed consent, confidentiality and reciprocity?
2. Look for information on the ethical review committees in your country. See if you can get an application form and practise completing one. Ask yourself what will be of importance for the committee. If an ethical review committee is involved in your research project, what is/was of importance for the committee? Do you agree with the committee that this is a real issue of concern to your

participants? If so, do you feel competent to manage these issues while conducting the research? If not, can you still obtain adequate training to become competent to carry out your research, and will your supervisor (or team members) be available to help you?

3. Run through the various issues raised in this chapter and anticipate any relevant problems that you have not yet identified while constructing the research proposal.

4. Think about the project from your perspective as a researcher and detect whether there is anything in the research project that may bother you from an ethical point of view. Try to find someone in whom you can confide and, if necessary, use to let off steam during the project.

5. Think of the parties involved in your research, such as participants, institutions, funders, science and society. Then try to list the benefits for each party, like knowledge, material resources, training, esteem, empowerment or success. Create a list of any possible dangers and risks for each of the parties involved. As a thinking model, creating such an overview may make you aware of the ethical issues in the project.

4
DATA COLLECTION

When browsing qualitative research literature it seems that almost anything that holds human experience can be used as data, whether texts such as interview transcripts, documents, diaries, letters, and notes taken during focus groups or visuals such as video-recordings, photographs, drawings and paintings. When we use already existing sources that have not been solicited by the researcher, we simply take the information as provided in the documents, and may include reflection on its quality. However, when we attempt to collect new data for our research projects, the demands of systematic and valid data collection are imperative. And although some of our data collection methods resemble daily activities, such as conversations or taking part in an event, researchers need skills and experience to produce good quality data. During analysis you are dependent on your data to make sense of your research subject, so quality of the data is imperative.

LEARNING AIMS

By the end of this chapter, you will be able to:

- Expand on the meaning of the word 'data' in qualitative research
- Understand the essence of the data collection methods most often used in qualitative research
- Reflect on strengths and weaknesses of different data collection methods
- Choose an appropriate data collection method in a specific research situation
- Develop a topic list and know how to use it
- Discuss the different uses of methodological, observational and theoretical memos
- Write memos
- List several advantages of video and audio recording during data collection
- Control the transcription of raw data in terms of content and anonymity
- Store data in the best possible way and prepare the data for analysis in a specific project

Data

In qualitative research, there are many ways in which data may be collected. Researchers can use verbal material from daily life, such as chat-sessions and advertisements. Social scientists can also request organizations or individuals to make their correspondence such as letters, minutes, e-mails and records available for study. In addition to these unsolicited sources, researchers may specifically ask participants to produce material, for instance to keep a diary, write a paper, take photographs or make a video. It can also be decided to conduct interviews or focus groups and invite people to participate in them. Likewise, researchers can request permission to observe and take part in the daily lives of the people they study. Which method is preferred depends on the research questions and the project's purposes – what the researcher wants to know and why – and the practical possibilities and limitations.

The above-mentioned activities result in data. Considered as empirical data are stories told by participants, quotes, observations by the researcher, photographs, case descriptions and so on (Sandelowski & Barroso, 2002a). Data are necessary in empirical research to give evidence or justification for everything you present later on as your findings, such as descriptions, new ideas, relationships between subjects, interpretations and explanations. The stance taken in this book is that qualitative data reflect people's experiences of daily life and that by studying these data social scientists are able to understand aspects of the social world.

However, qualitative data are not exact representations of life experiences. There are two reasons for this. First of all, solicited qualitative data are the result of an inter-action between the participant and the researcher in one way or another. In the interaction the full picture may not be revealed, for instance participants leave things out, they omit certain actions and sometimes present themselves in a way they wish to be perceived. In other words, data are produced in a specific context with a specific aim, and this will colour them in some way.

A second reason that data are not similar to the experience itself is that data depend on the participants' ability to reflectively distinguish aspects of their own thoughts, ideas, observations and experiences and to effectively communicate what they perceive through language (Polkinghorne, 2005). Telling someone about an excellent dinner party at a friend's house is not the same as that person actually tasting the delicious food and enjoying the company. In other words, people do not know everything about themselves, they do not want to share everything, and they are not capable of putting everything into words. With these limitations in mind, we use mainly textual data in our qualitative inquiries.

This chapter concentrates on solicited data that are produced and collected by researchers within the scope of their research. Many research activities that apply to interview transcriptions, such as data management and data analysis, can be used for other materials as well, though they are not necessarily suited for visual data.

Qualitative data collection

In the following section, various data collection methods are discussed. It is not, however, a complete overview of everything you always wanted to know about data collection in qualitative research. Here we deal with data collection methods, because you need to know what is demanded of data that are appropriate for a qualitative analysis. In each of the following sections several publications are mentioned for further reading. The four methods that will be discussed are: participant observation, qualitative interviewing, focus groups and the production of visual material.

Participant observation

A definition of participant observation is:

> The process in which an investigator establishes and sustains a many-sided and relatively long-term relationship with a human association in its natural setting for the purpose of developing a scientific understanding of that association. (Lofland & Lofland, 1995: 18)

Participant observation is a classical research strategy in both cultural anthropology and sociology. It is an approach to research which takes place in everyday situations rather than in laboratory conditions. This is why the method is also known as 'field work'. Direct observation of the people under study is enabled by the researcher taking part in the participant's everyday life (Lofland & Lofland, 1995; Spradley, 1980; Schatzman & Strauss, 1973). Where participation was at first viewed as a means to observe, nowadays participation is considered essential in detecting meanings, feelings and experiences.

Participant observation is just one method of conducting qualitative research: to describe what happens, who or what are involved, when and where things happen, how they occur, and why things happen as they do from the point of view of the participants (Jorgensen, 1989). Although participant observation is useful for studying almost every aspect of human existence pertaining to human meanings and interactions from the insiders' perspective, such as organizational life, family relationships, rituals, changes and continuities, and social-cultural rules of conduct, it is particularly useful when (Jorgensen, 1989):

- little is known about the phenomenon
- views of insiders and outsiders are opposed or stereotyped
- the phenomenon is somehow hidden from the view of outsiders.

Horowitz (1995) chose participant observation as a method to examine a social welfare programme for teenage mothers (see Box 1.5). The three reasons mentioned above for choosing participant observation all seem to apply to her study. There was a scarcity of knowledge on teenage mothers from the perspective of the mothers themselves. Outsiders' views of teenage pregnancies were rather stereotyped in terms of education and race of the girls involved. An insider may be able to recognize that the girls could be responsible mothers too. The phenomenon of teenage mothers is not fully known as many girls may remain within their own family environment or relocate to a shelter where they remain unseen.

Participant observation is an umbrella term that covers several methods and techniques. The researcher observes people's activities, accompanies participants, takes part in their activities, reads documents, provides aid or does small jobs, and interviews participants (Delamont, 2004). The method is challenging for researchers as it taxes their social skills as well as their memories. A researcher continually selects, is insider and outsider at the same time, joins and observes, participates and takes notes. The researcher in effect has to become an accurate measuring instrument.

What is it that participant observers discern? Three elements can be distinguished (Spradley, 1980):

- *What people do*: cultural behaviour such as events and interactions.
- *What people know*: cultural knowledge and opinions.
- *What people create and use*: cultural artefacts such as art objects, clothing, buildings and tools, as well as symbolic marks.

Even when the field and the exact location of the research have been chosen, researchers will still have to determine what, where and how much of each of the various elements they will want to observe. Not everything can be observed. Sometimes researchers decide to be where the action is during their field work. Horowitz (1995), when working on the teenage mother programme, focussed on classes, staff meetings concerning the goals of the programme, and excursions with the participants. A possible pitfall of this tactic is that only unusual or extreme incidents are observed, while the mundane and taken-for-granted world is usually just as interesting.

Every field worker has to log observations and take notes (Lofland & Lofland, 1995; Schatzman & Strauss, 1973). Facts that can be directly obtained through the senses (How many people are present? What is the colour of their clothing? What language do they speak?) are easier to agree upon with others than experiential aspects (What is the atmosphere like? Were they having a misunderstanding? Did she react disappointedly?). The literature provides a lot of clues for the making of field notes, for example (Spradley, 1980):

- identification: who says what
- write everything down literally
- take concrete notes, not abstract ones (not 'then the lecturer intervened', but rather 'then the lecturer took the chalk and wrote on the blackboard that everyone should be quiet').

There is a continuum to be sketched with regard to the balance between participation and observation in the researcher's role. One could be more of a participant or more of an observer, and anything in between. Which roles researchers adopt depend on what they want to learn about the field and on what the field has to offer (Hammersley & Atkinson, 2007). The success of the role taken depends on the researcher being accepted by the people in the field. Relevant questions are whether the people under study are willing to share their experiences with the researcher, and whether the researcher can put himself or herself in their place. Horowitz (1995) wondered if she would be accepted by the mainly-black staff and teenage mothers, and if she, being an elderly woman of Jewish descent, would identify with both groups.

How researchers should behave in the field and what a solid research relationship entails is bound to the ethical standards that we touched upon in Chapter 3. Overt performance and honesty about the intentions towards the researched is preferable to covert action. Field workers get their data by being admitted to the situation they want to study and, once there, in persuading people to let them stay. Many settings have a gatekeeper who imposes rules on those who want to study there. Gatekeepers, like school principals, nursing home directors or social workers in a teenage mother programme, know how the target population thinks, behaves and, importantly, how to live according to the rules. Therefore they have the power to help researchers understand and establish relationships within the research population. They also have the power to negotiate conditions that are acceptable to those they serve (Sieber, 1992).

Gaining entrance and building and maintaining trust with participants is one of the key issues in participant observation. But so is leaving the field. Simply stated, it is time to leave when the studied area has become uneventful, when theoretical saturation is attained (see Chapter 6) and when researchers feel confident about their knowledge of the subject (Snow, 1980). Leaving the field means that relationships are ended entirely, or at least become less intense, and this might be felt as a loss of grown friendships by the researcher as well as by the researched. It also means that researchers have completed data collection and are now faced with the challenge of writing the definitive version of their understanding of the people they studied. The ending of relationships on the one hand and the writing on the other hand can give rise to researcher's doubts, including some of the ethical issues mentioned at the end of the previous chapter, namely: Is harm prevented and is my message credible?

The qualitative interview

In interviews the researcher is the main instrument, just as in participant observation. There is extensive literature available on the topic of interviewing (for example, Kvale, 2008; Seidman, 2006; Rubin & Rubin, 2004; Gubrium & Holstein, 2002; Weiss, 1994; McCracken, 1988). A definition of an interview is:

> ... a form of conversation in which one person – the interviewer – restricts oneself to posing questions concerning behaviours, ideas, attitudes, and experiences with regard to social phenomena, to one or more others – the participants or interviewees – who mainly limit themselves to providing answers to these questions. (Maso, 1987: 63)

As is clear from the definition, a qualitative interview takes place in a reciprocal relationship. Interviews provide an opportunity for researchers to learn about social life through the perspective, experience and language of those living it. Participants are given the opportunity to share their story, pass on their knowledge, and provide their own perspective on a range of topics (Hesse-Biber & Leavy, 2006). A conversation, any conversation, is made easier when both conversational partners get along. This is referred to as 'rapport' in qualitative terminology, and holds that both partners have a genuine interest in the asking, answering and listening during an interview. Rapport is sometimes confused with liking each other, but it is possible to establish rapport and seriously work on the interview without liking or sympathizing with each other.

Interviews can be distinguished from one another by their predetermined structure. The more the interview is planned beforehand, the more the interviewer determines the direction of the interview. Alternatively, the more open the interview is, the more the interviewee can determine the contents and flow. A preliminary structure determines:

- which questions will be posed
- the formulation of the questions posed
- the sequence in which questions will be posed
- the answering options for the participants.

Since qualitative researchers are often looking for a true understanding of what is happening, the interviews are usually not entirely pre-structured with respect to content, formulation, sequence and answers. Neither are they left entirely open. Rather, thorough preparation results in a list of topics and/or questions to be asked at some point in the interview (see 'Instruments used' in this chapter). This type of interview is known as a 'semi-structured' or 'half-structured' interview. When the four components are at least in part dependent on the course and situation of each individual interview, we refer to it as an 'open' or 'qualitative' interview (Weiss, 1994). The different types of interviews are shown in Figure 4.1.

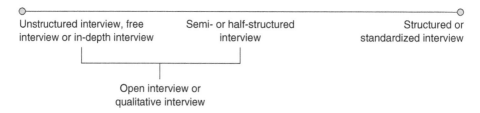

FIGURE 4.1   INTERVIEWS DISTINGUISHED BY THE EXTENT OF PRE-STRUCTURING (WEISS, 1994)

Interviews can also be categorized on the basis of their content and/or target group. For example, the term 'topic interview' means that the interview will encompass only one subject of interest. In comparison, the life-history or life-story interview makes one's entire life history the topic of inquiry. The term 'elite interview' is used when high-ranking or well-known people are interviewed, and the term 'expert interview' is reserved for interviews with informants who have expertise on a certain subject (Gubrium & Holstein, 2002).

Like participant observation, interviewing is a demanding enterprise for researchers, as they have to decide on the spot which questions to ask, how to formulate them and in which order they should be posed. Later on, an interviewer immediately evaluates whether the answer provided by the participant is sufficient, or if further enquiry is warranted (Gorden, 1980). If it is, additional considerations include what the best reaction of the interviewer is and what it may yield in terms of information. 'Probing' refers to verbal or non-verbal behaviour of the interviewer when the interviewee's reply to the question is not relevant, clear or complete, and can consist of posing questions, keeping silent or giving non-specified encouragement ('uh', 'yes', 'yeah') (Gorden, 1980). Sometimes probes are distinguished from prompts, the latter referring to issues that the interviewer wants to direct attention to (Ritchie & Lewis, 2003).

Matthews (2005) states that researchers do not ask questions to elicit answers to specific questions but rather to make it possible for participants to talk about something in their own words. I will not go as far as Matthews, but in essence her remark is right: the goal of an interview is to see a slice of the social world from the informant's perspective and the interviewer is merely facilitating the process. Interviewees are invited to share their ideas and opinions and may do so to a large extent on their own conditions. The interviewer facilitates the process of remembering and articulating, and shows respect for what the interviewee has to say. Detailed and rich information is mostly obtained in a conversation in which both partners genuinely enjoy participating and feel respected by the other person. It is the interviewer who is mostly responsible for creating trust and openness. As mentioned in Chapter 3, ethical aspects need to be considered and the interviewer must balance research aims with each participant's individual interest.

Crucial for a successful interview is that the questions fit the interviewee's frame of reference. One aspect of this is that the questions match the research topic exactly as it was introduced by the interviewer and to which the participant has agreed to participate. Both conversational partners then know more or less what the interview will be about. Another aspect of fit is that the topic needs to be of concern to the participant and the questions need to be posed in a language that is understandable. During the interview it is paramount that the interviewer to some degree accommodates the participant's need to spend more time on certain issues, listens with interest, and does not interrupt the flow. Jumping from one question to another, irrespective of what has been said before, is detrimental to the interview (Morse & Field, 1996). A calm, attentive interviewer can achieve wonders.

Focus groups

Qualitative interviews with more participants at a time are referred to as group interviews. Focus groups represent a specific set of group interviews that particularly emphasize the interactive patterns among group members and how they come to generate mutual understandings and ideas (Duggleby, 2005; Morgan, 1997). A definition is given below:

> A focus group is a group interview – centred on a specific topic ('focus') and facilitated and co-ordinated by a moderator or facilitator – which seeks to generate primarily qualitative data, by capitalising on the interaction that occurs within the group setting. (Sim, 1998: 346)

Focus groups use interviewing techniques with discussion taking place under the guidance of a moderator (Gibson, 2007). Tasks and activities can be employed as well, like drawings, role-play and vignettes. An assistant moderator usually does not actively take part in the discussion, but takes notes, observes group interactions and supervises recording equipment. Group size should be tailored to trigger lively discussion and at the same time allow everyone to participate. A number of six to ten will usually do, but depends on the participants and the subject of interest. Regarding group composition, homogeneity is often preferred for instance on gender, ethnicity or 'with' or 'without' a certain experience. Recruitment, sampling and scheduling of focus groups can be quite demanding, since a number of people are required to show up on a certain date at a certain place and 'no-shows' are a well-known phenomenon (Gibson, 2007).

Focus groups are an excellent way to collect data on group norms and to find out what is (and is not) expressed in a group context (Kitzinger, 1994). Referring again to Harry Potter: while in the wizard society at large 'he-who-must-not-be-named' was still a taboo topic, Harry, Hermione and Ron did mention his name as a strategy to break the spell (Rowling, 2008). In the research context certain groups may consider talking about a particular topic as offensive. This should be taken into account during any enquiry related to this topic and the questions or approach adjusted accordingly. Focus groups may also be used when the communication and construction of certain knowledge is the main interest of research. Focus groups show us in situ how people determine and/or change their point of view in terms of sources, arguments and evidence.

When data collection takes place in a group, ethical reflection is necessary on two counts. First, the disclosures by participants are to group members as well as to the researchers. Second, there will be a level of stress and distress as a consequence of group discussion taking place (Gibson, 2007). For the benefit of the moderator and participants alike, the moderator should prepare how to monitor stress levels and how to manage such a situation if one arises (Gibson, 2007).

With respect to the quality of the data, the strengths and weaknesses of focus groups must be taken into account. Group discussions can elicit rich, experiential information if managed sensitively, and participants can feel good about sharing their experiences. Conversely, if participants feel that their point of view is not respected, they could become upset or angry (Carey & Smith, 1994). Everyday forms of communication such as anecdotes and jokes tell us something about what people 'know', and this is what differentiates focus groups from individual interviews, which tend to be more formal (Kitzinger, 1994).

However, censoring and conforming can take place. Censoring means that the dominant norm of the group is not to mention or talk about a certain topic or to express a certain view on it. Conforming means that people agree with the dominant opinion of the group, sometimes even going further in voicing their own opinions (Sim, 1998). An example of this might be feeling strongly that perpetrators should have a fair trial, that they should be punished or imprisoned, that they should have life long sentences or be hanged.

Since the information elicited is very much a function of each group interaction, the group interaction data should be taken into account when analysing the data (Carey, 1995) (see Chapter 7). Group interaction data reflect the interactive patterns within focus groups (Duggleby, 2005). They show us which subjects the participants agree or disagree on, and which subjects they prefer not to talk about at all. The transcripts show the verbal elements of focus group interaction data as to how people verbally settle issues, share experiences, construct an argument, and which arguments and speakers weigh more than others. Another source of interaction data are observations documented in field notes. The assistant moderator can note non-verbal behaviour (nodding, applause, frowning, raising hands for turn-taking and so on) as well as linguistic and atmospheric elements, like a heated discussion, talking at the same time, talking loudly and so forth. These notes can be connected to the verbal exchange on the recordings.

Sometimes focus group data are considered to be of less value than individual interview data: the contribution of its members consists of what they chose to share in a particular group; therefore it is unlikely that in another mix of group members the exact same information would be collected (Carey, 1995). Remember that this is exactly why focus groups are organized: it is because we want to simulate how a group progresses when brought together. This stems from the assumption that people in general do not develop their opinions and views in a vacuum but operate in groups all the time. A focus group is a social setting and therefore the data may be a better reflection of 'reality' than data collected in a non-social setting (Carey & Smith, 1994).

Visual data

Visual data refer to the recording, analysis and communication of social life through photographs, film and video (Harper, 2007). There is a distinction between extant visual images that have not been produced for the research and research-generated visuals that have been produced by the researchers or at their request (Bryman, 2008). Here we focus on research-generated visual data. In anthropology photographs have been used to capture cultural phenomena and illustrate and explain cultural events. In sociology the accent has long been on documentaries showing work, social class, social problems, urbanization and so on. The sociologists were attracted by the involvement of the documentary makers with the subjects and the insider's knowledge they showed (Harper, 2007).

The quality of scientific research using visuals as data is of concern. With manipulation of images by software packages being so easy, one aspect of the debate is whether the picture is 'true' in the sense that it is a real image of reality at that moment. The photographer can arrange a scene and leave things out if preferred. However, it is widely acknowledged that pictures are merely productions of the photographer who operated the camera. Therefore a photograph can offer only a partial view on reality and cannot be considered an unmediated visual report.

The generation of visual material can be used as a stand-alone method. The choice of this method is most useful when observing spaces, places, the environment and objects. The same applies when photography or video is used to collect data on, for example, everyday life of community members, like video-taping a playground in a school for the deaf to learn about hearing-impaired culture (Alexander, 2008). Visual materials can also be used in combination with other methods to generate data, for instance when photographs are showed to a participant in an interview or a film to members of a focus group. Participants are then asked to comment on the images. These methods are commonly referred to as 'photo-elicitation' interviews (Collier, 2001).

People can be interviewed on the basis of extant photographs or photographs taken by the researcher. Schwartz (1989) took thousands of pictures in a rural community and catalogued them herself. She presented a selection of pictures to members of different generations to examine how they interpreted certain scenes and changes in the village. She also found out that visibly taking pictures in the streets brought her into contact with most of the villagers, which made later contact easier. In market research, photo-elicitation is a well-known technique to examine associations that people are not explicitly aware of themselves, like the ideas and emotions that are connected to a certain brand of products, such as shoes, watches or perfumes.

A different application of visuals is when the participants are asked to take their own photos to be used later as interview stimuli. The use of this method can reveal for instance the world from a child's point of view, from that of a person with a mental or physical disability or from the perspective of someone who has difficulty verbalizing. Pictures can be analysed for their content as well as for the meanings of the images and the reason they have been taken (Radley & Taylor, 2003). This method was used by Clark-Ibáñez (2007) when studying inner-city childhood in South Central Los Angeles. She gave the children who participated in her research disposable cameras to take pictures of the people and the things that were most important to them. They took photos of friends, family members, doll collections, trophies, fan books, refrigerators, computers, trees, kittens and so on.

Clark-Ibáñez found that there was nothing inherently interesting about the photographs and that they did not necessarily represent reality. More importantly, the photographs acted as a medium of communication between researcher and participant and added a lot to the conventional interview. They eased the relationship between researcher and interviewee and lessened some of the awkwardness of interviews by providing a photo to focus on. Photo-elicitation interviews became an excellent method to engage young children as well as their families. All viewers joining the discussion had their own perspectives and realities about the details in the photos.

Photos taken by the participants empower them to raise issues that would otherwise not have been addressed, and as such draw out meaning that would otherwise not have been found. An example is a student in the study of Clark-Ibáñez (2007) who photographed a tree across the street that she could see but could never really touch. For her the tree symbolized her confinement to the house, which she was unable to leave due to being an illegal immigrant. The photos illuminated viewers' lives and experiences. Photographer interviewees can point interviewers to elements in the picture that they would otherwise have overlooked.

Needless to say, the use of visuals is bound to ethical behaviour as described in Chapter 3. Consent is required when creating visual materials in private locations, and although it is allowed in public settings such as zoos and airports, people may still find it obtrusive and could object. When using images in presentations and publications, agreements must be reached about the availability or display of the photographs with regard to the anonymity of others. The use of photographs carries potential problems that researchers must be aware of. Clark-Ibáñez (2007) communicated that the children involved were the first to view the photographs in order to give them the opportunity to take out any 'mistakes'. Photographs can show intimate and delicate scenes of home life that would otherwise not have been seen, which should raise awareness of confidentiality in the researcher's mind.

Instruments used

This part of the chapter focuses on the instrument used during qualitative interviews. Different terms are used, such as conversation guide, interview guide, interview schedule or topic list, that reflect the somewhat fuzzy nature of the instrument and its application. To develop a measuring instrument, the research questions are converted into topics which may be raised in the interview and into questions which may be posed (Mason, 2002). Hence, the topics and the questions will correspond with the main research questions. The development of a topic list involves linking the research questions to the topics and vice versa, checking the legitimacy of every single question on the topic list.

When most of the topics have been decided, the next step is to group them into blocks of questions that belong together and to organize those blocks into a logical sequence that will facilitate the participant as much as possible. Thinking in blocks of questions is useful, since the interviewer can introduce the blocks with a lead-in question to the interviewees. The blocks are reflected in the layout of the instrument as well. Nonetheless, this order should not be imposed on the participant. The interviewer should be prepared to use the instrument in a flexible way and to pose the questions in an entirely different sequence if necessary.

Topic lists may take different shapes. Some researchers use long, relatively structured lists, whereas others settle for short, bulleted enumerations of relevant topics.

The main goal is to make the list a useful instrument for you as an interviewer. The development of an adequate interview instrument is part of the preparation stage of your research (see Chapter 2). Let's have a look at two examples. Box 4.1 displays one part of the topic list from research on medical students' perceptions on women in medicine and contains a comparison between male and female students (Lempp & Seale, 2006). These researchers use an hour-glass model: they start with a general question (any gender differences), then further detail (training experiences, medical specialities, respect) and then broaden again (future of women in medicine). Notice that the questions are accompanied by bullets for further probing.

BOX 4.1   EXAMPLE OF A FLESHED OUT THEME ON A TOPIC LIST

Women in medicine

- in your experience are there still any gender differences within the medical pro-fession?, i.e. are the training experiences of female medical students different from male medical students during the studies? (can you give examples, how, why?) (or, are students treated equally during the training?)
- do you think that women are more suited to certain kinds of medical speciali-ties than men? (which/why?)
- do you feel respected as a medical student in the class room/clinical setting (by patients, other professionals, doctors?)
- if no, why not, can you describe what happens?
- if yes, can you describe what happened? (or have you been humiliated/best or worst learning experience?)
- in your opinion, what are the likely scenarios for the future of women in medicine?
- finally, in relation to the issues discussed, is there anything else you want to add or you think is important which should be included in this study?

(Lempp & Seale, 2006: 7)

A different example comes from Lee and Kim (2007), who explore government per-ceptions on information systems/information technology (IS/IT). They distinguish three blocks of interesting areas, namely basic demographics and organizational details, current status of IS/IT in the department, and IS/IT planning and manage-ment. To explore the current status of IS/IT in the department, they generated the questions and topics given in Box 4.5. In contrast with the first example, these authors have a more structured instrument with fewer probes for examples and even some closed questions. It is possible that they have chosen this format to fit the tar-get population, being government employees with little time and therefore a need for clear and concise questioning.

BOX 4.2   EXAMPLE OF A PART OF A TOPIC LIST

Current status of IS/IT in the department

What is your opinion about the effectiveness of your current information systems in your agency?

Would you please tell us any major IS/IT that your agency is using in relation to the public service?

If the agency has implemented a major new information technology, answer the following questions.

We believe you have experienced changes triggered by this new information technology.

What do you think is the impact of information technology?

Does it ever influence your organizational structure?

Does it change the contents or procedures of your workers' tasks? If so, how?

(Lee & Kim, 2007: 138)

Always prepare a clear and engaging introduction to your interview. If you are a bit tense about the interview, it will help you when the introduction does not need much thinking. Introduce yourself as well as your research. You must thank the interviewees for participating and probably for welcoming you in their homes. Remember that you must ask for permission to record the session, and point out to interviewees that they may stop the interview if needed. It is useful to give an indication of the time that the interview will take and to ask whether the interviewee has this time available for you. Also very important is that you explain the intention of the interview. Interviewees are often accustomed to structured interviews and will expect a question and probably some answering categories. Do point out that you are interested in their opinions, experiences and ideas, and that it is their story that is of importance. Your questions only help to retrieve information. The question that you start with will therefore set the stage, and you should try to formulate it in the best possible way.

So how does the topic list function during interviewing? First of all, it reminds you of the topics and questions that matter. The topic list reduces the amount of instant improvisation and acts as a prompt if you lose track. Second, the instrument focuses data collection. Poorly prepared interviewers sometimes stray off focus and just ask what they think is appropriate. This will undoubtedly lead to missing data on areas of interest and a high level of unnecessary information (Morse & Field, 1996). Third, the experiences of previous interviews are processed in the emergent topic list. Questions that fall short are removed and missing questions added. Interviews conducted at the start of the research will therefore not be completely comparable to the last ones. And they should not, since at the end you will mainly ask questions to confirm your provisional ideas. Fourth, the instrument is a forerunner for what you are after and for what you think will be of interest later on. If you planned correctly at the beginning it will help you when structuring the analysis stage, although in qualitative research there will never be an exact match between questions prepared, answers given and ultimate findings.

Writing memos

Many relevant impressions, spontaneous ideas, evaluations, solutions and thoughts are often forgotten, because field work and analysis demand so much attention. It is therefore advisable to write memos or notes. Memos can function as a link between thinking and doing and they are comparable with the use of yellow Post-it notes. Memos form a kind of project log: a chronological overview of the decisions made and how they guided future actions of the researchers. Memos are useful for monitoring the development of the research project, asserting quality of the research (see Chapter 9), writing the report (see Chapter 10) and discussing progression in a team of researchers.

In the literature several types of memos or notes are distinguished, for instance between observational memos, methodological memos and theoretical memos (Schatzman & Strauss, 1973). Observational memos are also known as field notes. The researcher uses them to describe observations made in the field (see earlier in this chapter). Theoretical memos reflect how findings are derived from the data. As such, memos are pathways into your data that form an intermediate step between analysing the data – in particular coding – and the reporting phase (Hesse-Biber & Leavy, 2006). Methodological memos contain all thoughts relevant to the methods used.

Among others, methodological memos record the researcher's learning experiences during the research with regard to methodological issues. For instance, when several participants tend to ask you what you mean after asking the exact same question in the interview, a methodological memo can be used to record that the question should not be asked in this manner again and that the topic list must be adjusted. In this way memos have a special function in tracking the evolution of a research project. Memos can be used by independent experts, so-called auditors, who reflect upon the quality and thoroughness of decisions taken during the research (see Chapter 9).

Methodological memos can hold researchers' reflections on their own role during field work. This is useful when writing a methodological account and valuable for exchanging experiences within a team of researchers from different disciplines (see Chapter 9). When used in this way, the memos resemble a field-work journal in which the researcher reflects upon personal experiences and impressions pertaining to the research. These are sometimes thought to be invaluable when interpreting the data during analysis.

Memos are not often documented in research reports. Box 4.3 offers diverse examples of different types of memos. The first one is an illustration of an ethical issue that occurred during research into trauma patients' perspectives of their motor vehicle crashes. The second one is an example of a methodological memo in which the researcher reflects on conflicting feelings in a study into donor relatives. The last example is a theoretical memo from research into nursing home residents with dementia and their relationships with staff members, and contains some preliminary interpretations of observations.

BOX 4.3   EXAMPLES OF MEMOS

This informant indicated in the interview that she may have been trying to kill herself. I had to convey this information to her physician and ask for a psych consult. I couldn't believe that no one else had picked up on this. Her behavior was almost too blatant. I never thought I would run into this and I don't want to break the confidentiality of the researcher/informant relationship. I hope she understood when I told her why I had to discuss this with her physician. (Stinson Kidd, 1993: 324)

This was a very difficult interview to maintain the researcher's role and not to slide helter skelter into the nurse's role for the reasons of expressing my own anger at the poor caring skills employed by so many of the care professionals (...). (Sque, 2000: 29)

Quite a lot of residents on this ward experience grief. They cry because they want to go home. They ask for help to return home. The carers react to the grief by administering medication, verbally correcting the behaviour, and ignoring the behaviour entirely. These reactions are in accordance with the care plan. The grief is defined in various ways by the care givers: as fake, as unnecessary or as part of the disease. (Bosch, 1996: 52)

To fulfil the functions described above, memos need to be kept systematically and not in a haphazard way. Modern software for qualitative analysis offers possibilities to create memos and to link them to specific elements of a research project, such as documents, fragments of texts and codes. The use of computers is dealt with in more detail in Chapter 7.

Preparing data for analysis

In this chapter we dealt with some of the most used methods for data collection in qualitative research, namely participant observation, qualitative interviews, focus groups and visual aids. These methods produce, for example, field notes, cassette tapes, digital recordings, transcribed interviews, videotapes or transcripts, photographs, drawings and maps. As a consequence qualitative research is primarily text-based, which determines to a large extent the way in which analysis is conducted. Texts contain the natural language of those under investigation, and more often than not are detailed and unstructured. The unstructured character of the data is the result of only slight structuring at the outset, as was described earlier in the chapter. Topics deemed relevant for the research appear at different places in the research material and often use different terminology. One function of the analysis is to create structure to this disorder.

Data as they are originally generated are also known as 'raw' data. Getting these raw data ready for analysis requires preparation. Preparing the data is part of 'data management', a term which refers to the systematic, adequate storage and retrieval of data and of preliminary analyses. Proper data management contributes to transparency and facilitates the possibility for others to see what has transpired during investigation and analysis (McLellan, MacQueen & Neidig, 2003) (see Chapter 9). Four aspects of data preparation are addressed below.

One aspect of data preparation is the organization of the storage of different data files so that they can be easily retrieved. Most often the researcher will have more than one data source available during analysis, such as a file containing the researcher's observations, a log, digitally recorded interviews and photographs. The data in these various files are supplementary and the researcher uses all of them to comprehend the studied phenomenon. A neat archive will prevent many hours of searching for that one note or that particular quote or interview. Documentation is vital to research, will continually change and is dynamic in nature. Documenting analyses that have just been carried out and ordering researcher memos are very important as well (Miles & Huberman, 1994).

A second aspect of data preparation is the transcription of audio and visual sources. Image and sound recordings are usually transcribed so that the researcher may work with texts, sometimes in combination with the original recordings. Visual and audio recordings hold great advantages for the entire research (Chapter 9), and the analytical phase in particular, as recordings:

- benefit the quality of the data, as they allow the researcher to focus on the interview or observation without having to worry about taking notes.
- improve the quality of the data, as the researcher does not have to select what to take notes on and what not. Additionally, there is no distortion of the data resulting from this selection process.
- provide more of an insight in the subject under study because both the questions and the answers are registered, making it clear who is talking about a certain topic in response to a certain question.
- benefit the quality of the research as they enable discussion of the literal interviews or observations with peers, involving both the researcher's observation- and interview-techniques as well as interpretations of certain parts of the data.
- are considered to be an important guarantee of data quality and at the same time show the reviewer that the researchers care about quality.
- provide literal quotes that can be used in the final report for the readers to judge the relationship between the original data and the researcher's interpretations.

During the transcription of recordings, the data are altered. Non-verbal behaviour such as facial expression, posture, tone, rhythm and intonation is lost. The way in which the transcription is conducted depends on the goals of the research and of analysis in particular. In order to compensate for the loss of information, researchers can create elaborate memos, as discussed above, in which they describe impressions, observations and oddities. The memos play an important role in the depiction and interpretation of the data. However, the language-oriented types of research, such as conversation analysis and discourse analysis (see Chapter 1), require a different kind of transcription. In such an analysis, pauses, emphasis, alternation and so on have to be marked with a specifically designed transcription system. Transcription is dealt with in more detail in Chapter 10.

A third element of data preparation is taking out all information that can identify participants and violate the promise of confidentiality. This means that with a view to ethics as described in Chapter 3, the informants will not be identified on transcripts of interviews, notes or memos. The best method is to assign each participant or site a unique code number or pseudonym that will be used with all data. All names, places and other unique identifiers need to be taken out. This should be borne in mind when sharing the data with the participants in order for them to make accuracy checks.

A fourth and final part of data preparation is the manipulation of data that might be necessary for processing qualitative data analysis with the computer. Some programs need a few software-specific operations before the texts can be entered or imported and processed (Lewins & Silver, 2007). More and more data preparation including transcription is seen as a critical research activity which influences the analysis and the claims that a researcher intends to make (Forbat & Henderson, 2005). It is to analysis that we turn in the next chapter.

Readings I learnt much from

Gorden, R.L. (1980). *Interviewing: strategies, techniques and tactics*. Homewood, IL: Dorsey.

Lofland, J. & Lofland, L.H. (1995). *Analyzing social settings. A guide to qualitative observation and analysis*. Belmont, CA: Wadsworth.

Schatzman, L. & Strauss, A.L. (1973). *Field research: strategies for a natural sociology*. Englewood Cliffs, CA: Prentice-Hall.

Spradley, J.P. (1980). *Participant observation*. New York: Holt, Rinehart and Winston.

Doing your own qualitative research project

Step 4: Collecting your data

1. In your view, what is the best way to collect your data? When you have chosen a data collection method, try to elaborate on how you are going to use it in as much detail as you can. Think for instance about the introduction of your research, the instruments used, your role as an interviewer or observer, taking notes and storing the data.

2. Think about how you are going to introduce your project to the people you want to involve in your project. Assume that data collection takes place by means of interviewing, but many of the issues raised below are also applicable to other methods of data collection. Make a list of what you need to ask, what you need to inform them about and what promises to make. Practise (on a friend) before you contact real participants to discover unanticipated requests. Approach the participants as soon as you are ready, since getting access can lead to delays if not dealt with efficiently.

3. Prepare or adjust the topic list or observation scheme that will be used (see 'Instruments used' in this chapter). Pay attention to the introduction of your interview or visit to the field. Practise on a friend and adjust the list when necessary. This will take some time since the preparation of data collection is intensive.

4. Spend time on finding out what data management will mean for your project. What type of data will you collect? How should you store the data? Will audio and visual materials be transcribed, who is going to do that, and who will give instructions about transcription guidelines? Are you planning to use software for qualitative data analysis? Does the data need to be prepared for using this specific program?

5. Schedule some extra time after each round of data collection to write a memo with a brief summary, key findings and an evaluation of that day's session. This is extremely useful when working in a team of researchers as it enables you to catch up on each others' progress.

6. Reflect on the experience of the first round of data collection. Possible bottlenecks in recruitment become evident at this stage and solutions can be thought of. Weaknesses in your instruments can be rectified, such as questions that were not used, questions that need to be added, changing the sequence, and so on. Try to talk regularly with others about decisions and progress. Peer debriefing will sharpen your arguments, improve your interview and observation techniques, decrease potential bias and increase your self-confidence.

7. Record, for instance in memos, how data collection took place. This will help you to write your methods section in the final report. Think about the average time that an interview lasted, who conducted the interviews, where they took place, how many people would not cooperate and for what reasons. What can you say about the participants' responses to you as a researcher, why did they want to cooperate, what could have influenced the quality of the data, what have you learned during data collection?

8. When the interviews have been transcribed, check that the guidelines on editing and anonymity have been adhered to.

5
PRINCIPLES OF QUALITATIVE ANALYSIS

In the previous chapters, analysis was conceived as the processing of data in order to answer the research questions. Before explaining analysis in more depth, we first define it more precisely. Segmenting and reassembling are considered the chief activities of qualitative data analysis, and these are demonstrated with two examples. Then, having a better understanding of what data analysis entails, the general and more abstract principles underlying the qualitative analysis process are outlined, namely constant comparison, analytic induction and theoretical sensitivity. From these three principles follow the 'thinking' activities that social scientists are engaged in when segmenting and reassembling qualitative data. The three principles are incorporated into a vision on analysis that is further converted into a step-by-step model: the spiral of analysis. In the chapters to come the spiral of analysis is further explored in a practical sense; the 'doing' activities are added.

LEARNING AIMS

By the end of this chapter, you will be able to:

- Appreciate the importance of segmenting and reassembling in qualitative data analysis
- See how the need for segmenting flows logically from the use of flexible instruments
- Understand the meaning of the phrase 'the relationship between the data and the concepts is initially open'
- Differentiate between text segments, codes, categories and concepts
- Explain the principle of constant comparison and give an example
- Recognize the importance of analytical induction for the verification of propositions
- Expand on the meaning of theoretical sensitivity and its role in qualitative data analysis
- Reproduce the input and output of analytical activities in the spiral of analysis

What is analysis?

In the literature, several definitions of analysis can be found. One of them that relates to qualitative analysis reads:

> Analysis is a breaking up, separating, or disassembling of research materials into pieces, parts, elements, or units. With facts broken down into manageable pieces, the researcher sorts and sifts them, searching for types, classes, sequences, processes, patterns or wholes. The aim of this process is to assemble or reconstruct the data in a meaningful or comprehensible fashion. (Jorgensen, 1989: 107)

The emphasis in this definition is on two basic activities of qualitative data analysis, namely segmenting the data into parts and reassembling the parts again into a coherent whole. Reassembling refers to looking for patterns, searching for relationships between the distinguished parts, and finding explanations for what is observed. The aim of reassembling is to make sense of the data from a theoretical perspective.

Both activities, segmenting and reassembling, are carried out from the angle of the research questions and research purpose. Segmenting and assembling are only of use when they have relevancy to the research. The theoretical niche as reflected in the research questions and purposes determines what you will convey to others at the end of the research project as your most important findings and answers to your questions. This last element is stressed in the next definition of qualitative data analysis:

> Data analysis is the process of systematically searching and arranging the interview transcripts, field notes and other materials that you accumulate to increase your own understanding of them and to enable you to present what you have discovered to others. Analysis involves working with data, organizing them, breaking them into manageable units, synthesizing them, searching for patterns, discovering what is important and what is to be learned, and deciding what you will tell others. (Bogdan & Biklen, 1992: 153)

The emerging character of the analysis is not clear in either definition. Data are not mechanically separated and organized in predetermined categories; rather which categories are generated is mainly decided upon during the analysis process on the basis of what appears in the data. Sorting, naming and categorizing go hand in hand. Slowly but surely, the basic organizational blocks take shape in the analysis process. Likewise, the relationships between the basic blocks are generated during the analysis procedure based on the data, the interpretations of the data, and the preliminary categories. This view on analysis leads us to formulate the following definition:

> Qualitative analysis is the segmenting of data into relevant categories and the naming of these categories with codes while simultaneously generating the categories from the data. In the reassembling phase the categories are related to one another to generate theoretical understanding of the social phenomenon under study in terms of the research questions.

It is stressed throughout this chapter that qualitative data analysis consists of a stream of activities from segmenting the data to reassembling them, and that each of these activities has components of both thinking and doing. Key concepts are elaborated on as we go through the whole analytical process. In the next chapter the key concepts are addressed in detail.

Segmenting data

Researchers segment data in what are thought to be relevant and meaningful parts. Segmenting is also referred to as unfolding, unravelling, breaking up, separating, disassembling or fragmenting, and the process is followed by reassembly of the data. The parts are organized into categories or groups. This categorization is not a purely technical task, since the researcher constantly considers the bits and pieces of the data and interprets them. Pieces of data are compared in order to determine their similarities and differences and whether they should be grouped together or not.

Segmenting is considered to be the first modification of the data after data preparation (see Chapter 4). In disassembling the data it becomes clear what topics appear in the raw data. Topics of relevance can be found all throughout the data, and often multiple parts pertaining to the exact same theme are found in different places. This is a consequence of the use of open or semi-structured instruments (see Chapter 4), for interviewees do not usually give straightforward answers to the interviewer's questions. Moreover, it is quite common for participants to answer questions in a different order than the one deemed logical by the interviewer. Participants do not stick to the observation schedule of the field worker in their daily activities either.

Therefore, the texts – transcribed interviews, field notes, focus group reports – are more or less cut into pieces during analysis. Then the pieces that are believed to belong together are combined. This is illustrated with an article about mining: 'The men of the mine: retired miners descend into memory' (Heuts, 2004). The following extract was taken from an interview with Hans Klinkenberg, a former Dutch miner (73, lamp carrier, benchman, underground supervisor):

> '"Never go underground, son," my father said. "That's no life." My father literally worked himself to death. (...) But everyone wanted to go underground, because of the high wages. (...) The pupils who attended the OVS (a miners' school) and were not yet allowed to go underground did the dirtiest work. They worked the washing and sifting plants, where the stone had to be separated from the coal. You couldn't see your own hands because of the dust. Everyone had bronchitis, by the way. Black lung was supposedly unheard of back then. There were dusts masks. But because it was so hot underground you tended not to wear them more often than you did wear them. If you worked in a space 40 centimetres high, you were supposed to spray. But that meant you would end up mining with your belly in the mud. In hindsight, I was lucky. (...) When the mines began to close in the mid-sixties, many lost their jobs. (...) And the miners who found alternative employment were often unhappy. They missed the freedom and solidarity that ruled underground.'

In this interview we learn about the miners' wages (they were paid well) and about the nature of the job (filthy, full of risks and unhealthy). The ex-miner also talked about the risks that were taken in disregarding safety precautions. We also hear about the bond between the miners. In the following interview with Jan Hellebrand (68, hewer, blaster and foreman), we are given more information about these subjects, in slightly different words:

> 'Too many people died too soon. I'm glad the mines are closed. The camaraderie kept you going. You didn't talk about the bad things. It was a rotten job. The taste of salt remained in your mouth all day when you had had to drive a shaft through a 4-metre thick layer of salt. I never took bread with me as it was inedible because of the heat and dust. Just an orange. If the pumps failed, you ended up standing or lying up to your waist in water. And if there was a power failure in the mine, you knew that it would be full of gas. There were safety precautions, but sticking to them prevented you from achieving your maximum potential. We did piecework. The rotten thing about the mines, in hindsight, was that you were paid so well for working underground. That's why people literally worked themselves to death. It was very tempting to work extra shifts or double shifts. My father, his brothers: they all died from the dust. (...) I was banned from working on the coal front in 1983. A heart condition and problems with my lungs. I've spent months in convalescent homes. But it was too late. I had black lung and my arteries were clogged. And I always wore my dust mask. (...)'

The good wages for working in the mines return as a theme. But the other side of the coin is also mentioned: notice how a world of experience is hidden behind the expressions 'too many people died too soon', 'the rotten thing about the mines, in hindsight, was ...' and the fact that black lung occurred whether you obeyed the safety precautions or not. This interview also mentions the camaraderie again.

The interviews with Gerrit Duijkers (71, benchman, underground technical supervisor) and Rein Bettink (80, hewer, machinist) were also illuminating, though not reproduced in full here. If we focus on the theme of the 'atmosphere' among the miners, and cut and paste together all the pieces on this subject, the interviews teach us the following:

> 'And the miners who found alternative employment were often unhappy. They missed the freedom and solidarity that ruled underground.' (Klinkenberg)

> 'I'm glad the mines are closed. The camaraderie kept you going. You didn't talk about the bad things.' (Hellenbrand)

> 'It was a responsible job. We kept an eye on each other. When I went down the shaft on my own every weekend, to check the mine for gas, I had to phone up every half-hour. And you could see who was working below because their badges were missing. There was a great feeling of camaraderie, even when I became a supervisor. We got the job done together. From the hewing to the chattering, and washing each others backs under the shower. The comradeship was far-reaching.' (Duijkers)

> 'Working in the mines was not unpleasant. I was as strong as a lion. It was dangerous, but the atmosphere and the traditions made up for a lot.' (Bettink)

The different interviews are compared with each other, and the researcher decides that there are various fragments that relate to the same theme, even though the interviewees use different words to describe the theme (solidarity, camaraderie, comradeship, atmosphere, getting the job done together, keeping an eye on each other and so on). The information leads to the posing of new questions: What made the atmosphere so special? In what way was comradeship shown? Who felt bonded to whom, and to what extent did they experience this? How was the sense of belonging able to soften the negative impact of the work?

The process of naming fragments by giving them a summarizing label, such as 'atmosphere' or 'comradeship' in our example, is called coding. A label is called a code. This will be discussed in more detail later on in the current and following chapters.

The segmenting of data entails making distinctions between relevant fragments in the data. Fragments that the researcher believes should be put together are then sorted into meaningful groups. Groups or categories inductively emerge from the data and are then named or coded, although in a deductive approach to analysis, some categories may be decided upon a priori (see Chapter 6). It is up to the researcher to choose which codes are to be ascribed to which categories. Social theory is considered a chief source of inspiration here since it indicates interesting topics and relevant debates. By unfolding the data, researchers specify which building blocks their research contains, and they gradually gain an idea about the theoretical concepts that are needed to discuss the chosen field.

Reassembling data

Reassembling occurs as the analysis progresses. Reassembling of data is commonly described by a variety of terms, such as synthesizing, structuring, integrating, putting together, recombining and modelling. Before considering the relationships between the building blocks of the research, the building blocks themselves have to be fairly clear. Reassembly requires continuous consideration of the data, of the evolving relationships between the categories, and of the credibility of those relationships. The end result, possibly a coherent model or integrated explanation, serves as an in-depth view of the social phenomenon that is studied (see Chapter 8 on findings).

This process will be clarified using an example: research into the quality of nursing home care (Boeije, 1994). The purpose of this research was to determine how nursing home staff, consisting of nurses and aides, viewed the quality of care they supplied to the residents. Several aspects that the staff deemed important in the provision of care soon became clear during participant observation and from conversations. These aspects included giving the residents attention, stimulating the residents' independence, and maintaining their privacy (see Figure 5.1).

FIGURE 5.1   ASPECTS OF QUALITY OF CARE IN NURSING HOMES

Later in the study other aspects of care emerged which the staff felt were important, such as humane treatment, continuity and helpfulness. Statements, anecdotes,
examples, views, expressions and events that related to these themes were sought in
the observations and interviews. Text fragments stemming from field notes, interviews and documents were constantly compared to ensure that they dealt with
the same subject, and to determine in what way they differed from other subjects.
The themes were then all described and named (coded). Some codes were obvious
because team members used them in their everyday language. However, ultimately
the researcher classifies the themes and chooses the codes.

Each aspect of care could be illustrated with examples from everyday practice. For
example, continuity of care was described, on the basis of many remarks about the
subject, as the establishment of an enduring relationship between a resident and a
staff member. The more nurses know about a resident, the more they can personalize
the care they give. Furthermore, the care can result from the trust that people have
built up in one another over a longer period of time. Note that this description and
the interpretation are based upon the researcher's observations concerning continuity.
The researcher gives her interpretation of the nurses' perspective of continuity as an
aspect of quality care.

Throughout the research, one subject recurred when the researcher asked about
the background of the aspects deemed to be important for nursing home care. This
was the residents' self-worth. The nurses understood this to be how residents see
themselves, whether they perceive themselves to be worthy, and whether they feel
their lives are meaningful. The importance of this and other concepts were tested
each time a new nursing home was selected for research. Slowly but surely, a model
developed, which encompassed the various concepts. At this point, it was still unclear
where self-worth would fit in the preliminary theoretical model (see Figure 5.2).

The everyday aspects of care, such as giving attention, stimulating independence
and being helpful, became more pronounced as more data were obtained. These
aspects were observed by the researcher. For example, when a nurse was having a
conversation with a resident (giving attention), when team members encouraged residents to wash themselves rather than assisting them (stimulating independence), or
when nurses responded to requests for help as quickly as possible (helpfulness).
Nevertheless, in order to 'observe' these aspects, it was necessary for the researcher to
take a certain theoretical approach to viewing the daily practice of caring. The literature

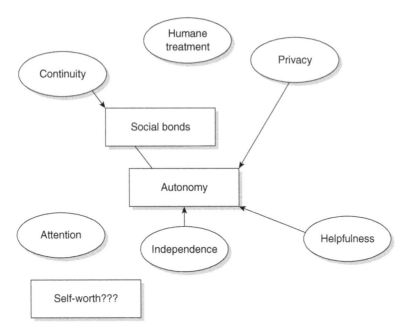

FIGURE 5.2   PRELIMINARY MODELLING OF ASPECTS OF QUALITY OF CARE IN NURSING HOMES

study is, of course, helpful in arriving at such a theoretical approach (see Chapter 2). The core conceptual elements must be noted during data collection and during data analysis; this is also known as 'theoretical sensitivity' (examined in more detail later in this chapter).

Other aspects also manifested themselves, namely autonomy, appearance and social contacts. These aspects could be linked to Western values concerning individuality and to existing theories, such as the theory on stigma and spoiled identity (Goffman, 1963). It became clear that these aspects were the bridge to the resident's self-worth, which became the core concept in the theoretical model (see Figure 5.3).

The relationship between, for example, continuity, social bonds and self-worth is demonstrated. Continuity in the staff on the wards of a nursing home contributes to the residents' social contacts. Staff must be prepared to make real contact with the residents, by listening to them and sometimes telling them something about themselves. Frequent changes in staff mean that residents have to bond again and again, something that not all residents are capable of doing due to their physical or psychological functioning. The fact that many residents only stay for a short while (usually because they pass away) makes staff members more reserved in their relationships with residents, as they regularly have to say goodbye to a resident. Despite these difficult circumstances, staff members think that social bonds are very important for residents. If they become isolated, the residents get the impression that no one cares about them anymore. This leads to a reduced self-worth, whereas the staff members regard it as their task to maintain self-worth.

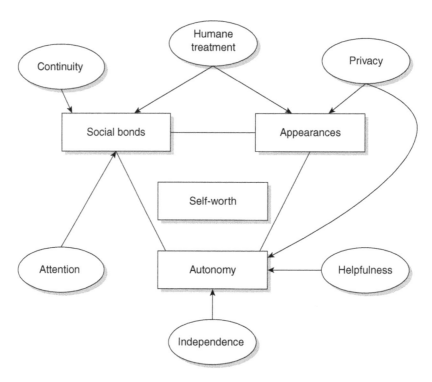

FIGURE 5.3   FINAL THEORETICAL MODEL OF QUALITY OF CARE IN NURSING HOMES

Once again, finding these links demands theoretical sensitivity on the part of the researcher. The choice for self-worth as a 'core concept' in the model is supported by data, arguments and the literature as well (see Chapters 6 and 7). The relationships between the different concepts in the model are based upon certain observations in the research. Subsequently, these observations were verified in the same research with observations of other nurses, other wards and other nursing homes. The researcher only reaches a decision about the core concept after many rounds of data collection and analysis, and after having given the subject a great deal of thought. It is quite feasible that another researcher would decide otherwise. Later on, the model was expanded to include the problems encountered by staff members when trying to realize the aspects of care that they deem important for quality care, and with the strategies the staff use to cope with these problems (Boeije, Nievaard & Casparie, 1997).

This example shows clearly why the analysis of qualitative data is considered to be so difficult. As Sandelowski (1995: 371) states, 'researchers must first *look at* their data in order to discern what to *look for* in their data.' The open research procedure described in Chapter 1 is not just applicable to data collection but also to data analysis. The word 'open', with regard to data analysis, means that a system of categories and concepts is created with the intention of gaining knowledge about the field of research and ultimately of answering the research questions. Prior to empirical data collection, theoretical concepts derived from the literature and results of previous research focus the researcher's lens (see Chapter 2), but the concepts that will come to play an actual role during the analysis and in the final results are not known in advance. In other words, the terminology that will be used in the findings to describe and explain the field of research is developed during the process of conducting the research. This is exactly what makes analysis so challenging: the relationship between the data and the concepts is initially open (Wester, 1995).

Three starting points

In the literature, three basic procedures are frequently used when qualitative data analysis is discussed: constant comparison, analytic induction and theoretical sensitivity. These three procedures need further explanation. They are starting points or principles as opposed to methods and techniques, which are more concrete and applicable. Methods and techniques are invaluable when doing research, and they are probably the reason why you decided to read this book. Nevertheless, it is important to understand the background and meaning of these three procedures, as they serve as a framework for understanding analytical methods.

Constant comparison

Constant comparison is the main component of the analytical process in the grounded theory approach (see Chapter 1). Constant comparison and theoretical selection, as described in Chapter 2, go hand in hand. Together they constitute the cornerstones of the research, as their purpose is to describe the variation that is found within a certain phenomenon, and wherever possible to indicate in which situations different variations of the phenomenon manifest themselves. The method of constant comparison arose from the idea that phenomena will manifest themselves in different ways when circumstances differ. It is thought that the circumstances of a specific manifestation can be found by systematically comparing the research material.

Every time new data have been gathered and data collection is temporarily halted so that the data can be analysed, new codes might be formulated, the content of an existing category might change, and new questions and propositions might arise about the relationships between the categories. All these outcomes can be considered interim products and results. These interim results are then tested in a new round of data collection, for which the cases studied are chosen strategically. By means of this process, new data collection provides the researcher with cases that are suitable for comparison. As well as being useful for testing, these comparison cases can also inspire the researcher to formulate new ideas, which can be incorporated in the research. This ongoing search for comparison cases goes on until no new insights are gained from them for the further development of the categories. This phase is called 'saturation' (see Chapters 2 and 6).

Constant comparison of data does not automatically lead to adequate descriptions of the field or to theory. The data do not 'speak for themselves' but the researcher plays an active role, whereby thinking, creativity, theoretical knowledge, knowledge of the field and combining the different elements are of chief importance. The literature offers very few guidelines to the researcher for constant comparison (Boeije, 2002). Wester (1995) is an exception, as he has developed the method of constant comparison into a strategy for qualitative research. The outcome of his approach of constant comparison of cases is an analytical framework – a theoretical model – that covers the field of research. His approach consists of four phases:

1. Exploration: the discovery of concepts
2. Specification: the development of the concepts
3. Reduction: determining the core concept
4. Integration: developing the final theory

In the exploration phase, researchers explore the field and try to depict it accurately in a number of codes. Parts of the same document are compared with one another, to ensure that fragments that the researcher thinks are about the same subject are given the same name or code. This applies equally to new documents: they are compared with each other at a fragmented level. An example in this chapter is the study on miners, in which fragments on 'comradeship' are assigned the same code.

In the specification phase, the researcher selects a number of key codes from all the codes that have been developed so far, and searches for differences and similarities in the fragments that have been awarded that code. So each code is reviewed, as well as the quotations to which it has been assigned. Based on the comparisons, the category represented by this key code can be developed further. Also in this phase the less important codes are subsumed under the key codes. Taking the example of the miners, this phase would involve developing a more detailed description of comradeship among the miners.

In the reduction phase, the goal of the analysis is to describe the core concept and the relationship this concept has with other concepts. At this stage documents are compared as a whole to provide information about the relationship between certain codes. For example, the researcher could ask each of the ex-miners whether he had experienced comradeship, and if so, to what extent and what it meant to him. Subsequently, it could be determined which factors had influenced that experience.

Finally, in the integration phase a theory is developed, and constant comparison is used to search for cases with which the theory is then tested. Furthermore, the cases are assessed to see whether they can be included in the theoretical framework, and if so where.

The highly abstract process of constant comparison can be clarified with the example in Box 5.1, which is an adjusted extract from *TopGear* in which different cars are described and compared (Master, 2007: 71–86). It is clear that the journalist does more than simply give a factual account of the cars. The goal of the magazine is to provide information, but above all a pleasurable reading experience. The author supplements the descriptions with all sorts of experiences, feelings and judgements. The text is a perfect example of the process of constant comparison in the exploration stage.

BOX 5.1 DRIVES

Volvo V7: Here's to a sequel that outclasses the original

There's a pal of mine who owns an old Volvo V70. And I've never really got it. OK, so the boot's huge, and it's comfortable and economical, but seriously, there were better estate cars out there when he bought his. This new V70, though. Well, that I could understand a bit more. Still not exactly my cup of tea, but I can see where it begins to make sense. (...) Equally, the ride is much better than the old version's. It's still not up to Mercedes' standards (acknowledged as the class best), but it doesn't feel as uncontrolled as it used to – over bumpy back roads, the new V70 feels more secure beneath you.

Mazda 2: Split personality

The new Mazda 2 is a great runabout in town, but get it on an M- , A- or B-road and suddenly it doesn't make sense anymore. Buy a Smart because you live in a city. Buy a Land Rover because you live up a muddy lane. Simple. But why buy a Mazda 2? You need to figure out exactly what sort of driving you'll be doing before you can answer this, because although the Mazda 2 comes with only two engine options, they're suited to entirely different things. (...) there's the 1.3 or the 1.5. Normally at TG [*TopGear*], we'd say don't even bother with the 1.3 because the 1.5 has more power and, therefore, is obviously the better one. But that's not the case with the Mazda 2, because the smaller engine offers up plenty. And if you do your driving in town it makes a lot more sense. (...) So the cheaper, fizzier 1.3 makes more sense. In an urban sort of way.

Toyota Land Cruiser: U.N.breakable

This is the new Toyota Land Cruiser V8 diesel. It costs a fiver short of £56k, and yet it looks about as sexy as a pair of wellies or a woolly hat. It is fully equipped with all the latest gadgetry and luxury car standards and yet is probably going to be bought by people who actually want to use it to drive across deserts, possibly while being sniped at by hostiles. This is a pretty confusing car. (...) You see, the United Nations have bought some 12,000 Toyota Land Cruisers over the years, and you'll invariably see one on any Middle-East crisis newscast (...) They

(Continued)

(Continued)

get painted Daz white, hammered to hell and back, and still the UN has an insatiable passion for this full-size SUV from Toyota. (...) Why? Because they never break; there's a reason why the outback is littered with the carcasses of old Land Rovers and not broken Toyotas. (...) That reputation is pure gold. It comes from a long history – the first Land Cruiser was in 1954, and it was pretty much the car that Toyota itself was founded on. Luckily, that proud heritage is kept right on in the new car, because when it comes to out-and-out reliability, off-road ability and manufacturing quality, the Land Cruiser is seriously good.

What does this comparison provide us? First of all, it provides descriptions. After reading the text, we know something about the cars. A description of just one car would have made far less of an impression than this description of several cars. The information increases because we compare it. 'Boring' is only significant when a 'colourful' or 'sexy' car is contrasted with it, and 'simple' has no meaning until it is contrasted with 'gadgetry and luxury'.

Second, the comparison provides a number of criteria with which the cars can be systematically compared with each other, such as their size, comfort, economics, radiation, security and usability. Which of these criteria would be important in a real social science research project on cars would depend on what the research question is addressing, for example, status and power, automobility or cars and emotions.

Third, the descriptions raise all sorts of questions, such as: Why are there so many different brands of cars produced? What are the main reasons for customers to choose a specific car? How do modern customers weigh automobility and pollution criteria with other criteria they find important, such as reputation and size? How are people, machines and spaces of mobility and dwelling connected? What are the social, material and affective dimensions of car cultures? What are car emotions? This may even lead to propositions, such as: 'In cultures of automobility, the inability to drive leads to feelings of social exclusion and disempowerment.' And believe it or not, emotions about cars have been the subject of serious scientific work (for instance, Sheller, 2004).

Analytic induction

Analytic induction is connected to the name of Florian Znaniecki, who first developed this principle in 1934. It can be interpreted as a search strategy: researchers try to find the best fitting theoretical structure for their research material (Bryman, 2008; Wester, 1995). The strategy can be used to develop a definition of a phenomenon. In that case, the researcher systematically determines which characteristics are present every time a phenomenon occurs. However, analytic induction is most commonly used to develop a theory about the causes of certain behaviour. With this goal in mind, hypotheses are continually tested on new material by explicitly searching for instances that do not support the hypotheses. Whenever such an inconsistent or deviant case is found, either the description of the phenomenon is changed in order to exclude the case (it does not fit the population that the researcher is going to draw conclusions about), or the hypothesis is restated (Hammersley & Atkinson, 2007).

Maso and Smaling (1998) have developed an application of analytic induction. In their opinion, this application is appropriate for research aimed at developing theories; in other words, research that is aiming for explanations. There are four phases to the application:

1. Incubation
2. Confrontation
3. Generation
4. Closure

In the incubation phase, a theoretical framework is developed based on the literature. This framework consists of concepts, propositions and hypotheses. A proposition, in this case, is an idea that is still so vague it cannot yet be formulated as a hypothesis. A hypothesis is a proposition that has been refined to a conditional statement, an 'if … then' relationship (Maso & Smaling, 1998). The theoretical framework includes propositions and hypotheses that pertain to the possible answers to the formulated research questions. The framework plays a central role in the remainder of the research process.

In the confrontation phase, the theoretical framework is pitted against the information that was derived from the observations immediately after the first round of data collection has been completed. The concepts, propositions and hypotheses of the theoretical framework are most important in this phase: they are modified, rejected, adapted and elaborated upon according to the results of the confrontation.

In the generation phase, the new material plays the leading role: new ideas and hypotheses are proposed as a result of the new material. These new propositions and questions are then also compared to other new material and so forth. This process aims particularly to find negative evidence; that is, evidence that does not support the propositions in order to gain more in-depth findings. The last two phases are then repeated again and again. In this way, preliminary outcomes are supplemented, corrected, clarified, rejected or confirmed.

In the closure phase, an initial answer to the research questions is formulated, and includes clear evidence of the source of the analysed data so that the value of this initial conclusion is clear. With this interpretation of analytic induction, Maso and Smaling (1998) demonstrate that a consistent application of these phases leads to a highly systematic research approach.

The following example demonstrates this approach. It is a student research into dyslexia and choice of education (Dam & Rooij, 2002). Dyslexia, formerly known as reading or word blindness, is a disability that is characterized by difficulties in transforming symbols into sounds and vice versa, and causes problems when reading and writing. The students assumed that linguistic competence is more important for arts and humanities courses than for the sciences. They formulated the proposition that students who know they are dyslectic will adapt their choice of education to match their affliction, and not choose a linguistic subject. Their research material showed that this proposition is largely correct. The choice of career is influenced by dyslexia, although it does not deter everyone from choosing an arts course.

Subsequently, the students formulated the proposition that dyslexia would be more of a hindrance for those following arts courses than those following science courses. They also posed the question 'How do people with dyslexia perform in their chosen arts studies?' It turned out that some of the interviewees had to quit their studies; others explained that the successful completion of their studies was due to pure determination. Based on these results, the students posited that dyslectic individuals have to possess a great deal of willpower or determination to complete their arts course. This proposition was then tested with a new round of data collection. The students also made a second proposition based on the original data, that successful completion of the studies would not only be dependent on the dyslectic individuals, but also on the cooperation and understanding of the environment where they studied, an example being the willingness of the institution to extend the length of examination time.

In arguing in this way, researchers gradually build a theoretical frame that fits the data and is tested in the subsequent rounds of data collection. Every time the initial frame is adjusted, so as to keep matching the newly found data and account for all relevant aspects involved.

Theoretical sensitivity

Theoretical sensitivity is a term that originated in the grounded theory approach. Strauss (1987: 21) describes it as 'sensitive to thinking about data in theoretical terms'. Theoretical sensitivity is the researcher's ability to develop creative ideas from research data, by viewing the data through a certain theoretical lens. Analysis requires an ability to interpret research data, and to derive ideas and themes from them. The word 'theoretical' indicates an ambition not merely to describe but also to theorize. A code is not just a name for a category; it has to lead to a meaningful interpretation of the data. To name categories accurately, insight is required into the research area, current research issues, the common explanations for phenomena, and the theoretical models that are usually used. Armed with this knowledge, a researcher can look at the data properly, in other words, with theoretical sensitivity or theoretically charged.

Glaser and Strauss have had a heated debate about this issue. Glaser attaches great importance to the researcher's theoretical sensitivity in the analysis of gathered data which he believes to be attained through immersion in the data (Glaser, 1978). He has developed a large number of models or moulds, which he called 'coding families', to stimulate the researcher's thinking. These coding families are intended for use by researchers who want to reassemble and organize their data. Strauss and Corbin (2007) propagated the use of a single mould, which they called the 'coding paradigm' and which they claimed is suitable for all data. The mould consists of several parts, namely conditions, context, interactions/strategies and consequences. These four elements should be sought for in the data. Strauss and Corbin attempt to provide the researcher with tools for structuring the data, but Glaser contends they do so at the expense of the richness of the data and the researcher's talent. In his opinion, the application of Strauss and Corbin's mould leads to forced modelling (forcing), as

opposed to the approach by which relevant categories arise as a result of the interaction between the data set and the researcher (emerging).

A stepwise approach: the spiral of analysis

In the preceding sections, the principles of qualitative analysis have been presented,
as well as several phased applications of these principles. All efforts are directed at
transformation of the raw data into findings (see Chapter 8). The list below consol-
idates these views and approaches for starting a qualitative data analysis:

- A thorough review of literature and social theory precedes the empirical part of a
  qualitative research project. The literature determines the researcher's niche or field
  of study, contributes to the formulation of research questions and purposes, and
  supplies suitable concepts that function as spotlights in the research process, often
  referred to as sensitizing concepts (see Chapter 2). A literature review may result in
  the formulation of a skeletal framework that guides the research process. Knowledge
  of the literature heightens the theoretical sensitivity of the researcher.
- The approach to analysis that we will be using is based upon the principle of constant
  comparison as developed in the grounded theory approach and the stages devised by
  Wester (1995). Many researchers regard constant comparison to be the researcher's
  most important mental activity, in both more descriptive and explanatory research.
  Constant comparison is inevitably linked to an approach in which data collection
  and data analysis are alternated. During phased data collection, the researcher looks
  for cases for comparison that can deepen the preliminary analyses.
- Coding is seen as the most important aid in conducting an analysis. Coding is used
  to segment and reassemble the data. Researchers can make use of the considerable
  body of literature that is available on coding as well as the experience that has been
  gained with coding in research practice.
- For a research project to be successful, structuring of the analytical process is
  crucial. The application of analytical induction to test propositions is a systematic
  approach. A qualitative research process does not have a linear course; it is more cyclical
  in nature and sampling, data collection and data analysis proceed simultaneously. Since
  this can be quite difficult and confusing, a step-by-step approach is needed.
- Analysis forces the researcher to engage in two activities: thinking and doing.
  Doing stimulates thinking, and vice versa. The researcher has to *do* a lot of things
  for the findings to 'emerge' from the data, such as reading, searching, interpreting,
  writing, conferring, coding and drawing. As well as doing things, researchers have
  to *think* a lot about the data and what they mean. Categorizing data, devising
  codes and discovering links between the categories can be brain-racking.

These five starting points are joined to develop a way of structuring the analysis,
called 'the spiral of analysis'. In Chapter 1 an overview was given of the qualitative
research process (Figure 1.1). The role of qualitative data analysis was not explored,
but now the spiral of analysis can be integrated to form Figure 5.4. The diagram runs
from the bottom upward.

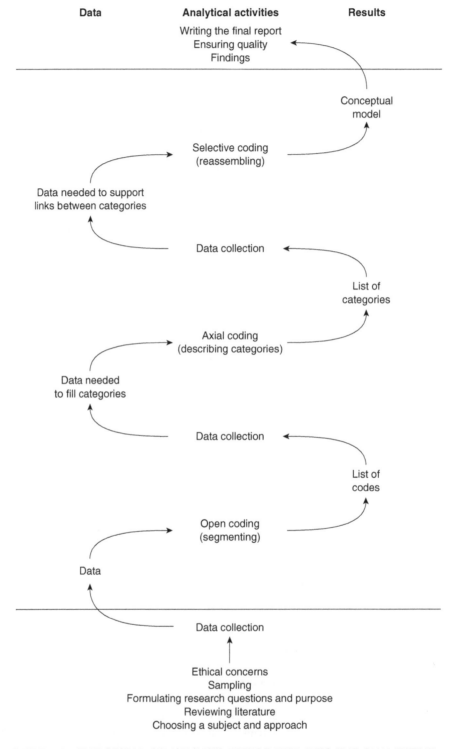

FIGURE 5.4   THE SPIRAL OF ANALYSIS INTEGRATED INTO THE QUALITATIVE RESEARCH PROCESS

The left-hand side of the diagram shows the role of data in the analysis, which is considered the input of the analysis. The middle column contains the analytical activities of the researcher. The right-hand side describes the output of the analysis, that is, the interim results of the research. Three types of coding are distinguished within analysis: open, axial and selective coding. In order to show that data collection and data analysis are alternated, the former has been added to the activities column. The diagram shows three separate rounds of data collection. There may be more or less, depending on the project. The spiral of analysis is the basis for Chapter 6, in which each analytical step of the model will be covered separately. In Chapter 7 we turn to integrative procedures that mainly serve to support the phase of selective coding and to the support that software packages can provide.

Readings I learnt much from

Glaser, B.G. & Strauss, A.L. (1967). *The discovery of grounded theory: strategies for qualitative research*. Chicago, IL: Aldine.
Maso, I. & Smaling, A. (1998). *Kwalitatief onderzoek. Theorie en praktijk* [Qualitative research: theory and practice]. Amsterdam: Boom.
Wester, F. (1995). *Strategieën voor kwalitatief onderzoek* [Strategies for qualitative research]. Muiderberg: Coutinho.

Doing your own qualitative research project

Step 5: Reflecting upon the nature of qualitative analysis

1. How would you have approached your textual (and possibly visual) materials if you did not know about coding? Do you think coding is a kind of natural way of proceeding with textual data, and if not, are your own ideas worth putting into practice?
2. Have you planned for a more inductive or a more deductive approach to data analysis? Is it clear what your concepts are derived from, and have you planned for an analysis that fits your starting point in relation to the literature review?
3. If you have not yet written a section on how you plan to analyse the data, attempt to do so now. Answer questions such as: Are you going to use software, and for what purposes? How will you assure quality of your analysis? Are there any concepts that you will use? How are you planning for the interchange between data collection and data analysis? Writing about the analysis before you actually engage in it is difficult, but give it a try because it will help you to be in touch with the analysis practice later on.
4. In some projects, a complex data set is generated; for example, because interviews are conducted with groups holding different opinions; because different cases are involved; or because observations are repeated at different time intervals. Try to

anticipate the amount and complexity of the data set by planning for comparisons between the different parts that make up your data.

5. Perhaps you have formulated propositions or conjectures based on the literature review, conversations with experts in the field or a pilot study. Write them down and monitor whether they remain relevant or lose importance, whether they can be answered, and whether the answers in turn lead to new questions and conjectures.

6
DOING QUALITATIVE ANALYSIS

Qualitative analysis entails segmenting and reassembling the data in the light of the problem statement. But how does a researcher approach analysis in a concrete project? Where to start? How is coding done? How can creativity be preserved when using 'routine' procedures such as open, axial and selective coding? How routine are these procedures anyway? How to proceed and remain in control when using software for qualitative data analysis? The spiral of analysis (Figure 5.4) is the foundation for the methods and techniques discussed in this chapter. We start with open coding and axial coding as means to break up the data into smaller parts, and then proceed to selective coding which facilitates reassembly of the data. At the end of the chapter we look back at what we have been doing by transforming the data through coding.

LEARNING AIMS

By the end of this chapter, you will be able to:

- Describe the functions of open, axial and selective coding
- Position the three types of coding in the spiral of analysis
- Employ open, axial and selective coding in a small- or moderate-scale research project
- Identify different sources of codes
- Appreciate the comparison of codes assigned by different researchers
- List the four elements of the coding paradigm
- Recognize a core category in your own research
- Focus the analysis based on the relevant criteria
- Detect possible sources of bias during analysis
- Argue how alternating data collection, analysis and sampling support exploration and verification

Introduction to coding

Analysis consists of segmenting the data and reassembling them with the aim of transforming the data into findings. Findings can consist of descriptions that are more or less theoretical as well as interpretive explanations of the research subject (see Chapter 8). Findings of qualitative research always include interpretations of the empirical data. It is a mistake to consider raw data as findings. In the analysis phase of the research project data are sorted, named, categorized and connected, and all these activities entail interpretation. When you interpret someone's words or actions, you explain what you think it means and how you think it should be understood. Jorgensen summarizes the analytical process as follows:

> The analysis of qualitative data is dialectical: data are disassembled into elements and components; these materials are examined for patterns and relationships, sometimes in connection to ideas derived from literature, existing theories, or hunches that have emerged during fieldwork or perhaps simply commonsense suspicions. With an idea in hand, the data are reassembled, providing an interpretation or explanation of a question or particular problem; this synthesis is then evaluated and critically examined; it may be accepted or rejected entirely or with modifications; and, not uncommonly, this process then is repeated to test further the emergent theoretical conception, expand its generality, or otherwise examine its usefulness. (Jorgensen, 1989: 111)

Interpretive analysis is shaped in many different ways, but we can distinguish two types of analyses: one is oriented towards the themes or categories present in the data, and the other is oriented towards the cases, such as organizations, activities, events, situations or participants. As with many other terms in qualitative research, several different terms are used to describe the two categories: some refer to code-based and case-based analysis (Lee & Fielding, 2004), or cross-case analysis and within-case analysis (Merriam, 1998), while others refer to cross-sectional or categorical indexing and non-cross-sectional indexing (Mason, 2002), or to issue-focused and case-focused analysis (Weiss, 1994), and variable-oriented and case-oriented analysis (Miles & Huberman, 1994).

The start of many, if not all, of these types of analyses comes down to coding. Why? Because everyone has to start with reading the data and then separating the data into meaningful parts. The latter is, in essence, what we know as coding. Coding was developed as a technique in the grounded theory approach, and has been increasingly refined since (see Chapter 1). At first the data may appear to be a bulky, diverse collection of accounts, but coding is a tool with which to create order. In this book coding is presented as the most important tool for qualitative data analysis. The three types of coding that are distinguished, namely open, axial and selective coding, will finally lead to the production of the definitive findings.

Segmenting and reassembling (see Chapter 5) occur largely through the coding process. Charmaz (2006) understands coding to be the process of defining what the data describes. In more detail she conceives it as:

Coding means categorizing segments of data with a short name that simultaneously summarizes and accounts for each piece of data. Your codes show how you select, separate, and sort data to begin an analytic accounting of them. [...] Coding is the first step in moving beyond concrete statements in the data to making analytic interpretations. We aim to make an interpretative rendering that begins with coding and illuminates studied life. (Charmaz, 2006: 43)

When coding, the researcher distinguishes themes or categories in the research data and names them by attributing a code. A code is a label that depicts the core topic of a segment. While coding, a researcher is looking for descriptions and sometimes for theoretical statements that go beyond the concrete observations in the specific sample. Charmaz, cited above, refers to coding as part of constructing a grounded theory. In that case special demands are made on codes because they need to be developed into concepts that together will constitute a theory. However, not all research, and consequently not all analyses and coding sessions, have to lead to a grounded theory. Lewins and Silver offer a much more pragmatic definition of coding:

Qualitative coding is the process by which segments of data are identified as relating to, or being an example of, a more general idea, instance, theme or category. Segments of data from across the whole dataset are placed together in order to be retrieved together at a later stage. (2007: 81)

In this case a code may 'represent a deeply theoretical or analytical concept; it could be completely practical or descriptive; or it could simply represent "interesting stuff" or "data I need to think about more"' (Lewins & Silver, 2007: 83). Bear in mind the different uses of coding and codes while conducting your own project or reading someone else's.

Since the use of different terms in qualitative analysis can be quite confusing, frequently used terms as they are applied in this book are described in Box 6.1. They will be further elaborated on throughout this chapter.

BOX 6.1   IMPORTANT TERMS IN QUALITATIVE ANALYSIS

Analytic:	Conceptual – expressed in concepts – or theoretical
Category:	A group or cluster used to sort parts of the data during analysis and designated with a code
Code:	A word or string of words used as a name for a category generated during analysis
Concept:	A term referring to a category and used as a building block in a theory
Interpretation:	An explanation of the meaning of what is observed in empirical data
Pattern:	An orderly sequence consisting of a number of repeated or complementary elements
Theme:	The matter with which the data are mainly concerned
Theory:	A coherent framework that attempts to describe, understand and explain aspects of social life

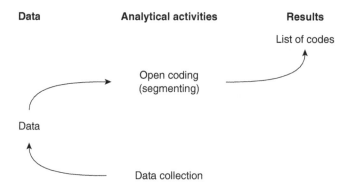

FIGURE 6.1   THE SPIRAL OF ANALYSIS ENLARGED: OPEN CODING

Strauss and Corbin (2007) distinguish three types of coding: open coding, axial coding and selective coding. These three types are expanded on in the following sections. Each section starts with the position of the type of coding in the spiral of analysis. Subsequently, details and frequently asked questions are addressed.

Open coding

Open coding is the process of 'breaking down, examining, comparing, conceptualizing and categorizing data' (Strauss & Corbin, 2007: 61). This means that all data that have been collected up to that point are read very carefully and divided into fragments. The fragments are compared among each other, grouped into categories dealing with the same subject, and labelled with a code. Open coding usually takes place at the beginning of the research project and starts during the collection of the first round of data. Little to no selection is made in terms of relevance of the research material, because it is still largely unpredictable what will be of value and what will not.

A code is a summarizing phrase for a piece of text which expresses the meaning of the fragment. It is by codes that fragments can be compared and filed. 'Qualitative codes take segments of data apart, name them in concise terms, and propose an analytic handle to develop abstract ideas for interpreting each segment of data.' (Charmaz, 2006: 45). Coding can be performed with paper and pencil, writing codes in the margin of a text, but coding can also be employed with the available computer programs. In Table 6.1 an example of open coding is provided from a student research project on dyslexia and choice of study and employment (Dam & Rooij, 2002). It concerns an interview with a male nurse who is dyslexic.

Exploration of the data by open coding constitutes the start of conceptualization of the field of research. Codes provide an analytic handle on the data. Open coding encourages a thematic approach since it forces the analyst to break up the text into pieces, to compare them and to assign them to groups that address the same theme. Open coding contributes to a clear organization of the data as well, since it results in an indexing system that fits the researcher's

TABLE 6.1   EXAMPLE OF OPEN CODING OF AN INTERVIEW WITH A PERSON WITH DYSLEXIA

Code	Interview transcript
	I: How did working as a psychiatric nurse work out for you?
Falling short	P: Especially in psychiatry I fell short, because I was asked to make analyses, in other words reports and behaviour along with it, and I really fell short. I obtained my diploma as a psy-
Importance of language	chiatric nurse, and then I moved on as this area was not the
Choosing a career	right choice for me.
	I: Because you ran into problems with reporting you have moved on to something else?
	P: Yes. I did continue to work in nursing, but in general nursing
Career change	instead. Reporting is also important there, but less so.
Job match	I: If you would be given the choice, regardless of aspects of language, what would you like to do most?
Preferred job	P: I felt most comfortable working on the ambulances.
	I: What was the role of language there?
Importance of language	P: It was again very important, but the forms had a specified format, reporting had to be accurate and very brief and it was not that important. I do remember that I did okay as long as I kept my sentences short. And that was enough for the
Aids	ambulance-world. I also had to transfer everything orally, but that was not a problem for me.
	I: But if you had not finished your report on time, how did colleagues respond to that?
	P: Well, it was not a matter of finishing, but I made more spelling
Flaws	errors, and the sentences were illogical. But they thought I didn't know better. The first time they mark it with a red pencil, but
Convey message	then they just read over it, because they know what the essence is, what is meant. [...]
Discovering dyslexia	I: I: How did you find out you were dyslectic?
Reading exercises	P: I never knew I was dyslectic until I had to write those reports. I used to visit the library three to four times a week. I've read many books, into the middle of the night. That has probably
Choosing a career	saved me and it has enabled me to choose this career.
	I: How has this been as you've aged?
	P: I have stopped reading, and I fill out the forms in short sentences,
Indifference	and occasionally there is a spelling error, but that washes over my broad back. I do not care at all. If it is really important, I have
Aids	it checked or use the spell-checker on the computer. But I must admit that since I stopped paid employment, I am increasingly
Reduced writing skills	wondering how some things need to be written.
	I: I wonder to what extent you experience your dyslexia as a handicap?
Experiencing no handicap	P: I haven't really experienced it as a handicap. I was just worse at language than others, but other than that it didn't matter. As a nurse, I was just as good as the others. I have never noticed
Equality	anyone looking down at me for making so many mistakes in my language. I have to add that as an ambulance nurse you have
Job match	your own responsibilities and you report to a superior and not to your colleagues. If I read a booklet, the sentence structure is completely strange to me. That is all I notice about my dyslexia,
Unaffected life	but it does not really affect my life. It's a society of reporting, reading and writing, and that is a society which badly needs
Languaged society	language and is very fast-paced.

Source: Dam & Rooij, 2002

analytical needs. A code enables the easy retrieval of the fragments that have been assigned a specific code.

The process of open coding involves the following steps:

1. Read the whole document.
2. Re-read the text line by line and determine the beginning and end of a fragment.
3. Determine why this fragment is a meaningful whole (text which belongs together and deals with mainly one subject).
4. Judge whether the fragment is relevant to the research.
5. Make up an appropriate name for the fragment, i.e. a code.
6. Assign this code to the text fragment.
7. Read the entire document and code all relevant fragments.
8. Compare the different fragments, because it is likely that multiple fragments in a text address the same topic and they should therefore receive the same code.

FAQ 1

Q: Can coding be done using a computer?
A: Yes, that is certainly possible and there are several advantages in using a software package designed for qualitative data analysis. Some researchers prefer using paper and pencil, others use their word processing program, but software packages for qualitative data analysis are becoming more readily available. When using a computer program for qualitative analysis, the researcher goes through the same steps as when coding manually, but the steps are automated instead. Any number of codes can be assigned to a single segment of text of any size, and to overlapping or embedded segments as well. Software also offers opportunities that are not really possible without a computer, or at least not with the speed of a computer, such as code searches, matrices or frequencies of codes (see Chapter 7).

The result of open coding is a list of codes, also referred to as a 'coding scheme'. Within a software program codes can be listed or organized in different ways. There are non-hierarchical and hierarchical coding schemes, in which higher-level codes can contain sub-codes. The codes can be sorted alphabetically or in an order determined by the researcher. When indicating a hierarchical structure of a coding scheme, we speak of the code tree in this book. For the dyslexia example, an alphabetically sorted list of codes may resemble Figure 6.2.

Multiple codes may be assigned to fragments if they contain information of multiple topics which are relevant to the research. However, when retrieving fragments, the same fragment will of course show up for every code that it is assigned to. This is convenient if the researcher really wants to retrieve the fragment for more than one code, but it is not helpful in reducing the amount of material. This

Aids
Importance of language
Choosing a career
Career change
Convey message
Discovering dyslexia
Equality
Experiencing no handicap
Falling short
Flaws
Indifference
Job match
Languaged society
Preferred job
Reading exercises
Reduced writing skills
Unaffected life

FIGURE 6.2   EXAMPLE OF A CODE TREE IN THE DYSLEXIA RESEARCH

is why it is sometimes better to choose to file the fragment with one code only. Such a choice shows an awareness of the relationship between the various emerging categories at this stage of the analysis: the fragment is seen as being part of one category and not the other.

FAQ 2

Q: What should I do with fragments which are irrelevant in my view?

A: Some researchers recommend deleting pieces of text that you believe are not relevant by crossing them out. However, the reverse can apply: bits of text which are not coded will eventually be left out of the next phases of analysis. They have not been labelled, and thus the researcher will not look for them anymore. Some computer programs explicitly offer the option to save pieces on which there is doubt, or for which the researcher has yet to come up with a tag but that do seem interesting. This tool usually includes the word 'free', as in free quotations.

Anyone who starts coding will quickly realize that it is more than simply writing down a word in the margin. The main activity during open coding is to ask questions about the data, such as: What is going on here? What is this about? What is the problem? What is observed here? What is this person trying to tell? What else does this term mean? Which experience is represented here? Asking these kinds of questions about your empirical data will familiarize you with the data and lead to a better understanding of them. In open coding, doing (actually assigning a code) and thinking (coming up with good questions and codes) converge.

FAQ 3

Q: To be honest, I don't understand the difficulty in the whole coding procedure. I've grouped together all the answers received for the first question on my questionnaire, and labelled them 'application'. Then, I clustered all of the answers on the second question, and labelled them 'work satisfaction'. And so on and so forth. Am I doing something wrong?

A: The way in which you approach coding reflects your research purpose and design. You probably knew what you were looking for, so you can be more explicit about the themes or categories to be considered at the outset of the coding process. This reflects a more deductive approach to research, including coding – this is rather more common in applied research, which strives for specific and immediate objective comments or specifically identified outcomes (Lewins & Silver, 2007). Most likely you have used a relatively structured questionnaire with little to no additional questioning beyond what was specified beforehand in the questionnaire. The results of the research will resemble a topical or thematic survey (see Chapter 8), and merely consist of a summary of the answers which were most frequently given.

Even though such a research design is irrevocably qualitative, this chapter – and in fact the whole book – is concerned with a more inductive approach to research and design. This approach identifies and develops new concepts, while existing theoretical concepts will not a priori over-define the analysis (Lewins & Silver, 2007). This implies that data collection takes place in a less structured fashion, and the answers to your questions and 'what you are looking for' may be found scattered through the different documents. In parallel, initial data analysis is less structured, since the frame of analysis has yet to be developed. This way of working forces researchers to find relevant themes and name them, and this is exactly what makes coding a very demanding task.

FAQ 4

Q: What is an appropriate length for a fragment to be coded?

A: There is no simple answer to this question. What is important is that the fragment is a coherent piece of text. This becomes apparent when one reads the fragment and considers its comprehensibility. Most fragments which consist of only one line do not meet this criterion. On the other hand, fragments which exceed half a page may bypass the purpose of open coding, which is to unravel a text, reduce the amount of data and organize the data.

FAQ 5

Q: Is it necessary to code the interviewer's question with the fragment?

A: Many researchers do not code the question, but merely register what the participant had to say. There are arguments in favour of coding the question as well. Doing so enables an evaluation of the answer given, i.e. was it really an answer to the question? Providing the question may improve the interpretation of the answer given, because it gives it context. It may not be necessary to code the questions with every single fragment, but only when it facilitates understanding the text segment.

How do researchers come up with codes? Many words from daily language may be used as a code. A code does not have to be complex or difficult to understand. Specific codes derived from the participants' terminology are known as 'in vivo' codes or field-related concepts (Strauss & Corbin, 2007). These codes then are identified within the data. 'Falling short' is an example of an in vivo code in the study on dyslexia. In vivo codes are not just catchy words; rather they pinpoint exactly what is happening or what the meaning of a certain experience or event is. Charmaz (2006: 55) describes in vivo codes as:

1. General terms everyone 'knows' that flag condensed and important meanings.
2. Terms made up by participants that capture meanings or their experiences.
3. Insider shorthand terms specific to a particular group that reflect their perspective.

Analysts must develop their theoretical sensitivity in order to notice useful in vivo codes for their research material (see Chapter 5).

Another source of codes is the concepts derived from social theories that researchers have come across during disciplinary education and while reading the literature. These kinds of codes are commonly known as 'theoretical concepts' or 'constructed codes' (Flick, 2006). They are, after all, the constructions of social scientists. Examples of theoretical concepts in the dyslexia research can be 'equality' and 'languaged society'. Of key importance are the sensitizing concepts which can be used as a code (see Chapter 2).

FAQ 6

Q: I have yet to start collecting my data, but I already have several codes. Is that possible?

A: Yes, that is possible. In this case codes may be derived from the professional arena as well as the literature (see above). When you already have several

(Continued)

(Continued)

codes beforehand it suggests that you are using a more deductive approach to coding. This might either stem from an applied research with an immediate aim for practical understanding (see FAQ 3) or it might stem from a clear theoretical frame that you want to verify on new cases. The research will therefore start with some predefined, higher-level areas of interest which are explicitly looked for in the data (Lewins & Silver, 2007).

An example of a deductive project that applied existing theoretical ideas is the earlier example on football hooligans (Spaaij, 2006). The author wished to verify the proposition that the nature of football hooliganism depends on the fault lines within a society by applying social identity theory. In addition to his empirical work, he wished to add the local influences on hooliganism to the existing theory. The possibility of changes over time in hooliganism was also investigated. This part of the research had a more explorative character. Within his deductive approach he allowed for emergent themes to be incorporated.

FAQ 7

Q: I am using the computer for my analysis. Can I import the codes I already have before I start my first round of data collection and coding?

A: Yes, codes can be generated at any point during the research independently of data (Lewins & Silver, 2007). Specialized software programs offer more than one way to work with codes. One is to generate a list of codes prior to commencing field work and attaching fragments to them later on. Another way is first importing the text files and then coding them. Each time a new code is needed, it is added to the code tree. Often researchers use both methods: they generate a small code tree before coding the data and adjust it and add codes to it when they actually start analysing their empirical material.

FAQ 8

Q: Can abbreviations be used as codes?

A: Yes, a researcher may use codes and abbreviate them. An advantage is that this provides even shorter names. A disadvantage to using abbreviations is that you have to remember what each abbreviation stands for, something which may prove to be difficult. To my knowledge very few researchers use abbreviations, even though Miles and Huberman (1994) use them frequently in their book on analysis.

Both descriptive and interpretive phrases may be used as codes (Miles & Huberman, 1994). It is quite possible when first entering the field that codes are needed to describe what is seen and heard. In that case, predominantly descriptive codes are used to label the observational reports. In this stage of the research, field workers particularly pay attention to the people involved (numbers, groups, activities, appearances, types of interaction), the physical environment (rooms, furniture, sounds, lighting) and the sequence in which events recur (work, play, breaks, discussions).

Figure 6.3 provides an example of a code tree that was constructed as part of a study on opportunities and obstacles of informal interactions in organizations

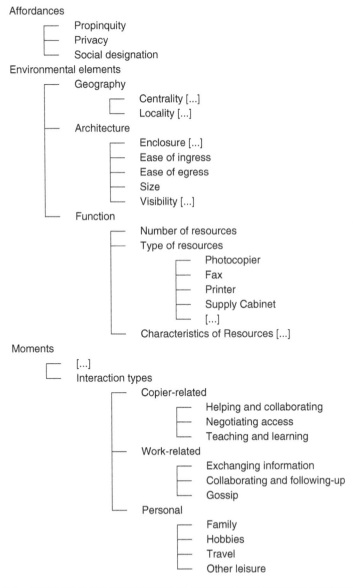

FIGURE 6.3   EXAMPLE OF DESCRIPTIVE CODES FOR OBSERVATIONAL NOTES (FAYARD & WEEKS, 2007)

(Fayard & Weeks, 2007). The authors chose photocopier rooms in order to examine if these rooms encouraged social interactions between employees, of what kind these interactions were, and what conditions provoked interactions. Note that only a part of the code tree is represented here.

After this initial phase, it is important to discern the meaning of the observations. This is where interpretive codes come into play. If it is exclusively 'facts' (activities, places) that are coded, then the meaning of the text would be lost. Experiences, perspectives, impressions and views are important in qualitative research (see Chapter 1). The researcher needs to gain experience in theoretical sensitive coding, which means that skills need to be gained to understand the key point in a piece of text, grasp what it is all about, notice meaningful expressions, and read between the lines. In the study on dyslexia, a remark such as 'I have never noticed anyone looking down at me for making so many mistakes in my language' (see Table 6.1) is very likely to harbour a lot of information on inferiority, superiority and unequal treatment. It is the researcher's task to be alert to these kinds of statements and to interpret them. Another example of this is given below, taken from an interview on binge drinking:

Interviewer: Why do you engage in binge drinking?
Interviewee: Well, when I go out and meet my friends we immediately start drinking. You have to do something you know. And with alcohol the chances are high that something exciting is going to happen. This is permanently lacking throughout the rest of the week.

One could code the entire fragment as 'reasons for binging', and simultaneously code parts of the fragment as 'social contacts' and 'excitement'. The key issue is that only assigning the code 'reasons for binging' results in loss of the main message that is being communicated. That message could very well be that life is dull and boring and that the weekend should compensate somehow. This meaning would be more apparent if we were to assign the fragment with the code 'compensating boredom' or 'evoking excitement'.

Charmaz (2006) particularly advises coding for action and process. This is made easier by coding with gerunds (verbs ending in '-ing', e.g. eating, swimming). You gain a stronger sense of action and process when you read 'choosing a career' instead of 'choice of career' and 'discovery of dyslexia' is more static than 'discovering dyslexia' which implies that an activity is involved. So you should keep your codes active and close to the data. Examples of questions that can help are: What process is at issue here? How does it develop? How does the participant act while involved in the process? When, why and how does the process change? What are the consequences of this process? (Charmaz, 2006: 51).

FAQ 9

Q: Sometimes I would like to see the broader context of the text fragment that I have coded. Is this possible?

A: Yes, with most computer programs you can go directly to the position in the document from which the fragment was taken. When analysing with paper and pencil, this is certainly more labour intensive. A summary of each document can be helpful, providing a quick résumé of the most important findings of an interview or observation. Context information is valuable for interpreting the fragment against the broader background of the entire document.

FAQ 10

Q: I have formulated a number of sensitizing concepts based on my literature study. Yet I still feel that I cannot properly use them in open coding. Why does this happen?

A: During open coding, the researcher starts analysing at a fairly detailed level in order to form a foundation of the analysis in the data. The data describe daily events and experiences and in order to name them appropriately, concepts of a low level of abstraction are needed to match the data. Sensitizing concepts often have a general character, and still need to be applied to the field of research (see Chapter 2). They possess a level of abstraction which transcends that of regular fragments. It is therefore no surprise that these concepts may not be usable in the open coding phase. In later phases of coding, in which analysis takes place at a higher level of abstraction, these codes may turn out to be useful.

In open coding, researchers should not globally examine the text but do so in detail. In research on dyslexia and job choice, for example, codes such as 'motivation', 'discrimination' and 'language' are not specific enough at this stage of the analysis. Such codes will come to harbour a large number of very diverse fragments and the disassembly of the data will be insufficient. The result is that fragments which have received the same code will have to be differentiated later on. In short, this means postponing the analysis. However, a coding scheme which is too detailed is not recommended either. When every distinguishable fragment in a text receives a different code, the researcher goes beyond comparison and categorization. This approach may easily result in hundreds of codes.

FAQ 11

Q: Is there a usual number of codes for the open coding phase?

A: This is impossible to say. A coding system is uniquely developed for each separate research project, and is related to the modus operandi of the researcher. It is important for researchers to develop their own coding system. For a small-scale study (with a narrow research question, a limited number of participants and

(Continued)

(Continued)

restricted data collection), 50 codes may be sufficient. For a large-scale investigation, there may be as many as 100 to 200 codes. Keep in mind that this is a rough estimate only.

An indication of whether an 'appropriate' number of codes has been awarded is the number of fragments hosted by one code. If there is only one fragment assigned to a single code, this code should probably be discarded or merged with another code, and the fragment filed under this other code. If there are more than 20 fragments assigned to a certain code, the diversity of these fragments should be evaluated. If the diversity is deemed too large, the fragments may have to be divided into two or more categories. More specific sub-codes can then be assigned to these smaller groups of fragments. Another indicator is the ratio between main codes and sub-codes: 10 to 20 main codes seem to be an acceptable starting point. The number of sub-codes can vary strongly between researchers, as it depends on how detailed the researcher's coding is (see next section).

FAQ 12

Q: Is it necessary to code all sorts of personal information of the interviewees, such as gender, age and study or profession?

A: No. Codes such as 'age', 'place of residence' and 'profession' are useless because they will not become a part of later descriptions nor of the theoretical model. This information about participants is best kept in a separate file about the composition of the sample. Some computer programs offer the option of assigning variables or attributes to a document; for example, an interview could receive variables representing age and gender of the interviewee. This is a wise thing to do for reasons of comparison, for instance, whether female binge drinkers engage in disorderly behaviour and if so whether this behaviour is different from that of males. Then again, it is not the demographic variable itself that is of interest per se, but the mechanism behind it. For instance, female binge drinkers run into different types of trouble than male binge drinkers, and it is relevant to describe the differences and the causes.

In this phase of a research project, it is recommended that researchers work in a group instead of on their own. Having others to confer with contributes to a well-developed coding system, thereby ensuring that certain fragments are systematically awarded the 'correct' code. This is known as 'inter-rater reliability'. Asserting inter-rater reliability does not tell us anything about the adequacy of coding, but it does cover the systematic approach to coding. Every fragment dealing with a certain topic will end up with the same code; they will not be awarded one code at one time and another code the next. In the end, this procedure does give an indication of the adequacy of the coding scheme, since it is assumed that the members of the group discuss the interpretation of the texts, exchange their views and come to an agreement.

FAQ 13

Q: Can software for qualitative data analysis calculate the inter-rater reliability?
A: According to Lewins and Silver (2007) who did an extensive comparison of different software packages, only N6 and CISAID can calculate a reliability rating. In other programs the evaluation of the level of reliability is not so much based on assigning the exact same code between independent analysts as on discussing how parts of the texts should be interpreted. MAXQDA2007 for instance offers the possibility for different analysts to code the same text. The coding of other raters can be turned off so as to not be influenced by them. Later on when all codes are made visible, a comparison can be easily conducted.

Eventually, all relevant data must be covered with the generated codes. Judging what is relevant is difficult at the start of the research. The research questions are the most important guideline for doing so. The phase of open coding can be ended if no new codes are necessary. Another term for this is 'saturation': the information from a new case can be separated into fragments that can be covered with one of the already existing codes. The entire process may repeat itself until the second or third round of data collection (see Figure 5.4, the spiral of analysis). Every time new observations provide a reason for generating a new code, open coding is resumed. Box 6.2 contains a summary of the most important elements of open coding.

BOX 6.2   SUMMARY OF OPEN CODING

Purpose: Exploration of the field, coverage of the field with codes, manageability of data files, familiarity with data
Phase: Especially in the beginning of the research
Activities: Reading and re-reading (close reading), asking questions about the data, comparing data with data, assigning codes to data fragments
Starting point: Data
Results: List of codes, memos
Validation: Saturation, meaning that no new codes are needed to label fragments that appeared in the data up until now

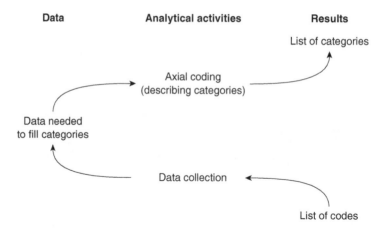

FIGURE 6.4   THE SPIRAL OF ANALYSIS ENLARGED: AXIAL CODING

Axial coding

The term 'axial coding' refers to 'a set of procedures whereby data are put back together in new ways after open coding, by making connections between categories' (Strauss & Corbin, 2007: 96). Axial coding is a more abstract process and consists of coding around several single categories or axes (see Figure 6.4). The term is somewhat confusing and personally I like 'focused coding' (Charmaz, 2006) better, but axial coding is the more commonly used term. 'Axial coding relates categories to subcategories, specifies the properties and dimensions of a category, and reassembles the data you have fractured during initial coding to give coherence to the emerging analysis' (Charmaz, 2006: 60). When researchers employ axial coding, the reasoning moves predominantly from codes to data, whereas in open coding the reasoning moves in the opposite direction, from data to codes. While in this phase of the analysis, new ideas are generated by conducting another round of data collection. Categories and propositions generated in the previous phase are tested by confronting them with the new material. In axial coding the distinction is made between the categories for which everything indicates that they might fulfil an important role in the definitive findings and the categories that can be gathered around these particular categories. The relationships between salient categories (axes!) and subcategories can be generated, modified, refined, elaborated or even rejected throughout axial coding.

Axial coding involves the following steps:

- Determine whether the codes developed thus far cover the data sufficiently and create new ones when the data provide incentives to do so.
- Check whether each fragment has been coded properly, or if it should be assigned a different code.
- Decide which code is most suitable if synonyms have been used to create two equal categories, and merge the categories.

- Look at the overview of fragments assigned to a certain code. Consider their similarities and differences.
- Subdivide categories if necessary.
- Look for evidence for distinguishing main codes and sub-codes and assign the sub-codes to the main code.
- See whether a sufficiently detailed description of a category can be derived from the assigned fragments and if not, decide to collect new data to fill the gap.
- Keep thinking about the data and the coding.

The primary purpose of axial coding is to determine which elements in the research are the dominant ones and which are the less important ones. As insights into the field increase and ideas about the observed social phenomena develop, confidence grows in making choices among the codes and the connections between them. The second purpose of axial coding is to reduce and reorganize the data set: synonyms are crossed out, redundant codes are removed and the best representative codes are selected. All activities are employed to gradually focus the research.

Sensitizing concepts come into play again during the phase of axial coding. As described in Chapter 2, sensitizing concepts have a rather general content at the beginning of the research. They give you ideas of directions to pursue and sensitize you to ask particular kinds of questions about your topic (Charmaz, 2006). The sensitizing concepts can be filled in during the analytic phase of axial coding to get their definitive content that fits in with how they are used by the participants in the field (Jorgensen, 1989). During axial coding, one tries to determine the properties of the categories. In doing so it becomes clear by which indicators a category can be recognized in the data. Note that with a definitive concept it works the other way around: its fixed content is reflected by its measure, i.e. the indicators that stand for the concept. Qualitative research is well suited to discover the contents of a concept when these contents are unclear. This function is also used in a particular type of mixed methods research that aims at the development of a measuring instrument (see Chapter 8).

In the dyslexia study (Dam & Rooij, 2002), the following main codes were awarded after several rounds of data collection: previous history, experiencing problems, choosing education, choosing a career, compensating, own responsibility and environment. The other codes were considered to be sub-codes of these; that is to say, they were considered instances, specifications, parts or stages of the main codes. The code tree is depicted in Figure 6.5.

The hierarchical sequence in the tree structure is simply a clear way to sort and organize the subjects, making it easy to retrieve the data pertaining to the subjects later on. It is possible that there are no fragments assigned to a main code, like 'experiencing problems', 'choosing a career' or 'strategies' in Figure 6.5. Such a code then functions as a hanger for others. But the main code can also contain fragments which clarify what is meant by the main category. For example, 'past history' can contain fragments that have to do with significant events in the lives of participants leading up to the discovery of dyslexia and 'compensating' can hold fragments in which participants explain what they mean by this term and when they feel they need to even out their flaws.

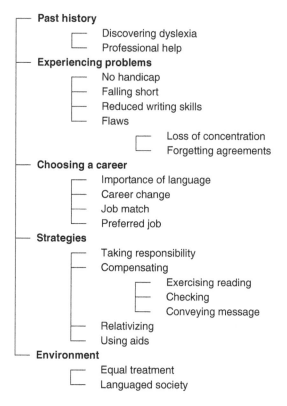

FIGURE 6.5 EXAMPLE OF A CODE TREE IN THE DYSLEXIA RESEARCH AFTER AXIAL CODING (DAM & ROOIJ, 2002)

FAQ 14

Q: In the beginning I felt comfortable using the hierarchical ordering of the list of codes. But now that I see connections between the codes I wonder whether I can use the software for linking the codes in different ways?

A: Different software packages offer different ways of escaping the structures of the main code listing (Lewins & Silver, 2007). In this respect you can think of codes to be retrieved in different combinations independent of the main structure. You can bring the different elements of your project – codes, memos, segments – into a mapping device, you can link fragments within and between documents, and you can regroup the documents and codes in sets or families leaving the original code structure intact (see Chapter 7).

At this point during the analysis it is important to remember that codes can be used for different purposes, whether more descriptive or analytical (see the beginning of this chapter). In the list of codes in Figure 6.5 you can see that some of the codes are more descriptive, such as 'past history' and 'flaws', and that others may be more analytical, like 'choosing a career' and 'strategies'. There is no set way in which to use a code; they must simply be meaningful for you or the research team in the sense that they indicate the nature of the data grouped by that code in some way (Lewins & Silver, 2007).

In the case of analytical use of codes, thinking about inter-rater reliability is important. When codes are to capture important properties of a concept, it is essential that different researchers agree when these properties appear in the data, i.e. what fragments are seen as evidence for these properties. Subsequently, they have to be coded with a concise and accurate label. When the codes are used in a more practical or descriptive way, the value of inter-rater reliability diminishes and can even become a hindrance. When you use a code as a 'box' to put in interesting data to revisit and think about, then it is not that important how you label the box. Spending a lot of time on agreeing on the correct code is a waste of time and a hindrance for creative labelling and may cause unnecessary delays to the project.

FAQ 15

Q: I only have limited time for my qualitative research and my sponsor has already provided a number of relevant themes. Can I go straight into axial coding and skip open coding?

A: In commissioned research the exploration of the field during open coding is sometimes seen as a waste of time, because 'so much detail is unnecessary' and because 'you do not have to start from scratch'. Much depends on the purpose of the investigation. For example, when the purpose of the research is to make an inventory of a number of predetermined topics, data will often be collected with a reasonably structured measurement instrument. In this case, the need for open coding is minimal. The data can be assigned to anticipated categories, leaving some room for adding categories by means of open coding (see also FAQ 3).

In the axial coding phase, the codes become increasingly disconnected from the data although the data never entirely disappear from sight. In the open coding phase the data were central and evidence was built-up to be used later on. Open coding logically paves the way for axial coding, as the basic data is transformed into a more abstract framework through – let's not forget – the researcher's hard work. Nothing emerges without effort. This organizing structure is grounded in the data, preventing friction between the data and the framework. By systematically segmenting the fragments assigned to a code the researcher gains the ability to describe the category at a more abstract level. An example may clarify this issue. In the study on the quality of care in nursing homes (see Chapter 5), staff members often spoke of the hospitalization of residents (Boeije, 1994). The fragments labelled with the code 'hospitalization' are listed:

- 'Being hospitalized is being used to an institution, that everything is done for you, and that you will see yourself as not being able to care for yourself anymore.'
- 'The process of hospitalization contributes to a decline in interest; everything that happens outside the institution is not of concern.'
- 'Hospitalization is the loss of autonomy, going along with the rhythm, not wanting to do anything else, adaptation to rules. Initiatives are no longer necessary.'
- 'Those people become very passive, they stop thinking for themselves.'
- 'Hospitalization means that people are fully self-directed, like "I should get my porridge now", and "I have to go to the bathroom now", and "I have to go to bed". Everything needs to be done at its own specific hour and time.'

The various fragments are compared to each other in order to extract the core of the hospitalization process as it is viewed by the staff. Hospitalization is depicted as a process that takes place over time. It is the process by which residents lose their autonomy and stop thinking for themselves, take no responsibility anymore and leave everything to others. The consequence is that their world is reduced to the confines of the nursing home. Hospitalization is an unwanted phenomenon with respect to self-worth. In the hospitalization process residents give up their 'selves', which is at odds with striving for self-worth. When residents are 'de-hospitalized' their self-worth increases again.

In order to ensure theoretical sampling (see Chapter 2), comparison cases were sought (other nursing homes with other staff members) for a new round of data collection. Emphasis was put on locating settings in which residents were not hospitalized. Also, cases were sought in which hospitalization was valued positively. This led to the discovery that some staff members thought it to be effective when residents had little say and went along with the working routines established on the ward. Note that hospitalization had become an important category in the research, because of its relationship with resident's self-worth and the quality of care.

FAQ 16

Q: I have performed open coding with the support of a software package. How can I use the computer in axial coding?

A: The computer is a great tool for creating a hierarchical code tree and for retrieving fragments that have been assigned a certain code. Both these tasks are relevant in the stage of axial coding. Software packages are able to trace the conceptual development of the data together with the various phases and processes of the entire project. During axial coding visual tools and various search options can assist in the discovery of themes, patterns and connections between the different categories (see Chapter 7).

We have addressed the role of the coding paradigm in the discussion about 'forcing' versus 'emerging' in Chapter 5. Remember that the coding paradigm was used as a mould for organizing the data and consists of four elements, namely context, conditions, interactions/strategies and consequences. The coding paradigm is meant to be applied during the axial coding phase (Strauss & Corbin, 2007). Application to the above-mentioned research could, for example, lead to the following distinctions:

- What is the *context* in which hospitalization takes place?
  - o For instance, placement in a relatively closed institution due to severe physical and/or mental limitations of the elderly; wider nursing home policy including staffing.
- Under which *conditions* does hospitalization take place?
  - o Fixed daily schedule; structures, routines and rituals; absence of variety of stimuli or impossibility of processing these stimuli.
- Which *interactions* take place?
  - o Staff and residents meet when a deviation from the daily schedule upsets residents; staff and residents negotiate possible deviations; residents delegate activities to staff members; staff members urge residents to adjust to the valid, same care pattern every day; caregivers urge residents to take initiatives.
- What are the *consequences*?
  - o For residents: passivity, loss of self-worth, rest, surrender. For staff: control, boredom, detachments, dissatisfaction, frustration.

Salient codes are raised to categories. They represent important themes in the data and can lead to more abstract, theoretical ideas. In the axial coding phase, both the definition and the properties of a category become clear. When coding, it can be useful to think about properties in terms of dimensions (Strauss & Corbin, 2007). For instance, 'equality' could be appropriate when studying dyslectics in a social setting. Dimensional categories of 'equality' could be 'equal treatment' and 'disadvantaged'. A different property of the social context may be 'nature', which could be dimensionalized as 'languaged' or 'physical'. It can be proposed that people with dyslexia tend to withdraw from social environments that are perceived as 'languaged'. It then becomes easier to argue what comparison cases are needed for further data collection to test this proposition. Thinking in dimensions contributes to theoretical selection and constant comparison (see Chapters 2 and 5). Dimensionalizing is useful, but only when done in moderation otherwise the researcher is in danger of losing track of the coding system because it becomes forced and unwieldy.

The logic of going back to the data and moving forward into analysis is that missing knowledge often comes to light when glossing over the categories that have been developed. If you detect a code that has only one fragment assigned to it while glancing over the tabular summaries of code frequencies, consider whether it is best to delete the code (known as 'uncoding') or to fill in the gap and gather more data about that particular topic. When your categories are still only briefly described and are not convincing, you should return to the field and gather more data to enhance the descriptions. Focused data collection is needed to fill conceptual gaps. Ultimately, simultaneous data collection and analysis help you to gain more insight into the research problem.

In this phase of the analysis, regularities or patterns emerge which rise above the level of a single text fragment. Usually such a pattern is difficult to capture in a code, although Miles and Huberman (1994) speak of pattern codes in this way. A pattern can be defined as 'an orderly sequence consisting of a number of repeated or complementary elements' (Fredericks & Miller, 1997). Patterns have an overarching character and cannot be placed within one category. In her study on family relationships, Mason gives 'reciprocity' as an example of such a overarching topic and remarks 'that it is unlikely that such a process of reciprocity will be neatly bundled into small chunks of interview text ready for the reader to categorize and index' (2002: 119).

In other words: the encompassing topics in which the researcher is interested are not readily observable in a piece of text. Ideas, patterns, explanations and types which do not 'fit' into codes are quickly forgotten. In order to remember and develop them, a researcher would write memos (see Chapter 4). Gradually, coding becomes aimed at explaining larger parts of the data and at bringing the different parts back together. Axial coding can be finalized when the distinction between main codes and sub-codes is clearly established and the contents of the categories are known. This means that the preliminary findings up till then do not change substantially when confronted with newly gathered data. The test again is saturation: newly collected data from comparison cases do not change the outcomes so far.

BOX 6.3   SUMMARY OF AXIAL CODING

Purpose:	Describe and delineate categories, determine relevance of categories, increase level of conceptual abstraction
Phase:	Halfway through
Activities:	Retrieve and compare fragments assigned to a certain code, define the category, determine relationships between main categories and subcategories, add, refine and check preliminary ideas and conjectures with newly added data
Starting point:	Codes developed during open coding
Result:	Categories are described and distinctions are made between main categories and subcategories, memo file containing ideas and verified assertions
Validation:	Saturation, meaning that the definition and properties of each category (axis) are clear and that no further adjustment is needed

---

Selective coding

Selective coding refers to looking for connections between the categories in order to make sense of what is happening in the field. Selective coding is aimed at integrating the loose pieces of your earlier coding efforts and can be considered a logical step after the segmenting of the data:

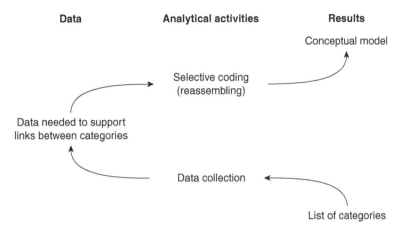

FIGURE 6.6   THE SPIRAL OF ANALYSIS ENLARGED: SELECTIVE CODING

> Efforts to code data will lead to sorting, sifting, organizing, and reorganizing these materials, usually into larger units and components. Sometimes this involves flashes of insight about how things fit together, while at other times it depends on less dramatic hunches, or simply hard work. Is a pattern or type discernible? Is some sequence or process apparent? Can you ascertain connections or relationships among concepts? [...] As you sort, sift, arrange, and rearrange the data and analytic labels and comments about them, it will be increasingly necessary to become more directly and explicitly involved in theory and theorizing. (Jorgensen, 1989: 110)

Often, but not always, the findings of a qualitative piece of work will aim at theory development. When this is the case, it is in the process of selective coding that certain categories are adopted as theoretical concepts, since they will most certainly become part of the theoretical model. For authors such as Strauss and Corbin the end result of qualitative research is a grounded theory, and for them selective coding equals 'selecting the core category, systematically relating it to other categories and filling in categories that need further refinement and development' (Strauss & Corbin, 2007: 116). Theoretical coding as an alternative term for selective coding is therefore a rather good choice for this sophisticated level of coding (Charmaz, 2006).

The term 'core category' originally stems from the grounded theory approach and refers to a category that is central to the integration of the theory (Strauss, 1987). In other traditions, the term may not be used at all. One of the most compelling examples of a core category is the awareness context of Glaser and Strauss (1965) (see Box 1.4). We have already come across some examples of core concepts in our illustrative studies, such as 'trust' in a research on residents in nursing homes (Bosch, 1996) and 're-connecting the person to humanity' in a study on care of psychiatric nurses for suicidal people (Cutcliffe et al., 2006).

The core category or core concept is a construction of the researcher which does not magically emerge from the data. The core category describes and explains the researcher's observations. A number of characteristics of the core category are provided by Strauss (1987: 36). These characteristics, which may facilitate the identification of the core category, are shown in Box 6.4.

BOX 6.4   CHARACTERISTICS OF THE CORE CATEGORY

The core category:

- is central, meaning that a lot of other categories are linked to it
- is the heart of the analysis: it indicates that the category accounts for a large portion of the variation in the behaviour in the data
- appears frequently in the data; otherwise stated, the indicators pointing to the core phenomenon must appear frequently
- is not easily saturated because there is so much material related to the core category
- can be formulated in a more abstract way, which can then result in the possible application to other fields of research
- facilitates analysis, makes the pieces of the puzzle fit together

---

Since the phase of selective coding marks the end of the analysis phase, it is useful to answer the questions listed below. When an answer can be given, it shows that you understand how the pieces of data fit together:

- Which themes have turned up repeatedly in the observations?
- What is the main message that the participants have tried to bring across?
- How are the various relevant themes related?
- What is important for the description (What) and the understanding (Why) of the participant's perspective and behaviour?

Researchers looking for explanations for the observed phenomena will probably ask the following questions as well (Lofland & Lofland, 1995):

- Under which circumstances does phenomenon A emerge?
- What facilitates experience B?
- What influences phenomenon C?
- When is event D absent?

Although by some, selective coding is mainly considered as the hunt for the core concept, the synthesis of data by establishing relationships is in itself just as vital as the selection of the core category. Connecting is also necessary when one chooses not to work with a core category and to focus on the main concepts instead. Reassembling is initiated during axial coding, but gains importance as the research progresses towards the final stages. In deciding which categories will stand out in the findings, the researcher can use the following elements as guidelines:

1. Research question and purpose: the most influential factors in determining how the data will be integrated and what the findings will look like.
2. Literature: the results are contrasted with the relevant literature and demonstrate how the sensitizing concepts have functioned.
3. Data: the outcomes are guided by what stands out in the data in terms of richness and the insights they have yielded.
4. Fascination: the surprising, fascinating and original parts should be included in the findings.
5. Actuality: the results occasionally grow in value if they fit the actual context of societal and scientific debates or events.

So far, attention has mainly focused on discovery of relationships between concepts. A second activity in reassembling is checking the relationships between the concepts with new data. Data have to contain the evidence for the asserted claims. In order to substantiate the conjectures, the researcher may initiate a new round of data collection. In analytic induction, testing the propositions with new research material is important right from the start (see Chapter 5). Theoretical selection (see Chapter 2) and in particular the analysis of negative cases provides the researcher with sufficient evidence to verify whether conjectures are justified. The crucial question is whether all the data, including the negative cases, can be described and understood within the conceptual framework.

There are several pitfalls in establishing and verifying connections between phenomena. When the researcher is not alert to these errors, they threaten the validity of the results and the eventual conclusions. Diverse procedures to ascertain quality of the research, including the interpretation of the data, are addressed in Chapter 9. Box 6.5 depicts some areas of possible misinterpretations that researchers should be aware of (Miles & Huberman, 1994).

BOX 6.5   POSSIBLE CAUSES OF MISINTERPRETATIONS WHEN CONFIRMING FINDINGS

- An unbalanced selection of the data: important information is missed and other information is weighed too heavily.
- Overemphasis of the first data or factual and dramatic events that made a lasting impression on the researcher.
- Selectivity, especially when the researcher is trying to validate the most important finding (and would rather not see it disproven).
- Interpreting co-occurring events as connection or even causality.
- Having trouble with estimating the value of various sources of information.
- Drawing unwarranted conclusions based on the frequency with which events occur.
- Putting a hypothesis aside too easily based on certain information.

FAQ 17

Q: During selective coding I have the feeling I am not 'coding' anymore at all. I feel as if I am doing all kinds of different things and I keep thinking about the data. I have not touched my computer for days, other than for writing texts, and I have neglected to update my coding scheme. Do I need to do that?

A: When your thinking goes on independently of the software support, congratulate yourself! Do not feel compelled to change the contents of your computer project to follow what you have already done. Other tools (see FAQ 16) might enable you to think outside the coding scheme. Unless for obvious reasons you want the code tree to reflect your latest work; for instance, when you need to present your provisional knowledge to others as a code tree, a matrix, or a map, or when you want to continue using the computer from where you are now and cannot do it otherwise.

Arriving at the end of selective coding, we are far removed from 'putting words in the text margin'. In the final phase of the analysis, the definitive findings are shaped. Instead of the chronological order in which the data were originally collected, the data now stand in the order implied by the data and the research questions. This new order is the surplus-value of the analysis. When the analysis provides a fresh, theoretical look at the phenomenon under study, the findings might be a source of inspiration and an invitation to the reader to think about and pose questions about the meaning of the findings.

BOX 6.6   SUMMARY OF SELECTIVE CODING

Purpose:	Determining important categories and possibly a core category, formulating the theoretical model, reassembling of the data in order to answer the research question and realize the research aim
Phase:	End phase of the research
Activities:	Determining core concept(s), determining relationships between the concepts and verifying them, writing, interpreting and positioning findings in the existing literature, thinking about the answers to the research questions and drawing conclusions
Starting point:	All available research material
Result:	Description of the most important concepts, coherent story in which the relationships between concepts become apparent, answers to the research questions
Validation:	Saturation, meaning that new data collection provides data which are consistent with descriptions thus far and fit the theoretical model

Reflections on analysis

Let us take a step back and look at what we have been doing this chapter. Thus far, this chapter has discussed two activities which, when taken together, form the core of the analysis. One, the segmenting of the data. This is largely achieved by means of open coding. The researcher puts markers into place which signify interesting parts in the research material. Two, the reassembling of the data in light of the problem statement. This is mainly achieved through selective coding. Axial coding occupies a certain in-between position and bridges segmenting and reassembling. In all three types of coding, thinking and doing go hand in hand.

Coding basically fulfils two functions. First, coding is important for data management. Interviews, field notes and other materials are generated throughout the research, and can be stored chronologically. But the researcher needs to develop an indexing system, to store the data based on the contents, from which the data can easily be retrieved. Coding supports this by reducing the amount of data, since only relevant sections are selected for storage and are assigned a summarizing and meaningful code. Coding also ensures that the data are filed in a way that enables easy retrieval: data are archived by code. In this manner, a code is a reference to passages in a text which relate to a common theme.

Second, coding is also important as a way to explore and interpret the data. It is a tool for mining a new research area. After all, coding is a way of constantly interrogating the data and asking questions about the meaning of the data. Coding is also the driving force behind categorization and conceptualization. Coding forces the researcher to generate categories and to be clear about what distinguishes them from each other in relation to their properties, as well as clarifying which indicators there are for each category to occur. Finally, coding plays a role in the reassembly of the data, so that the data are looked at from a new perspective and the research questions can be answered.

In the spiral of analysis the three types of coding are depicted as linear stages, but in practice the three activities are not neatly distinguished. It is possible that some areas of the field still need further exploration, while other areas are already subject to axial coding. Open coding and axial coding often merge into one another, as do axial and selective coding. It is does not matter which activity you are engaged in at a given moment, as long as you work systematically from the data to the findings.

The qualitative research process is characterized by alternating between data collection, data analysis and sampling. These activities cannot be strictly separated, as the researcher jumps backwards and forwards between them. Simultaneous data collection and analysis is seen as the backbone of the spiral of analysis (Figure 5.4). Its procedure is referred to as cyclical, spiral-shaped, iterative or recursive. In contrast, quantitative research is characterized by separate phases of data collection and data analysis; the two phases take place one after the other, also known as a 'linear' research process. Towards the end of the qualitative research process, data collection decreases in favour of analysis. An abstract representation of the models of qualitative and quantitative research is given in Figure 6.7.

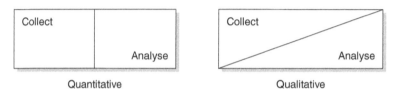

FIGURE 6.7   MODELS OF THE QUANTITATIVE AND THE QUALITATIVE
RESEARCH PROCESS (MAYS & POPE, 1995: 184)

There are several reasons for adopting a zigzag style of data collection and analysis approach. Working this way contributes to the explorative capacity of the research. Each stage of data collection is informed by the analysis of the previous data collection stage. The topic list or any other measuring instrument can be revised for the next round of data collection to be more specific and focused. As the amount of data grows, new paths can be followed. This could even lead to a fine-tuning of the research questions (see Chapter 2) and ultimately lead to more relevant outcomes. The principle of purposive sampling and in particular theoretical selection (see Chapter 2) supports this way of working, since the interim results of the analysis determine where the researcher will collect new data.

The interchange between data collection and analysis not only benefits the explorative aim of qualitative research, but also its explanatory aim. Conjectures and propositions about the connections between phenomena can be tested for accuracy when the researcher collects new data from new cases. This testing of provisional findings against new information can lead to modification, rejection or elaboration of the first ideas. This is part of analytical induction (see Chapter 5). The newly gathered data is compared with everything that has been learnt from the data that was collected and analysed previously – concepts, conjectures or assertions. What was thought to be a known result or assumption is then adjusted accordingly.

Finally, there is a third much more practical reason for the data collection and analysis to proceed simultaneously. Imagine returning from field work carrying tapes (or digital recordings) of at least 20 interviews, plus some exercise books full of field notes. Where would you start? Would you listen to the first interviews, already knowing their content? Would you instantly start writing the results from memory without having the basic material in front of you? Either method would double the work and most likely lead to frustrations. Postponement of analysis only adds to the pressure. The yield of the research will most likely be better if analysis is started right at the beginning, because the exploration and verification opportunities of an emerging design can then be utilized to their fullest potential.

Readings I learnt much from

Charmaz, K. (2006). *Constructing grounded theory. A practical guide through qualitative analysis.* London: Sage.

Jorgensen, D.L. (1989). *Participant observation. A methodology for human studies.* Newbury Park, CA: Sage.

Lofland, J. & Lofland, L.H. (1995). *Analysing social settings. A guide to qualitative observation and analysis.* Belmont, CA: Wadsworth.
Ritchie, J. & Lewis, J. (2003). *Qualitative research practice. A guide for social science students and researchers.* London: Sage.

Doing your own qualitative research project

Step 6: Open, axial and selective coding

1. After collecting the first data, the analysis can be started. Start open coding after the first two or three sessions of data collection. Although the sequence of the activities involved in this series suggests a linear process, it is emphasized again that data collection and data analysis alternate.
2. Have you decided upon the use of software yet? If you have decided to use a package, try to choose one that suits your purposes and start using it right from the beginning.
3. Do not forget to write memos as you go along. Write memos on methodological issues as well as on the contents of your project, in particular the development of categories and concepts.
4. Stay close to the data when conducting open coding. When you have reached saturation after a few rounds of data collection (see Box 6.2), you will automatically progress to axial coding. It is highly likely that some areas within your project will still need open coding as well.
5. If you work in a research team, use each member's capabilities and knowledge in coding and memo-writing.
6. When you have defined and delineated different categories, you should begin selective coding. Start processing all the assumptions and theories that have accumulated during the research project up to this point. Do use all the work of earlier phases. This is by far the most difficult stage of the research but also the most rewarding. Most importantly, you should capitalize on your theoretical sensitivity that can be stimulated by the integrative procedures presented in the next chapter.

7
INTEGRATIVE PROCEDURES

The integration of the data into a coherent, analytical format is a difficult part of every qualitative research project, even with the use of methods and techniques such as coding and memo-writing. Ten integrative procedures and heuristic devices are presented in this chapter to help you to extract the interesting elements from your data. They should be seen as thinking aids, and examples are given here as inspiration. To illustrate the decision-making processes during the analysis, we present a 'think aloud' report of a real-life analytical procedure. Modern software packages are immensely useful for coding and performing the more mechanical tasks, and are a useful tool when interrogating the data and heuristically thinking about the material.

LEARNING AIMS

By the end of this chapter, you will be able to:

- Pursue integrative procedures that benefit your analysis
- Create diagrams and know how to present them
- Capture social processes in a mould encompassing chronological stages
- Work out whether and how searches and counts are useful in your own project
- Incorporate the influence of group interaction in the analysis of focus group data
- See how visuals are used as a stand-alone method or as an elicitation technique
- Value code-and-retrieve and theory-building software tools in your project
- Reflect on the pros and cons of computer-assisted data analysis

Heuristics for discovery

The reassembling phase in analysis is without doubt the most difficult phase in the entire research process. It is this phase that requires the researcher to be theoretically sensitive, resourceful, open-minded, skilful and well-informed on the literature. No ready-made solutions are available for integrating the data. The literature on qualitative analysis does not tell us much about this analytic stage either. This is probably because this phase of the investigation is unique for all research projects and intrinsically bound to the contents of the specific research project. It is also generally assumed that the capabilities needed in this part of the project are the hardest to acquire. According to Cutcliffe and McKenna (2004), it is only the experienced qualitative researcher who can recognize the over-riding or underlying dynamic, principle or process in a data set. It is precisely this proficiency that is difficult to articulate or teach.

This so being, there are several methods and devices to help solve these problems. These 'heuristics' are rules of thumb, thinking models and creative instruments to turn your data around and look at them from different angles. The ten integrative procedures and heuristic devices presented in this chapter are:

1. Creating visual displays
2. Looking for the core category
3. Using moulds
4. Creating a matrix
5. Reading your memos
6. Searching and counting
7. Acknowledging the presence of feelings
8. Formulating a typology
9. Constructing arguments
10. Outlining the main message

No universal solutions exist for the reconstruction of data. There are, however, different kinds of thinking aids which may be applicable to your work. They are discussed in this section and in order to clarify them, examples are included where possible.

Creating visual displays

According to the motto 'You know what you display' (Miles & Huberman, 1994), drawing figures, flow charts, maps, decision trees and Venn diagrams (sets of interlocking circles) is an excellent way for researchers to test what they know and do not yet know regarding their topic. Creating visuals will raise awareness about the possible gaps in the available knowledge and stimulate thinking about how to fill these gaps. Maps and diagrams may help develop interpretations. In a project that is informed by social theory from the outset, a map may offer insight in all the adjustments and refinements made to the theory based on the current research.

TIP _____

Modern software can be used to visualize connections in maps and diagrams. The mapping tools enable a different and often more complex set of linkages that go beyond the hierarchical coding scheme (Lewins & Silver, 2007). Most packages allow an integration of the source data – documents, memos and codes – and the maps and support a visual way to rethink connections.

If a diagram is solely an aid for the researcher it is not necessary to include it in the presentation of the findings. However, a visual display may be added to a presentation and to the final report when it clearly illustrates the structure of the findings, most commonly a proposed theory. A diagram enables the researcher to present a lot of information in a concise manner. Figures must be kept as simple as possible, they should be analytically sound, and all elements should be clear, logically connected and simple to follow (Morse, 2006).

Graphical representations of both interim results and final results are common (Strauss, 1987). Examples of such depictions were given in Figures 5.1 to 5.3 about the quality of care in nursing homes. The diagram depicted in Figure 7.1 is taken from the study on alcohol use among adolescents during their social gatherings and night life (Engineer et al., 2003). It is an example of how a model can summarize a lot of information. The fishbone diagram depicts the most important risk factors for alcohol abuse and the resulting criminal and disorderly behaviour. While reading the text of the original report, the reader moves logically through the model.

Looking for the core category

Reassembling the data may be achieved by seriously looking for core conceptual categories. It is possible that one category is very central but remains unnoticed until one actually looks for it. It has to be a category which matches all of the characteristics described in Box 6.4. The benefit of a core category lies in the fact that the researcher may continue analysis from the new perspective, as if all pieces of the puzzle fall into place. Then the 'old' material and earlier steps are recycled in terms of the newly found theoretical angle. It is not possible or desirable to appoint a core category for every research project. In some studies, multiple categories may claim a leading role.

In the study on prolonged use of sedatives, Haafkens (1997) appointed 'rituals of silence' as the core concept. It became the most important social pattern of what led women to continue using tranquillizers over a prolonged period of time. As time went by, the study tells us, the doctor stopped asking whether the tranquillizers helped and the women stopped talking about or asking for feedback or opinions. The people in the women's social network who knew about their use would not offer their opinion. This allowed those involved to go on living under the assumption that the drugs were still working and not producing any negative effects. This mutual silence largely explained the prolonged use of tranquillizers and became the main theme in the study.

Using moulds

In Chapter 5 we touched upon the moulds or 'coding families' which were developed by Glaser (1978) in order to structure the data. The coding paradigm of Strauss and Corbin (2007) – a mould consisting of context, conditions, interactions/strategies

FIGURE 7.1 KEY RISK FACTORS OF ENDING A NIGHT OUT IN DISORDER (ENGINEER ET AL., 2003)

and consequences – was discussed in Chapter 6. A different mould may incorporate processes, stages or phases. Since qualitative researchers are often interested in processes and changes over time, a mould incorporating stages would be useful in dealing with the different materials.

A well-known example is Becker's phase model, in which he described the stages that a person should go through to start finding the use of marihuana pleasurable (Becker, 1982). He deduced that no one will become a user without:

- learning how to smoke the drugs in such a way that the effects are noticeable
- learning to recognize the effects and attributing them to the drugs (learning how to get high)
- appreciating the experiences.

Haafkens (1997) was inspired by this research, and distinguishes between five phases in the use of tranquillizers:

- The period which leads to the first prescription.
- The first six months of the use on prescription.
- The last six months of taking the tranquillizers.
- The decision to stop.
- The stopping in itself.

TIP

Some software packages enable the tracking of a sequence of events that is talked about throughout the text (Lewins & Silver, 2007). The tools allow hyper-linking between points in the text. You can either link several segments or pairs of segments. A sequential model (and other models as well) can also be visualized using the mapping tools of the software packages.

Creating a matrix

Miles and Huberman (1994) recommend the use of a matrix, as creating it facilitates thinking about the linkages between the various categories. A matrix displays whether and how phenomena appear when other phenomena are also present. A matrix may have a very simple shape. Whether a trait is present or absent or whether a phenomenon does or does not occur is noted in the rows and columns. In order to depict this, a category is divided into parts (see Chapter 6). Thus, connections become apparent. A matrix that looks simple can still be very informative and labour-intensive to create.

An example of a matrix about causes of aversive behaviour and feeding issues of nursing home residents is shown in Table 7.1 (Pasman, The, Onwuteaka-Philipsen, Van der Wal & Ribbe, 2003: 311). The rows contain the reasons why nursing home residents do not eat and the columns specify the domains to which the reasons apply. The cells contain words or short descriptions. This matrix is far from simple and summarizes an important part of the findings.

TABLE 7.1 FRAMEWORK OF CAUSES OF AVERSIVE BEHAVIOUR AND DOMAINS OF FUNCTIONING

	Domains		
Causes	**Physical**	**Psychological**	**Social**
Not able to eat/drink	Difficulty in swallowing Paralysis Acute illness	Grief Apathy	Distracting environment Insufficient time for feeding
Not understanding the need to eat/drink	Visual and audio problems	Apraxia Agnosia	Insufficient nursing skills
Not wanting to eat/drink	Declining/loss of appetite Afraid of choking	Not wanting to live any longer Disliking food	Unpleasant environment

Source: Pasman et al., 2003

A matrix may be used to document a profile of participants. In this manner, Haafkens (1997) summarized the life histories of the women in the tranquillizer study. The rows contained the interviewed women. The columns contained the following information: the year of the first use, the age of the woman at that moment, the most important biographical event, the reason for using the tranquillizer, the role of the doctor, the role of others, the nature of the medication and the pattern of use. The life history of a person is found by reading through the matrix from left to right. Reading through the matrix from top to bottom yields the variation in content of a phenomenon, for example the various reasons for using tranquillizers.

Reading your memos

Theoretical or analytical memos are created during the project to record any ideas that are related to the interpretation of the data (see Chapter 4). They reflect attempts to organize the data in a way to derive meaning from them and record the development of the interpretation. They allow researchers (and others) to track down the development of the concepts. In the memos is described, for example, how a particular observation has been interpreted, why codes are split or merged, how a sensitizing concept has slowly gained empirical weight, with which colleagues the interpretations are discussed and so on. A theoretical memo might contain just one statement or it might comprise several pages of relevant information.

The reading of memos helps to track the various categories and follow or understand the conceptual progression of the findings. Memos are particularly valuable in providing a chain of reasoning (Cutcliffe & McKenna, 2004): the 'evidence' found in the data, the inferences drawn from the data, the choices for the main categories and their properties and so on. Your chain of reasoning should be sound and convincing. Memos can then remind you of the development history of the various categories and the relationships between them, and alert you to missing or yet incomplete elements in your line of thinking.

TIP

When you use software in your project you can attach memos to different elements of the project, such as documents, codes and text fragments. Memos can be managed in a systematic and useful way, and their contents can be searched and retrieved. It might be useful to write memos as stand-alone documents in your project, especially for the overarching themes and patterns that are discerned at the end of the research (see Chapter 6). A memo not attached to other sources has the advantage that you can assign codes to them and use all the functions that are available to 'normal' documents (Lewins & Silver, 2007).

Searching and counting

Software packages offer the option of searching for words or codes either in a section of the data set or in the entire data set and determine their frequency. Two types are distinguished: searching and counting for specific words or expressions as they are used by the participants, and searching and counting how often a specific code has been used.

TIP
_____

Most software packages offer tools to easily search for words and view them in context. They also have tools for counting words and codes. Most programs allow you to search whether several codes co-occur in the data and whether certain words are used in each other's vicinity.

_____

First, there is searching for particular words as they occur in the texts as a way to interrogate the data. For instance, in the example study into the quality of care in nursing homes (Chapter 5), staff members often spoke about 'attention' paid to residents. To verify whether 'attention' was indeed often used in the interviews and in the field notes, the empirical material was searched for the word 'attention' and the hits were counted. When the occurrences were reviewed in context, it was confirmed that 'attention' was an important activity that occurred under several conditions and had several definitions attached to it.

Counting can also be used to explore large data sets and to compare the use of certain words and phrases in different groups. One example of counting words is keyword analysis, illustrated by Seale, Charteris-Black, Dumelow, Locock and Ziebland (2008). The authors compared joint interviews with individual interviews with men and women. One assumption was that in mixed-sex joint interviewing the perspective of one gender will be favoured, i.e. that of the overbearing male informants who see themselves speaking on behalf of the couple. To test this hypothesis the authors counted how often the singular pronouns ('I', 'me' and 'my') were used, as well as plural pronouns ('we', 'us' and 'our'). Analysis of the individual interviews showed that men were more likely than women to use plural pronouns that referred to both themselves and their partner. Women, on the other hand, used the individual interview to speak about their own personal experience, reflected in their more frequent use of 'I', 'me' and 'my'. In joint interviews 'we' became used more frequently by women to indicate inclusion of their partners, while no such change occurred for men. Keyword analysis is not a qualitative analysis in the strict sense, but it shows that counting should not be dismissed immediately, especially when large data sets need to be scanned for interesting subjects.

Second, there is searching and counting for the number of times a certain code has been assigned to the whole or parts of the data set. Due to the nature of the data collection, we have to use these frequencies with even more caution. The content and time spent on each topic varies according to the questions asked and the participant's own salient concerns. So when counting codes, you count your own concerns as well as the participant's. Your concerns can change during the research process as you come to understand the topic being studied. As a consequence, the outcome of a count will not lead to a reliable estimate of the true prevalence of the various social phenomena, and not even of their weight.

Then again, during analysis it is the researcher who assigns the codes, so that information stored will be retrievable. Generally, the frequencies with which the codes are used will give additional evidence. Instead of relying on implicit notions of frequency only, counting how often a theme appears in the transcripts or field notes may demonstrate that a theme is weighty and be considered supportive evidence. Here is one example of my research on veterans who developed post-traumatic stress disorder (examined later in this chapter). I coded for positive and negative experiences during their deployment in Cambodia. Negative aspects for instance consisted of 'bribing', 'witnessing misery', 'poverty', 'cruelty' and 'disparaging human life'. Positive aspects were 'beauty of nature', 'resilience of local people', 'children', 'hospitality' and 'travelling'. When I counted the fragments that were assigned these codes, I noticed a ratio of 3:1 for the negative aspects in relation to the positive ones.

The outcome of this counting was used with caution. The fragments I counted were all of a different nature and had a different impact. Is 'travelling' of the same nature as 'bribing'? Is that a 1:1 ratio? Maybe only one negative, unpredictable life-threatening event could spoil the entire exercise. What I want to demonstrate with this example is that you cannot rely on counting only, you have to interpret what you are counting in the context of the particular source that your segments are taken from and in the context of all your sources, all your analytical efforts, and all your interpretations.

Acknowledging the presence of feelings

Researchers' feelings during field work, such as embarrassment, unease, fear, guilt, anger and sadness, can be used in analysis. Feelings were previously discussed in Chapter 3, when researcher's stress during data collection and data analysis were addressed. We have learnt to ignore and suppress feelings because they are thought to bias our data collection and analysis. However, feelings can serve as heuristic instruments when one tries to become aware of them and tries to find out what possibly could have caused them. Feelings can be used to your advantage, especially when trying to place yourself in the shoes of another person (Harris & Huntington, 2001; Kleinman & Copp, 1993). When emotions are acknowledged they can be used as analytic tools.

It is possible to feel upset, for example when veterans tell you about the injustice and misery they observed when deployed in a war-zone area. You will be affected each time you read the transcript about mine incidents with children. By using your emotional reaction as an analytic tool you can try to understand how others feel, and why (see the next section). Your own feelings then serve as a means to see the world through the eyes of other human beings, who try to share their experiences with you. Your own feelings might mirror those who hold a particular role in the setting you are studying (Kleinman & Copp, 1993). Feelings can alert you to ask many questions about what it is that upsets veterans, what strategies they use to deal with their emotions, how they protect themselves against becoming traumatized, and how they deal with emotions in a culture perceived to be tough. Feelings should not be considered inappropriate in field work; rather they should be seen as advantageous in understanding the data.

There are times during analysis when it is appropriate to respect and acknowledge your own emotions, and these should be included in the field notes or memos. However, it is still comparatively rare for authors to include descriptions and analyses of their own intense emotions experienced during field work in the final report. This has to do with the common writing styles used in scientific reporting, although some writing formats allow you to write about your situation in the field and your personal background (see Chapter 10). The disclosure of feelings can be considered helpful when analysing qualitative data.

Formulating a typology

Qualitative research may result in the formulation of a typology. The four awareness contexts of Glaser and Strauss (1965) for instance, constitute a typology (see Box 1.4). The construction of a typology stimulates the analyst's imagination. In Chapter 6 we identified that two types of analyses are commonly distinguished: issue-focussed or cross-case analyses and case-focussed or within-case analyses. Until now we have mainly concentrated on issue-focussed analyses by using codes to find common themes through all collected materials. Classification into types helps identify connections between different phenomena within one case.

Types can be constructed on the level of an individual, for instance focussing on the beliefs, intentions, behaviour and the consequences of behaviour in women using sedatives. They can also be constructed on the level of groups or organizations, such as the relationships between culture, degree of organization, traditions and involvement in violence of football club supporters. This kind of connecting may illuminate how several elements of a case are linked and may show the flow of events over time.

TIP

To generate a typology it is useful to code relevant segments that pertain to a certain type. When using software, consider the use of hyperlinking tools to link distinct parts of the type within a text (the columns in Table 7.2) or to link the values on the criteria in all the available texts (the rows in Table 7.2). A useful software tool is the overview of codes that appear in one document. This index of coded segments per document provides a text profile that can help you to focus on the specifics of a type.

Types are useful tools for readers as well. First, because the names of the types usually reveal a lot about their contents. In most cases the types are easily recognizable and easy to work with. Second, a typology allows readers to compare the types with each other as well as with empirical cases in real life – organizations, persons, activities, situations – in order to trace differences and similarities. These comparisons provide knowledge on these cases and may provide clues about the reasons of possible deviations from the types or about the consequences attached to different types.

TABLE 7.2 TYPOLOGY OF TWO PERSPECTIVES OF PEOPLE WITH MULTIPLE SCLEROSIS

	Perspective	
Criteria	MS will never have the upper hand	I have nothing to do with MS
Feelings about MS	Confident, realistic	Bitterness, powerless
Identity	Integration of illness in life	Loss of former identity
Coping strategies	Normalizing, managing	Hiding, banishing
Dealing with the family	Openness, support	Isolation, distraction
Dealing with help	Organizing, control	Rebellion, resistance

Source: Boeije, 2002

The typology in Table 7.2 stems from research on the perspectives of people who have the chronic degenerative illness multiple sclerosis (MS). Most interviewees were found to live by a certain motto. These mottos were used as titles for different types which were distinguished in the data and of which two are described as an example here (Boeije, 2002). Putting a typology together forces one to think about the criteria by which different cases can be distinguished, whether situations, individuals, organizations, groups or activities. These criteria are put into the rows of a matrix and the cases in the columns. The values for each of the examined cases are systematically filled out in the cells.

Constructing arguments

This section describes the use of logic as a heuristic device for analysing your data. Logic has to do with reasoning, with what is considered proof and with drawing inferences (Cutcliffe & McKenna, 2004). The reader should be able to follow the progression of the findings in the research report, i.e. to trace the path from the data to the inferences. Cutcliffe and McKenna remark that one person's chain of reasoning may well be different from another's, yet both can be logical. These different chains of reasoning may even produce different conclusions. To think about your chain of reasoning during the reporting phase is a good exercise in thinking about your data. In your report reasoning takes place on at least two levels.

The first level is the logic you apply to the participants' accounts. While doing your research you try to dissect how participants view their world and how this view relates to their actions. When you claim for instance to have 'found' a type – 'MS will never have the upper hand' (Table 7.2) – this claim should be supported by arguments, such as observations, interpretations, regularities and theories. To substantiate your logical reasoning you have to ask all kinds of questions: What are the participants' arguments for behaving in a certain way? Are there any contradictions? What do they take into account? How do they weigh different aspects? Do they perceive these aspects as within their control? Do they have different experiences as well? In other words, your claim as a scientific writer must be based on plausible arguments (Smaling, 2002).

TIP _____

To support this heuristic aid, you can use the hyperlinking tool in the software to link contradictory statements, points in the data where strong arguments are demonstrated or where doubts arise.

_____

The second level of reasoning concerns the report as a whole in which you are constructing an argument. A strong argument persuades the reader to accept the writer's viewpoint (Charmaz, 2006). The most important argument is the overall message of your research: the one that elaborates the salient contribution. Therefore you can go back to the elements of your research proposal, but you cannot copy and paste them, because now that you have carried out the research you can add the insights you have developed into the argument. We know that in a scientific piece of work we have to present a straightforward research design including the gathering of adequate data, the conducting of a sound analysis, and the construction of the overall argument and the logical reasoning it involves.

All chapters, all sections and all paragraphs consist of smaller arguments. Each paragraph has a core message comprising a main issue and some side issues. This core message is connected to your argument in the section. And the argument of the section builds up the argument of the entire report. All of them are connected. The point you want to make in each part should be clear. Charmaz is helpful in formulating four questions to help you find arguments (Charmaz, 2006: 157):

- What sense of this process or analysis do you want your reader to make?
- Why is it important?
- What did you tell your readers that you intended to do, and why did you tell them that?
- In which sentences or paragraphs do your major points coalesce?

Charmaz suggests that working on the data, taking notes about an emerging argument, talking to colleagues, talking to yourself or thinking aloud may help formulate your initial arguments. Or take a rest and sometimes the right reasoning comes to you ('That's it!').

Outlining the main message

Suppose that the deadline to hand in your final research report is imminent. How would the main argument of the story be formulated and what would be the message to the reader? This question forces you to think about the preliminary table of contents and in particular the contents of the results section (see Chapter 10). When writing different drafts of your results your ideas and especially the order or logic of the presentation will develop (Jorgensen, 1989: 120). Jorgensen sees an outline as a heuristic device that helps you order your ideas and prepares you for writing the final report:

> Outlines may be very useful once you have notes and files in need of further organization. Outlines, however, are purely heuristic devices. You need an outline only to get a handle on the possible arrangement of ideas or an argument. The outline serves temporarily to organize your thinking and provide a definitive direction to the work. Be prepared to deviate from your outline.

Below is an example of the table of contents from the study by Cutcliffe et al. (2006) on the support of psychiatric nurses for suicidal people.

BOX 7.1   EXAMPLE OF A TABLE OF CONTENTS

1. Introduction
2. The study of suicide: a brief historical overview
3. Research method and design: modified Grounded Theory

    3.1   Ethical considerations
    3.2   Selection of the sample and data collection

4. Data analysis
5. Findings

    5.1   Core variable – 're-connecting the person with humanity'

6. Stage one: reflecting an image of humanity

    6.1   Experiencing intense, warm, care-based human to human contact
    6.2   Implicitly challenging suicidal constructs as a results of encountering contrary experiences

7. Stage two: guiding the individual back to humanity

    7.1   Nurturing insight and understanding
    7.2   Supporting and strengthening pre-suicidal beliefs
    7.3   Encountering a novel interpersonal, helping relationship

8. Stage three: 'learning to live'

    8.1   Accommodating an existential crisis, past, present and future
    8.2   Going on in the context set by the existential relationship with suicide

9. Discussion
10. Conclusions

There are sufficient aids to properly round off the final stages of the analysis. Of course, these aids do not need to be applied all at the same time. You should use them when they fit your data and only if you are convinced of their value. In choosing heuristic devices, a personal component is involved: when you are always sketching you will probably be drawn into visualization, when you are sloppy you will find it difficult to read and use the memos (if you can still find them), and when you enjoy seeing a bigger picture you will probably like to construct a matrix and an outline.

Think aloud analysis

Although you can learn a lot from books, some things are best learned by watching someone doing the job. Therefore I recorded my thoughts during an analysis to generate a 'think aloud' report. I would like to show the type of mental activities I was engaged in while analysing qualitative interviews with Dutch veterans who had been deployed to Cambodia on a peace mission. Half of the group had been diagnosed with post-traumatic stress disorder (PTSD), while the other half had not. I did not conduct the interviews myself. I started out with ten interviews of veterans who had been diagnosed with PTSD. The research question formulated for the entire project was 'How do Dutch veterans attribute meaning to their deployment on a peace mission in Cambodia and what are the similarities and differences between veterans diagnosed with post-traumatic stress disorder and the ones not diagnosed?'

Data management

The first thing I am going to do is rename the interviews of the group diagnosed with PTSD. They have these complicated numbers like 31–287 that even after some time do not ring a bell and I keep forgetting who is who. The texts are numbered as simply as possible with an abbreviation of an Interview Diagnosis Number (ID-01, ID-02 and so on). I generate a project in MAXQDA2007, the software I am working with, and import the texts. I suspect I will be using different codes for this group and for the group that is not diagnosed, and therefore decide to analyse the two groups one after the other so that I can concentrate on each group separately. Afterwards the two can be compared and combined.

Start open coding

The experience of control during deployment seems to have two dimensions: mastery on the one hand and powerlessness on the other hand. I decide to merge the codes 'comradeship' and 'collegiality', and decide to use the code 'comradeship' because this expresses the meaning of what the participants tell me. How they deal with each other while on a mission seems to be a mixture of working together professionally and friendship. The relationship between soldiers and officers is sometimes described as the formal soldier/officer relationship in which the officer is clearly the superior of the soldier, but sometimes the relationship is described as equal.

While analysing ID-04 I have to generate new codes because he gives a lot of information about the nature of the mission and what he perceived to be their ambivalent task in Cambodia. Because they were on a peace mission they were not allowed to fight and shoot except when seriously threatened themselves. I discover that many men in this group have some sort of conflict with their (former) employer, the army. I decide to generate an attribute (a variable) to cover the current relationship with the army either as neutral/all right or as a cause for conflict. Later on when I add the interviews with the veterans without PTSD I can create a matrix and compare the groups.

Half-time score

After coding four interviews of around 80 minutes each, I have generated around 75 codes organized in nine themes. On average I have assigned around four fragments per code. I tidy up the code tree and order it in a logical sequence. It now runs from the motivation to join the army, to motivation for deployment, their experiences in Cambodia, their home front, the comrades, returning home, and current experiences.

Theoretical memo 1

I remember having glanced over an interview with a veteran who did not develop PTSD in which he was talking about 'just doing your work' in a kind of instrumental and pragmatic way. In this group there is an interviewee who also says 'you just do your job' but he seems to use it in a different meaning. It is a demoralized expression of duty, a way of expressing that you just do your duty without thinking about it in order to get the job done. The veteran without PTSD seemed to use the word 'job' as employment, like any other job.

Theoretical memo 2

In the meantime I have studied an article about self-enhancement in the context of trauma and recovery, since I felt troubled by my lack of knowledge on the subject. Victims of danger and fear often feel guilty or blame themselves for not having done enough. Their confidence has to be restored, and this is what Taylor (1983) refers to as 'self-enhancement'. The interviewed veterans seem to restore their confidence by making comparisons, for instance with colleagues who are going through a divorce or even some who committed suicide. At first I did not grasp the meaning of these comparisons, but now I see them as attempts to restore confidence. In comparison with these other veterans they are doing quite well.

Continuation: open coding and axial coding

While coding ID-06 I still need new codes, which means that the exploration is still going on. For example, about carelessness, awareness of danger and risk, about exhaustion, and about the macho culture of the Marines. I am a bit wary of creating new codes because I already have so many of them.

Now coding is speeding up. I feel the need to find out where I stored all the fragments and to check if I have worked systematically. I guess I have not. I refrain from checking because it takes a lot of time. I am confident that when retrieving segments and writing, I can filter out the useful fragments.

Theoretical memo

While coding ID-06 I notice that the veterans confide mainly in male persons (sometimes before their partners), like an uncle, a father-in-law, a grandfather or a male friend.

I discover that the veterans are impressed by the children they met in Cambodia. Are they a symbol of innocence and disarmament? When something happens to these children it is experienced as very painful. They attach positive and negative emotions to children in general. To check this conjecture I do a lexical search to find the word 'children', and indeed children are mentioned in all interviews except one. The exception or negative case is an interview with an interpreter who had a different task and role than the other interviewees, and during the interview mostly concentrated on the negotiations with Cambodian rulers.

Methodological memo

The idea of bracketing or the role of presuppositions in the analysis becomes meaningful. It would have been a nice experiment to see whether I could have detected the interviews with the veterans diagnosed with PTSD and the ones without. I think there is only one interview in this group that would have left me in doubt.

Finding a core concept

I have read Janoff-Bulman's (1992) book, in which she builds an argument that extreme situations and life-threatening events can lead to shattered assumptions. She presupposes that we hold basic assumptions, namely that the world is benevolent and meaningful and that the self is worthy. A trauma can suddenly and powerfully threaten these assumptions of a safe and protected life and a just world. One response to threatening events is that the fundamental beliefs are destroyed. Of course the veterans in our study do not tell me that their 'assumptions are shattered' but there are many indications that they found themselves in a frightening place and that they are still filled with images representing malevolence, meaninglessness and self-abasement. In Cambodia they found themselves in an inconceivable, unimaginable world.

And then the puzzle is suddenly solved. With hindsight the veterans state that you cannot prepare yourself for deployment. This makes sense because you cannot prepare for the unimaginable. They all say their families do not and cannot possibly understand them. This is self-evident, taking into account that their families' basic assumptions are still intact and that they see the world through different eyes than the veterans in this group. The concept of shattered assumptions allows me to understand their accounts, and I am connecting several themes with the core concept, such as the training and preparation, the experience of danger and the ignorance they perceive when coming home.

Methodological memo

I am analysing ID-08 and I become a bit bored. With ID-10 I seem to have reached saturation in my categories. Now that I have analysed all the interviews of the veterans with PTSD I feel the urge to let it out and write it all down. So I start writing. This is really the best part of qualitative research.

Writing

The structure of the written report seems to make sense. I start out describing the life-threatening events and danger. This is central for the experience of trauma. Then I go on with the shattered assumptions because this is, I think, what happens after having experienced danger and fear. Next, I contrast shattered assumptions with the taken-for-granted world they used to know at home. Subsequently, I describe the negative things and the positive ones they encountered, and notice that they often go hand-in-hand but that the negative ones are much stronger. And I finish with dealing with family and friends when returning home in what once was a taken-for-granted world.

Each time I start writing again, I reread what I have written up till then to get my mind back into the project and see whether it still makes sense. Each segment that I retrieve is read and reread to see what is in it. When retrieving segments that belong to a certain category, I sometimes come across the same segment again. This is obviously because I coded it twice. When I retrieve a segment that I do not understand, I store it in a file to be read later on. When I retrieve a segment that I probably need in a different section, I copy the entire segment into that other section. I am afraid that otherwise I will forget the segment altogether, but it makes the concept of the manuscript very unclear and unwieldy.

It is important to describe the danger and life-threatening events that the veterans met, like shootings, minefields and accidents that involve children. I make inventories of the less important themes that are expressed. All veterans talk about the backwardness of the country and I just list what they mention, like poverty and the lack of asphalt roads, sewerage and appropriate health care. In this way all their impressions are used to give one image for the reader to have when interviewees refer to being in a primitive country.

Now that I have described the danger and life-threatening events, I come back to these issues to demonstrate shattered assumptions. I desperately need the expressions of the interviewees, since the subject is difficult and it is also hard to indicate data to be evidence. After having processed the fragments that were assigned the most important codes, such as shattered assumptions, negative and positive aspects of being there, taken-for-granted world and danger, I can fairly well assess which other codes I will be needing, like distrust, ignorance and misunderstanding of family, adventure, growth, returning home and the Marines' culture. I am trying to connect all themes, which means that the different parts of the manuscript will be interrelated and that there is consistency in the piece of work.

Half-time score

MAXQDA2007 showed me that I had coded 654 fragments and when I have processed all the categories that I need for this particular manuscript I think I might have read half of them. Because I did the coding myself I know exactly what is coded and what I can save for later publications. For instance, the conditions under which these veterans went on deployment, their education and training, their motivation and relationships with their families before departure. A comparison between the group with PTSD and without will be very interesting and I am burning with curiosity to find out how they compare.

Special devices: focus groups and visuals

Focus groups

Focus group data are special because there are group dynamics involved. The individual might be influenced by the group and the group as a whole might be influenced by the individual. Although the analysis of focus group data follows the same processes as the analysis of other types of qualitative data to a certain degree, we have to be aware of the specific group composition as well as the individuals finding their own meaning within the group (Duggleby, 2005). How to incorporate the impact of the group context in the analysis of focus group data is a matter not yet resolved (Vicsek, 2007).

Ultimately, there seem to be three levels of analysis, namely the intragroup level, the intergroup level and the individual level. First, there is the group itself. For intragroup analysis it is useful to have a combination of two analyses. One is of the group discussion on a particular subject, and the other is a more fine-grained analysis of the subject itself (Kidd & Parshall, 2000).

When analysing the larger units of texts, attention can be paid to group interactions, such as levels of agreement, consensus, conflict, censoring and characteristics of the discussion. Attention should go to tracking individuals' contributions as well, to see if or how they are influenced by group interaction. In an intragroup analysis the effects of group composition and characteristics are identified, such as a very talkative member taking part or the use of a small group due to absenteeism (Morrison-Beedy, Côté-Arsenault & Fischbeck Feinstein, 2001).

When analysing for content, the focus can be directed at different points of view when addressing the subject. Counting how often a subject is addressed during a focus group meeting needs to be approached carefully because of the effect it may have on the group. For instance, one group member may put a topic that is prominent to him or her at the top of the agenda, or during the discussion participants may select items that they consider of interest or importance to the other group members, such as themes they think would be good to discuss together (Vicsek, 2007). So when a theme appears to dominate the discussion, it could be a sign of its significance but it could also be an artefact of the method used. It is up to the researcher to decide how the outcomes of counting have to be interpreted.

The intergroup level refers to the comparison of the groups with an eye to group differences, the shared experiences and topics in each group, and the reasons for this. Situational factors that can be taken into account are the characteristics of the participants, the moderator, the environment, the time factors and the content (Vicsek, 2007). By comparing the groups it becomes possible to say something about how these factors might have influenced the results of a group discussion. An intergroup analysis can determine whether there is consensus on the range of issues deemed relevant to the participants. A form of consensus across groups can be identified in terms of the range of issues concerned.

And finally there is the individual level of the participants of the focus groups. The responses and behaviours of separate members can be examined at this level. It is possible to link the contribution of each specific group member by marking all statements of a member in the transcript. In this way the use of certain terms and the contribution of particular themes can be linked to certain roles, identities and personal attributes (Sim, 1998). If people were invited for a particular reason, such as their vision, opinion, or expertise, it is possible to address whether this is evident in the results. A more thorough investigation of group influence on an individual member taking part can be made. A sequential analysis can be conducted for any changes of proposed views or re-emphasizing certain experiences. For instance, social pressure can bring a group member to soften his view on a particular topic and conform to the group norm.

Not every study demands an analysis on all three levels. When analysing with respect to the influences of the group, group interaction data is needed (see Chapter 4). They will help the researcher to understand how contents are collectively created and how interactions build on one another. Group interaction data can be generated in different ways (see also Chapter 4). In reporting focus group results, excerpts of group interactions can be presented instead of quotes of individuals.

Visuals

Visual data are valuable because they communicate through images instead of language, showing aspects of the lives of the participants involved. The conceptualization of images – putting the meaning of the picture into words – is different from conceptualizing verbal data, which expresses thoughts, emotions, ideas and arguments. In Chapter 4 it became clear that neither verbal nor visual data can be considered exact representations of reality. When using visual images, whether media images (e.g. magazine covers), photographs or drawings, the researcher should be aware that people viewing the images may interpret them differently from those who created them.

Collier (2001) differentiates between indirect and direct analysis of visuals. Indirect analysis means that the images are used to trigger others to tell and explain what can be noticed in them, for instance in photo elicitation (see Chapter 4). Direct analysis means examination of the content and the character of the images as data by the researcher. Direct analysis can be employed as open viewing or open immersion and is based on initial grouping in a natural way. Different criteria can be used to organize and compare the images in order to detect themes and patterns. Direct analysis can also be employed in a more closed and structured way. Much of what then takes place is based on the assumption that visuals are often part of a collection or series.

Collier (2001) distinguishes two types of collections of images. A collection may consist of many different images of the same subject, for instance panoramic views of a park, details, different angles and aerial photographs. In the analysis they are put together to allow descriptions and interpretations to emerge, for instance how the various corners of a park are used differently by visitors or how the park gradually changed over time. Another type of collection consists of different images that help to identify what is depicted in a certain image. For example, an image of a child engaged in playing with a toy that is compared with photos of the child in class, the child playing in other locations or with other toys and photos of family members.

As the literature does not offer much in the way of guidelines for incorporating visual images into an interpretive analysis, I draw on my own experience with student projects in which we practised with the use of photographs and drawings. It was clear that pictures reduced the amount of description needed to understand what a situation looked like, whether a religious lesson in Koran texts, skiing lessons for small children, or women at home and at work. Photographs produced elements of what these situations were supposed to be; images as writing, in fact (O'Reilly, 2005). In this respect they added to the verbal descriptions and could be coded according to certain categories.

The photos also showed the environment, such as a classroom with rows of chairs and tables, a mountain slope, and artefacts like books, skis or computers. They also showed the number of people present as well as something about the relationship between the different photographed individuals, such as teachers and children. In picturing all this, the photographs give us a glimpse of how these situations were experienced, whether seriously or jokingly, weary, bored or eagerly, or intimately or casually. These elements could all be coded, although the meaning and 'proof' was debatable since the photographs could have been interpreted in many different ways.

It seems that today visuals are often used alongside other kinds of methods, maybe to overcome the difficulty in using and interpreting them. The use of different methods to study a research subject is referred to as 'methods triangulation' (see Chapter 9). Radley and Taylor (2003) are among the few who offer some valuable points for analysing visual material in combination with interviews:

- Set out all photographs to examine the kinds of images selected: what scenes, events, places, spaces, and objects have been visualized?
- Listen to the interviews with the photos at hand to find out more about the reasons for taking these particular photographs.

- Analyse what the pictures denote in terms of times, places and experiences. Sometimes this becomes clear if a participant has given the photograph a caption.
- In what way do the images represent a story that the participant wants to tell?
- What are the limits to which photographs can show what they are intended to exemplify?

In sum, to study human experiences and culture visual materials are of value. Open viewing can help to explore the field of study. Once identified, themes and patterns can be tested via structured analysis and complemented with indirect analysis as in photo elicitation.

Using the computer in analysis

Today many of the above-mentioned activities can be conducted with the use of software packages for qualitative data analysis. Most of these programs have been specifically developed for this purpose. In the literature the term CAQDAS, or computer-assisted qualitative data analysis, is used to indicate analysis supported by software. Some researchers still conduct their analysis manually. They copy documents, cut fragments, archive them in folders, create cards for each concept, stick Post-it notes to the wall to find relationships, draw maps and so on. Computers can make these activities much easier, although they have their limitations as well.

Software developers would like you to believe that the computer will allow you to search the data and present the findings with lightning speed. I call this the 'Furby-syndrome': Furby is a furry toy animal, and children love it when Furby talks back and even changes its facial expressions. They also enjoy having conversations with the toy because it is programmed to give adequate responses. Software for qualitative data analysis also gives you appropriate responses when you search for words, codes and frequencies and willingly shows text portraits, matrices, tables and colourful charts. But software cannot help you to judge the worth of a document, it does not break up the text into meaningful fragments, it does not decide what codes to assign, it cannot interpret any relationships between categories, and it does not come up with great ideas to capture in memos. The artificial intelligence part is still not that well-developed.

I am a big supporter of computer use in analysis, but it is the researcher who has to know what it is the computer needs to do. I expect that with digital technology still developing fast, the debate whether to use a computer or not will lose its currency. Vast amounts of digital documents, digital visual material, voice recognition software and simultaneous analysis of the transcript, as well as the audio-recording, are all within easy reach via the computer.

If the majority of the effort remains the work of the researcher, what then are the functions of computers in qualitative analysis? In this section the most used functions of qualitative analysis software packages will be described. In the following section the description will continue with a reflection on computer-assisted data analysis.

Tools

In writing about the tools of software programs I refer to the code-based theory-building software (Lewins & Silver, 2007). These packages assist the researcher in coding texts and retrieval along thematic lines as well as in memoing. They have incorporated search tools allowing the researcher to test relationships between categories and concepts. Within the search tools they have sometimes taken on language-based searching tools, like word frequencies, word indexing, the creation of keyword co-occurrence matrices, and proximity plots. Some programs enable the graphic visualization of connections and processes using mapping tools (Lewins & Silver, 2007).

In the description of program tools I draw heavily on my experiences with MAX-QDA2007. I will focus on the support of software with the analytical activities that were addressed in this and the previous chapter.

Filing

All materials that you use, whether field notes, interview transcripts or existing documents, can be imported into the database of your project. In MAXQDA this is referred to as a 'document system'. Just as in a real filing cabinet, you can systematically file your documents in 'drawers' of your choice (text groups), whether in type of data (for instance, interviews and observations) or chronologically (first-wave interviews and second-wave interviews) or participant groups (teachers and pupils, organization X and organization Y). The document system is very flexible and makes it easy to combine documents from different 'drawers'.

Editing

Most programs allow you to change your documents once imported. Not only can you remove, for instance, spelling errors, but you can also change the fonts, use underlining, italics or bold and colour words or text fragments.

Coding

One of the basic functions of software for qualitative data analysis is the coding function. In MAXQDA you work in the text browser to select an excerpt and award it a code. The codes are hierarchically ordered in a coding scheme (code system). New codes are easily generated. Needless to say, it is the researcher who develops the codes. Modifying coding, like merging, splitting, renaming, deleting and moving excerpts from one code to another is all very easy and can be carried out systematically. For example, if you change the code 'pet' into 'dog' in the code tree, the program will automatically change the code in all documents in which this code was used.

The codes are displayed in the margins of the working documents. You can assign more than one code to a fragment, overlap fragments, nest them and so on. If you want to stress the interconnectedness between the sub-codes and the main code, you can use colours. You can choose not to display all codes and make some of them invisible, for instance those of a particular colour or awarded by a particular user. This is a useful function if you work in teams and want to compare codes without being influenced by what the others have done.

Retrieving

In software for qualitative data analysis it is easy to retrieve your coded segments. It is also very flexible. You can retrieve from all your documents or from a selection. You can retrieve one code at a time or several codes at once. More advanced retrieval is possible with the use of 'boolean' searches, for instance fragments that have awarded code A and code B or fragments with code A and code B within only five sentences.

In MAXQDA you can award attributes to your documents; for instance, sex and age of an interviewee, or the number of members of a group when your document is a focus group transcript. You can also award attributes that relate to your analysis and codes. For instance, you assign the code 'happiness' and then decide to turn this code into an attribute. The number of times this code is used in a particular document is considered as the value on this attribute for this document. Later on you can retrieve fragments from documents in which, for example, the code 'happiness' was used more than five times ('happy people'). Then you can make all kinds of combinations, for instance, you can search in the group of female happy elderly and male unhappy youth. The attributes can then be used in software for quantitative data analysis.

It is very easy to get an overview of all retrieved segments in all documents. The program counts the frequency of a certain code and it shows you the line numbers and position in the documents. Per text this can give you a kind of profile in terms of codes that you can compare with other texts.

One of the criticisms about coding and in particular coding with the computer was that retrieved fragments were decontextualized, that is, taken out of the situation or conversation they had taken place in. However, in modern software one click on a retrieved segment opens the original text and shows you where the fragment was originally located.

Searching

Most programs have a function to search for words or strings of words in your texts. You can also search for words that are often found in each others' vicinity. The results of these lexical searches show you the context of sentences in which certain words were used. Once again, frequencies can be obtained.

Memos

Memos tend to get lost, since they are like the yellow Post-it notes we use on our books, desks and walls. Modern software incorporates the Post-its in our projects. In MAXQDA the memo icon is in the form of a yellow Post-it. This function enables you to write project memos, document memos, code memos and text memos. Memos can contain all kinds of remarks, and are easily adjusted and completed. You can give them colours or other symbols to remind you of their content and the type of annotation. Using the software, it is easy to generate an overview of memos.

Visualizations

Visualizations are novel. MAXQDA started with cross-case visualizations. It used a matrix to combine documents and codes and another matrix to combine only codes to search for co-occurrences. Recently per case visualizations were added. They make use of the colours that have been attached to certain codes and show which colour (=code) often pops up in a certain text (textportrait) or in what sequence the colours (=codes) appear in a text (codeline).

In addition to these features, there is a special graphical tool available within MAX-QDA called MAXMaps. This allows you to import elements of your MAXQDA project and draw diagrams and maps showing the relationships between the elements. Of course, you have to link the elements; the computer does not do that for you.

Writing

Memos and retrieved segments serve as the basis for writing the chapters in the research report. Systematically all fragments that you awarded a certain code are retrieved and can either be printed or transported to your text processor. You can use the fragments as a prompt to refresh your memory of what to write about or directly as quotes in your report. Again, the computer does not write for you, but it provides the basic material that you need to write about.

Methodological memos can be easily retrieved for writing the methods section of your report. Memos are also used to have all your ideas and brain waves at hand while writing. Other types of output are tables of, for instance, search commands, or visuals that can be used in reports and presentations.

Of course there is more. As we have seen already, text parts can be linked to other parts in the same text or in a different text or even to other sources (hyperlinking). Sometimes visual materials such as photographs can be imported and coded as for any other document. Team members can work on the project at the same time and merge projects later on. There are options for quick coding, in vivo coding and so on. However, the core function of software for qualitative data analysis is to facilitate the data management and analytic tasks.

TIP
_____

Lewins and Silver (2007) ascertain that most of the students they train in software find innovative ways of using the packages. They seem to work independently, using the tools in a way that benefits their work and can be legitimated by their methodological approach. Consider a cupboard that you can use for shoes, CDs, jewellery, clothes or books. It can be used standing up or lying down, underneath your bed, in the living room or in the hallway. With the use of software it is much the same: tools can be used in any way you consider appropriate for your project. I think this opinion from such experienced teachers in software as Lewins and Silver should boost our confidence!

_____

Reflections on computer-assisted data analysis

There are a lot of programs on the market that assist in qualitative research. Examples are QSR Nvivo, ATLAS.ti, HyperRESEARCH, MAXQDA2007, QDA Miner,

The Ethnograph, Transana, Qualrus and Framework. Information on specific software packages, such as tutorials and manuals, as well as demo versions, are available on the software developer websites. Programs are not static products; they are continually revised and developed. Some authors who have written books about qualitative analysis recommend the software they are familiar with. Examples are Nvivo (Richards, 2005; Bryman, 2008) and HyperRESEARCH (Hesse-Biber & Leavy, 2006).

A few authors have made attempts to compare the programs and help researchers to select the best one for their use (Lewins & Silver, 2007; Fielding & Lee, 1991; Tesch, 1991). There are also useful software sites that provide information on computer applications, education and conferences, and advice about the purchase of software such as the Computer-Aided Qualitative Data Analysis Networking Project (http://caqdas.soc.surrey.ac.uk). In my opinion, except for the software enthusiasts, most researchers do not have the time nor inclination for long deliberations about their choice of software.

You can make a choice by looking at a few criteria. The first one is to clarify your needs and subsequently your expectations of the program. Ask yourself what part of data analysis worries you and what would help you to do this task. St John and Johnson (2000: 397) suggest some helpful questions:

- What are the advantages and disadvantages of this package for my research?
- What purpose will this package serve for this research project?
- Will this package handle the kind and amount of data I intend to collect?
- Will this package enable flexible handling of data for this project?
- Will this package enable me to interact with and reduce data in a way that is consistent with my methods?

Another important criterion to consider is user-friendliness. How easy and comfortable it is to work with the package is one aspect. User interface and interactivity are key words here (Hesse-Biber & Leavy, 2006). However, this is partly a matter of taste. 'Interface' refers to the organization of the screen, whether it is appealing to you and whether it matches your way of thinking and working. For instance, do you like a structured interface that always looks the same, or is a flexible interface more convenient for you? Do you remember things by their colours or do colours confuse you? Interactivity means that there is a good, instant hyperlink (one click or double click) between an object in one pane and an object in another, for instance a code can easily be linked with its context and retrieved segment and there is instantaneous access to source data files once introduced into the project (Lewins & Silver, 2007).

Another aspect of user-friendliness is how fast you can learn to work with the program. Again, except for the enthusiasts, most researchers do not want to spend hours and hours before they can start using the program. So it is worthwhile to know the capabilities of the packages and to estimate the time and effort required to use the package. Programs that offer many capabilities are generally speaking harder to learn. On the other hand, they might have all the tools that you need.

A last criterion to consider when purchasing a program is its price. Websites are a useful guide in this matter. Many programs offer free demos that can be used for a certain period of time, offer upgrades, additional modules and special deals for students. Search for the 'best purchase' for your purpose, which means that for you the optimal balance is found between capabilities of the program and its price.

There are current debates about the strengths and possible concerns of data analysis software (Lewins & Silver, 2007; St John & Johnson, 2000; Fielding & Lee, 1991). Here are a few remarks from a user's perspective.

A particularly attractive advantage is that software packages free the researcher of many manual and mechanical tasks which in turn saves time. The examination of the data can be more complete and rigorous too. Once you have gone over the documents and coded them and wrote the memos, you can retrieve them at any time, and a complete and systematic overview will be given. According to Lewins and Silver (2007), one of the main aspects of computer use which has most changed the process of interpretive analysis is the ability to gain direct access to all relevant areas in the data in immediate response to the researcher's train of thought.

The ease by which data are handled might seduce researchers into using larger amounts of data (Seidel, 1991). This is not a problem for computers providing the memory capacity is large enough for the job. Data overload is actually a researcher's problem. Qualitative researchers often have a vivid memory of data collection. With too much data they run the risk of not remembering anything of the data themselves and of losing the overview. The consequence might be a more superficial analysis rather than the more complex analysis aimed at originally.

Software opens up opportunities to look at the data from different angles. The tools provided might reveal patterns otherwise not noticed. At the same time, by providing these tools the software in some way predetermines what will be drawn to your attention (St John & Johnson, 2000). This may be an extra time investment that does not need further consideration, or it could take your attention away from other more relevant parts of analysis. I will give one example drawn from my own experience. In the beginning, when MAXQDA was still called Winmax, there was only one colour involved in coding: green. In the new product, several colours can be picked to distinguish different codes. At first it never even crossed my mind to use the colours because I considered thinking about using the colour and clicking on it as extra mental and manual activities. But now I find myself using colours more frequently. First, simply because the option is available and this might even open up new opportunities. Second, other newly added visual tools, like textportrait and codeline, build on the code colours.

Some software developers argue that their packages support researchers to examine relationships between categories and engage in theory building. They point at tools like retrieval with boolean search operators, visual tools that show co-occurrence of different codes in a matrix or show code-profiles of texts, linguistic search operations and the use of attributes. All these functions seem to be 'under construction'. Lewins and Silver (2007) advise stepping away from the computer now and then to use paper and pencil. There is nothing wrong with scribbling diagrams or provisional frameworks on paper, and there is also nothing wrong with boolean searches and graphical representations of texts. In some way it is all a matter of taste, as long as it helps you to notice new things in your data.

Readings I learnt much from

Hesse-Biber, S.N. & Leavy, P. (2006). *The practice of qualitative research.* London: Sage.

Lewins, A. & Silver, C. (2007). *Using software in qualitative research: a step-by-step guide.* London: Sage.

Seidel, J.V. (1991). Method and madness in the application of computer technology to qualitative data analysis. In: N.G. Fielding & R.M. Lee (Eds.), *Using computers in qualitative research* (pp. 107–116). Newbury Park, CA: Sage.

Strauss, A.L. (1987). *Qualitative analysis for social scientists.* Cambridge: Cambridge University Press.

Doing your own qualitative research project

Step 7: Using heuristics and software

1. When coming to a closure of the data transformation that leads to the findings, you may benefit from several thinking aids. Have a thorough look at the heuristics described at the beginning of this chapter and apply the ones you think will be useful in your project.

2. Analysing focus group data and visuals is somewhat more pioneering than the analysis of the commonly used individual interviews or observations. You might consider searching for interesting publications of these sorts of data and examine how they have been analysed and how the findings were reported.

3. It is quite obvious when using qualitative software that you will need to use the code-and-retrieve tools. Take a look at the less evident tools that might be helpful for your project, such as searching, linking, visualizing and creating subsets of texts and codes. Make sure that you use the biggest surplus value of the software, which is that your texts, code system, memos and interim products are all linked to shape new constellations that might offer new insights into your research subject.

8
FINDINGS

We have addressed many topics related to qualitative research and to qualitative analysis in particular. Having worked with the data during analysis, one could assume that you know how the findings of a qualitative research are conceived and what they will look like. In practice this is not so easy, and social scientists are often puzzled as to what can be considered to be the outcomes of a qualitative research project. This chapter will focus on the different types of findings that a qualitative effort can produce. Findings can exist in their own right to add to theoretical knowledge or to professional practice, but they can also be used for re-analysis in a meta-synthesis. Mixed methods research is also addressed, in which qualitative research has a specific role and is chosen for its distinctive findings in comparison with the statistical findings of quantitative research.

LEARNING AIMS

By the end of this chapter, you will be able to:

- Grasp the relationship between data, interpretations and findings
- Identify and prevent common mistakes in reporting qualitative findings
- Adjust the degree of data transformation and the findings to the research purpose
- Define qualitative meta-synthesis and indicate different elements of it
- Elaborate on the advocates' and adversaries' points of view with regard to combining different qualitative traditions or approaches
- Reflect on the debate about the paradigm–method fit
- Address a mixed methods design and explain the role of the qualitative part in it
- Direct instrumental and conceptual use of findings

Results of qualitative research

Findings in qualitative research are conceptualized differently from findings in quantitative research. This relates to the methods and the particular role that theory plays as described in Chapters 1 and 2. In quantitative research the findings are conceived as the result of statistical calculations based on a set of data. Findings resulting from calculations do not require manipulation by the researcher and are therefore easily replicated by others. Processing the data in qualitative research explicitly requires the researcher's interpretation and consequently qualitative findings comprise the interpretations and can be defined as 'The databased and integrated discoveries, judgments, or pronouncements researchers have offered about the events or experiences under investigation' (Sandelowski & Barroso, 2002a: 214).

The link between data and interpretations complicates what can be thought of as findings. In quantitative research, interpretations of numerical analysis results are commonly put into the discussion section of the formal report. In qualitative research, however, it is the researcher's interpretations that constitute the results. Misguidedly putting the interpretations into the discussion section of the published research project is to be avoided because the actual findings would then be difficult to find in the report.

When presenting the findings of a qualitative research, different sources of mistakes can be detected (see Box 8.1). These mistakes confuse not only the findings of a particular study, but also what can be expected of qualitative research in general. When presenting qualitative research to the scientific world and demonstrating its value, it is essential to make it absolutely clear what are considered to be the findings of a qualitative study and to what quality standards they live up to.

BOX 8.1   MISTAKES IN QUALITATIVE RESEARCH

Data are not findings

Data represent something different from findings (Sandelowski & Barroso, 2003b). Data are viewed as the empirical material on which scientific findings are based. This empirical material needs interpretation, enables discoveries, enables conclusions to be drawn and makes inferences possible. In Chapter 4 it was acknowledged that data are not pre-existing either and that the researcher's involvement is what shapes the collection of the data. But the active involvement of the researcher in producing the data does not turn the data into findings.

Analyses are not findings

All interim products in the analysis, such as code trees, matrices, diagrams and memos that were described in Chapters 6 and 7, are means of transforming the data and to discovering and generating findings. Processing and manipulating the data are means by which to arrive at interpretations that demonstrate (from a particular theoretical viewpoint) how people make sense of their situations and act on them. The analyses themselves, or 'the making of the findings' (see Chapter 10), are not findings themselves.

Under-analysis

Under-analysis or 'premature closing' (Wilson & Hutchinson, 1996) means that the transforming of the data has not moved beyond the exploration of the data. This often happens with codes that are so general that they could apply to any subject, instead of being situation specific (Wilson & Hutchinson, 1996). When reading the results of reports that have been affected by under-analysis, the reader gets the feeling that there is much more to the data than the researcher has drawn out. Sometimes the studied phenomenon is simplified and stripped of its nuances, details and complexities with the use of one pattern or one metaphor (Thorne, Paterson, Acorn, Canam, Joachim & Jillings, 2002). Although one single conceptualization can suffice – the core concept dealt with in Chapters 6 and 7 – it must convincingly fit the data and not be insubstantial in any way.

Lack of thick description

Matthews (2005) points at findings that claim certain feelings or judgements of participants without showing what it is that the participants have feelings about or what these judgements are based on. When the report lacks examples and descriptions about the context that produced these feelings, views or judgements, the findings become unconvincing. For instance, when it is claimed that some veterans who were deployed to war zones are troubled in daily life because of vivid memories and re-lived experiences, the nature of these memories and experiences needs to be described. If they are not, the story does not come to life, it remains abstract and unconvincing.

Forcing a framework

Forcing a framework on the data is sometimes referred to as 'importing concepts' (Wilson & Hutchinson, 1996). It means that an existing framework is imposed on the data, for instance a three-staged behavioural change model consisting of contemplation, planning and action. The existing theoretical concepts over-define the analysis at the cost of identifying and developing new concepts and theories. When a researcher attempts to impose a framework rather than to ground it in the data, inferences will be forced onto the data and there will simply be no evidence for the framework (Matthews, 2005). Sensitizing concepts on the contrary are very useful because they help to find indicators in qualitative data for concepts that are otherwise difficult to measure.

Over-generalizations

Over-generalization can take on two different forms: First, it refers to studies that seem to draw inferences about the entire sample based on a selection of cases within the sample, mainly the most dominant and eloquent participants (Thorne et al., 2002). If there is no explanation given, it will naturally appear that the perspective of those few cases has biased the researcher's interpretations. This effect is even stronger when the cases are exceptional, strange or otherwise not representative of the population. A second variant of over-generalization bears on reports that formulate theoretical and practical implications that go far beyond what the findings permit (Thorne et al., 2002). That is, inferences about a population that, when the sample is taken into account, are not permitted. This issue of generalization is dealt with in Chapter 9.

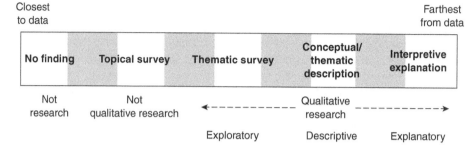

FIGURE 8.1   TYPOLOGY OF QUALITATIVE FINDINGS (ADAPTED FROM SANDELOWSKI & BARROSO, 2003B)

In the process of analysis, data are worked upon so as to make sense of them in the light of the research question, all of which has been the subject of the book so far. The many examples given have demonstrated the variety in results of qualitative research. Sandelowski and Barroso (2003b) have tried to come up with a typology of the results (see Figure 8.1). Their criterion is the degree of transformation of the data. On the left of the figure are findings that represent the least transformation of data, and on the right are those that are most transformed. In other words, the level of abstraction of analysis and interpretation of data is highest on the right-hand side.

Although the typology is not intended as a tool for evaluating the quality of studies, a study's classification might be hard to disentangle from a judgement of its quality. This accounts especially for the studies on the left side of the typology that are not classified as qualitative research or even as research. The different categories in the classification are summarized from the Sandelowski and Barroso article (2003b) and annotated in Box 8.2.

BOX 8.2   DESCRIPTION OF THE DIFFERENT TYPES OF FINDINGS

No findings

In a no-finding report the data are presented as findings. The researchers simply reproduce the data – interviews, field notes, focus group transcripts, photographs and so on – with almost no interpretation of the data. In this book empirical materials are only considered 'data' because they are in some way related to the research questions. But data do not contain ready-made answers for the reader to guess at. The transformation of the data into answers is the researcher's job.

Topical surveys

In topical surveys the data are minimally transformed. In the reports, nominal or categorical groupings are used to present and possibly reduce the data . Also lists and inventories of topics covered, for instance in focus groups and interviews, belong

---

to this type. The topics used are often preselected as a formation for data collection, and structured instruments are used. The system for ordering the topics into groups is based on simple descriptions, sometimes influenced by number of occurrences (frequencies) rather than interpretations.

Thematic survey

In the thematic survey a greater degree of transformation is found. Often themes are discerned in the data that represent repetitive responses or a subtle pattern in the data. Sometimes the existing literature is used to label and organize the data. More effort is put into exploring themes, and describing and interpreting them instead of merely listing topics. More attention is paid to the nuances and subtleties and to the language used and the way participants express themselves.

Conceptual/thematic description

Reports with a conceptual/thematic description contain findings rendered in the form of one or more themes or concepts either developed from the data or imported from existing theories or literature. These themes represent a pattern in the data that the researcher, by analysing the data, had to find and extract. Conceptual descriptions move beyond a topical or thematic description of events, phenomena or cases toward interpretively integrating parts of the data. Concepts and themes from existing literature are used to transform the data and to provide new insights instead of merely organizing the data.

Interpretive explanation

The defining feature of findings classified as interpretive explanation is the transformation of data to produce grounded theories, ethnographies or otherwise fully integrated explanations of some phenomenon, event or case. The explanations are composed of linkages between different categories that represent the studied phenomenon in a new way. The core of this type is an explanation that fully covers variations in both sample and data.

Capturing the differences between research projects is important, especially with respect to analytical efforts. At the heart of the above-mentioned classification is the degree of data transformation – that is, the analytical effort – and the classification is therefore considered to be a useful aid. Not all studies aim for the same goals, and as such they do not demand the same analytical efforts. The instrument might help you to clarify your study's purposes. It is perfectly acceptable to aim for a thematic survey if that is what your commissioner needs or if that is what you think you can do in the available time. It is also acceptable to aim for an interpretive explanation, but you must be aware that the analysis process is demanding.

Meta-synthesis of qualitative studies

In this chapter we are particularly interested in the nature of qualitative findings, in their origins, and in the factors that influence the ultimate findings. It is with this in mind that we look at the lessons learned and at the results of meta-synthesis endeavours. With so much qualitative research being undertaken, one could assume that it is possible to synthesize everything that is already known and simply ask what really needs to be examined or draw the conclusion that no new research is necessary.

Qualitative meta-synthesis is defined as 'a kind of research integration study in which the findings of completed qualitative studies are combined' (Sandelowski & Barroso, 2003b). As these authors point out, findings from completed studies form the raw data for a research integration project. In quantitative research, meta-analysis is a well-known approach in which results of previous studies are examined, critically reflected upon and re-calculated to consider and extend the range of existing knowledge. To prevent confusion with the quantitative meta-analysis, the qualitative counterpart is usually referred to as 'meta-synthesis'.

As an example, Thorne and colleagues (2002) undertook a meta-synthesis in the field of chronic illness from the perspective of the patients themselves. With an extensive body of qualitatively derived knowledge, they presumed that they could agree on the common features of what it was like to live with a chronic illness. In their approach they distinguished three phases, namely meta-theory, meta-method and meta-data-analysis. Finally, the stages gave rise to a meta-synthesis. The definitions of these four distinguished activities are cited from Thorne et al. (2002) in Box 8.3.

BOX 8.3   FOUR STAGES OF META-SYNTHESIS

- *Meta-theory* involves examination of the theories that led researchers to iden-tify relevant research topics, frame research questions in certain ways and determine such factors as inclusion criteria, angle of vision and interpretive lens.
- *Meta-method* involves thoughtful examination of the manner in which the methodological approach that was used to gather and interpret data shapes the findings that emerge from a particular study.
- *Meta-data-analysis* involves reinterpretation of the actual findings from the original qualitative studies in light of data and findings from other studies.
- *Meta-synthesis* refers to testing for the degree that overarching conceptualizations and the theories that derive from them surmount the analytic challenges that have been detected within the body of research.

(Thorne et al., 2002: 438)

In the meta-theory stage, Thorne et al. (2002) found that findings are deemed to be influenced by the disciplinary and theoretical perspectives of the researchers, even if their research questions and sample populations are quite similar. The disciplinary orientation of the authors is reflected in the framing of the research questions, the data collection and analysis methods, the interpretation of the findings and the presentation in the report. The authors argue that when researchers start exploring a certain disciplinary-derived concept, such as psychologists looking for growth in adversity, that they will find evidence for its existence and stress the importance of it in their work. Accordingly, the authors concluded that this does not say anything about the importance of a concept, such as growth, in relation to other processes or concepts in different fields.

The meta-method analysis confirmed once again that certain disciplines prefer certain methods, like ethnography in anthropology and grounded theory in sociology. But other choices with regard to methods have an effect on the findings as well. One of these choices is sampling. It turned out that certain chronic diseases were much more 'popular' to study than others and therefore much more frequently studied. Also verbally strong individuals and physically ill people were preferred to people who had difficulty talking and expressing themselves and people with mental problems. As a consequence, what is known about the experience of chronic illness is drawn on a specific subsample of the entire population.

Meta-data-analysis implies that the entire results section of a qualitative report is examined. For qualitative meta-data-analysis to take place it should be clear exactly what the researchers have found out about their topic (see previous section). In carrying out meta-data-analysis in the project on living with a chronic illness, findings sometimes turned out to be full of mistakes (see Box 8.1). In another meta-synthesis project, difficulty arose in recognizing the findings because they were sometimes misplaced in, for instance, the discussion section instead of the results section (Sandelowski & Barroso, 2002a). The findings then run the risk of underuse just because they cannot be found where they are expected to be.

Synthesizing qualitative research is no easy job since it involves, among others (Sandelowski & Barroso, 2002a: 213):

- Discerning the influence of method on findings
- Deciding whether a study is worthy of being included in an integration project
- Preserving the integrity of each study
- Choosing the right approach to combining the findings
- Deciding what integration means in qualitative research.

Strategies have been developed to synthesize qualitative research, like the one by Dixon-Woods, Booth and Sutton (2007). They developed methods for searching (databases, keywords), for including papers in the review, for appraisal of the papers and for synthesis.

Muddling qualitative methods

A lesson learned from meta-syntheses is that qualitative research is not easy to classify as belonging to a certain tradition. In practice, not all researchers are concerned with the relationship between their research and different qualitative traditions as described in Chapter 1. They simply do qualitative research. This form of qualitative research is known in literature as 'basic' or 'generic' qualitative research (Merriam, 1998). These researchers may choose qualitative research methods for pragmatic reasons, for example, because of the nature of their research question, but they have no interpretivist or constructivist leanings (Sandelowski & Barroso, 2002a: 215). Or, they do have these leanings but do not acknowledge them or perhaps choose to neglect them (Greckhamer & Koro-Ljungberg, 2005).

A different phenomenon is the claim of researchers to have used a certain method that does not fit the actual content and form of the findings (Sandelowski & Barroso, 2003b; Thorne et al., 2002). Examples are grounded theory approaches that do not result in a grounded theory, ethnographies that do not add to cultural knowledge and phenomenologies that do not study lived experience. Both research teams involved in meta-synthesis found that researchers mentioning different methodological traditions and strategies were actually doing quite similar things. Slippages between methods, however, do not automatically make the findings worthless. The variety of branches, traditions, perspectives and approaches that were described in Chapter 1 are obviously still quite confusing for many social scientists.

Morse (1999) argues that different research methods are suitable for answering different research questions, and that different research methods lead to different outcomes. Within one field of interest, in her case comfort and trauma care, many different kinds of research questions can be asked. Her proposal contained four projects: a phenomenological study to explore the meaning of comfort; an ethnographic study to explore the context of comfort; a grounded theory to examine the process of comforting; and a conversation analysis to examine reassuring techniques in language and intonation. She demonstrated that these different methods produced different outcomes although the setting and the topic were more or less the same. Therefore Morse advises using methodological versatility in research methods.

Creswell (2006) is occupied with a different experiment. He wants to know whether the investigation of the same event with different research methods will lead to different outcomes. As a case in point he examines the campus response to a student gunman and uses five traditions to study the event: the biographical method, the grounded theory approach, phenomenology, ethnography and a case study. The conclusion he draws from this test is convergent with Morse's conclusion mentioned above: the traditions have their own philosophical assumptions, data collection methods, analytical strategies, rhetoric and presentational styles and the use of different methods leads to different outcomes.

Possible problems arise when the canons of a tradition are compromised through intentional or unintentional muddling methods (Wilson & Hutchinson, 1996). 'Muddling' refers to the incorporation of methods and techniques that did not originate in the tradition and that at first sight do not fit in. Some scientists argue that researchers need to make a clear-cut choice between the different traditions and approaches (Baker, Wuest & Noerager Stern, 1992). From a quality perspective (see Chapter 9), they are of the opinion that good research may only exist when researchers keep to the embedded epistemology, theoretical perspective and research methods which govern a certain tradition (Greckhamer & Koro-Ljungberg, 2005). They argue that ignorance with regard to traditions and approaches leads researchers to sloppily mix traditions, resulting in an inconsequent application of methods as well as unclear results. Other scientists argue that a refined combination of traditions may lead to innovation in scientific methodology, provided that attention is paid to the internal consistency of the study (see Chapter 2).

At least one question remains: do similar methods and techniques, like data collection methods and questioning techniques, really change when they are applied within, let's say, an ethnographic or a phenomenological study? The answer according to several authors is 'yes'. Working within a certain tradition shapes the entire research process, including data collection methods, data analysis and the report writing (Creswell, 2006; Merkle Sorrell & Redmond, 1995). Within an ethnographic study the interview style will differ from the style used in, for instance, a phenomenological study. This does not only concern the types of questions and the sequence in which they are posed, but the explanations and encouragements given by the researcher for the participant as well. The interview style must be different in order to provide the researchers with the information they need for an ethnographic or a phenomenological analysis. The difference in interview styles is also important for providing findings that are strived for in ethnographical and phenomenological studies, respectively (Merkle Sorrell & Redmond, 1995).

This section ends with a final look at paradigms. In Chapter 1 we considered paradigms to be the rules and norms that groups of scholars use in shaping their investigations. Here we have seen that paradigms not only play a part in the context of quantitative and qualitative research, but in the realm of the different qualitative traditions as well. Some social scientists have learned and liked to work as phenomenologists and think this is an appropriate way to examine social phenomena in their field of interest, while others may be grounded theorists or ethnographers. Paradigms are essential for the way social scientists regulate their work. In the next section we again meet the paradigms when addressing mixed methods research.

Mixed methods research

Mixed methods can be broadly defined as 'research in which the investigator collects and analyses data, integrates the findings, and draws inferences using both qualitative and quantitative approaches or methods in a single study or a program of inquiry' (Tashakkori & Creswell, 2007). The legitimacy of combinations of qualitative and quantitative research has been questioned mainly within the debate about the paradigm–method fit (Hanson, Creswell, Plano Clark, Petska & Creswell, 2005).

When research methods are chosen because of philosophical considerations, this is coined a paradigmatic choice (Smaling, 2000). This means, for instance, that for social scientists holding a constructivist view, it would be unjust to study human beings as if they were passive 'respondents' (as in quantitative research) instead of active participants who can co-examine as part of a team (as in qualitative research). Conversely, it would be incorrect for researchers holding an objectivistic view to bias the respondents' answers by introducing the researcher personally as is done in qualitative research. This implies that a certain worldview is followed by a taken-for-granted research method. Can the argument be reversed? When researchers choose to conduct qualitative research should they be considered constructivists, and when they choose quantitative methods should they be considered objectivists? These questions pertain to the debate about the paradigm–method fit.

Social science researchers are thought to be driven by paradigmatic considerations as well as by all kinds of pragmatic issues when stating research questions and deciding on key design features, like access to the field, available means and research populations. It is my belief that within a group of scholars, paradigmatic and pragmatic considerations have an effect on the opinion on what research questions are most meaningful and which procedures are most appropriate for answering them. These opinions are then put into perspective and cause the incompatibility of methods to be stressed less. In that case, the justification of mixed methods studies is that they provide better findings about a research problem than the use of either a qualitative or a quantitative approach alone.

Interesting design questions emerge when one considers how the qualitative and the quantitative substudy can be related to one another. Mixed methods designs are commonly distinguished on two criteria (Creswell, Plano Clark, Gutmann & Hanson, 2003). The first criterion is whether any of the two branches is prioritized or whether both have equal weight. This distinction is noted in the use of uppercase letters for the one prioritized. The second criterion is whether the studies take place simultaneously or sequentially, respectively noted with a plus (+) or an arrow (→). There are many conceivable combinations, but here we focus on three common shapes depicted in Table 8.1. Our interest is primarily in the function of qualitative research in these designs.

When looking more closely at the role of qualitative research in the mixed method designs, we can recognize the reasons for choosing qualitative research mentioned in Chapter 2. In a sequential explanatory design, qualitative research is mainly chosen for its explanatory power, and in the sequential exploratory design it is chosen mostly for its exploratory capacities. In a concurrent triangulation design the choice is mainly motivated by the fact that qualitative research complements quantitative research by providing different types of knowledge. Below the three different designs are described by means of an example.

Sequential explanatory (QUAN → qual)

Sometimes quantitative research provides unexpected outcomes, contradicting outcomes or outcomes that are not very well understood. Unexpected or unexplained outcomes can then be followed up with qualitative research. Qualitative data can also be used to embellish the outcomes of the quantitative study. The challenge in such a design is to integrate both parts in a way that the qualitative research answers the questions that puzzle the researchers after finishing the quantitative part.

An example of this is a longitudinal study by Lukkarinen (2005) in which the quality of life was examined in people with coronary artery disease (CAD) during the period following the onset of the disease, including therapy and rehabilitation ($N = 280$). The researchers were surprised that the patients in the youngest age group reported the

TABLE 8.1 THREE DESIGNS OF MIXED METHODS RESEARCH

Designs	Data collection	Role of qualitative research
Sequential explanatory QUAN → qual	Quantitative data are collected and analysed, followed by qualitative data. Priority is usually unequal and given to the quantitative data.	Qualitative data are used to explain unexpected and/or unexplained outcomes of quantitative research by examining the mechanisms that may underlie the outcomes. The qualitative part is used to augment quantitative data.
Sequential exploratory QUAL → quan	Qualitative data are collected and analysed first, followed by quantitative data. Priority is usually unequal and given to the qualitative data.	The qualitative part is used to develop theory and explore relationships between phenomena. Qualitative research is used to develop new test or assessment instruments and is useful in pre-testing these instruments.
Concurrent triangulation QUAN + QUAL	Quantitative and qualitative data are collected and analysed at the same time. Priority is usually equal and given to both forms of data.	The qualitative part is used to confirm and cross-validate the findings of the quantitative part. The qualitative part is used for research questions that quantitative research cannot deal with.

poorest quality of life. To find out how these unexpected results could be understood, 19 people were interviewed following their treatment. It turned out that patients who developed CAD in early adulthood (35–37 years) had the biggest drawback when they compared the situation before and after the diagnosis of CAD. Before, they were healthy, employed and active adults, and CAD made them change their lifestyle and caused financial drawbacks. In contrast, people who typically developed CAD in middle-age (45–71 years) felt their survival of serious disease to be a new opportunity in life. As a consequence, they rated their quality of life much higher.

Here the qualitative data analysis helped to gain insight into the participants' situational experience of quality and course of life, which was not detectable with the use of the questionnaire in the first, quantitative part. The combination of methods allowed the researchers to understand the results of precise, instrument-based measurements by contextual, field-based information.

Sequential exploratory (QUAL → quan)

A sequential exploratory design is chosen, among other reasons, when researchers aim at measuring phenomena with standardized and valid instruments in an area that still needs exploration. Qualitative research is instigated to discover topics that need to be covered to measure the phenomenon. The next step of this approach has a predominantly quantitative character, in most cases the generation and administering of a survey. The challenge is to translate the qualitative findings into appropriate items to create a valid and reliable measuring instrument. The details, expressions and nuances of the participants need to be preserved to some degree in the development of the instrument.

An example of this design is given by Imle and Atwood (1988). They wanted to develop an instrument that would assess and evaluate the learning needs and concerns of prospective parents. Qualitative methods were used to develop and define concepts that validly represented the needs and concerns normally experienced by expectant parents. The generated concepts were then used to develop a scale: the Transition to Parenthood Concerns (TPC) Scale. The challenge became one of creating scales and scale items to index the concepts in such a way that they would retain their qualitative validity for the target group and yet would meet the criteria for adequate psychometric performance.

Qualitative research can contribute to the pretesting stage of a questionnaire as well. The final draft of the questionnaire is distributed to potential respondents and their reactions are examined in order to discover problems in the questionnaire and to learn how respondents interpret the questions. Focus groups and individual interviews are generally used for pretesting questionnaires (Campanelli, 2008; Beatty & Willis, 2007).

Concurrent triangulation (QUAN + QUAL)

A third domain in which mixed methods can be used is research in which quantitative and qualitative data are generated simultaneously to examine a particular phenomenon from different angles, also referred to as 'concurrent triangulation design' (see Chapter 9). The purpose of such a design is often to generalize findings from the quantitative research to the entire population by means of a large sample and to understand the mechanisms that underlie the outcomes at the local or micro-interactional level by means of the qualitative research. The difficulty with triangulation is the question whether both methods measure the same phenomenon and how evidence resulting from both methods should be interpreted (Erzberger & Kelle, 2003; Moran-Ellis, Alexander, Cronin, Dickinson, Fielding, Sleney & Thomas 2006).

An example of a triangulation design is a study evaluating whether welfare rights advice, often resulting in financial gain, had an impact on health and social outcomes among a population aged 60 and over (Moffatt, White, Mackintosh & Howel, 2006). The researchers were confronted with quantitative data, including standardized outcome measures of health and well-being, that suggested that the intervention had no impact, while the qualitative data, exploring participants' views about the intervention and its outcome, showed wide-ranging impacts, indicating that the intervention had a positive effect.

Three aspects were found in exploring whether the outcomes of both components matched. First, the qualitative study revealed a number of dimensions not measured by the quantitative study, such as 'maintaining independence'. Second, some of the quantitative measures used did not adequately encapsulate participants' experiences and feelings. An example is the measure of mental health that lacked a way to express feeling 'less stressed' by financial worries. Third, during the interviews they discovered what the 'real issue' was. This appeared to be the way in which older people, despite their condition, were better able to cope with existing health problems after the intervention because of financial gain. In this example the combination of methods leads to a broadened and deepened insight into the research subject.

Currently it is popular to claim that the best possible design is one in which quantitative and qualitative methods are combined. It is undoubtedly true that most topics lend themselves to formulation of interesting research questions for both qualitative and quantitative research. But combining the two research types has to be motivated by good reasons, as the choice for a mix greatly increases the burden of the research (Creswell, 2008). Both the qualitative and quantitative parts need to be conducted in accordance with the rules of the art, which is demanding even for a team of researchers with different backgrounds and training. But using mixed methods is tempting when one wishes to innovate social science research and cross borders of preferred paradigms in certain scholarly networks.

TIP
_____

It is difficult for quantitative researchers to keep up with the progress in qualitative research methods and vice versa. Notice that several mainly quantitative journals publish special issues that are sometimes dedicated to qualitative research methods. Regularly these journals have a research section in which all kinds of methodological issues are discussed and debated. The reviews of new books that some journals offer are also an effective and efficient way of keeping up with the development of qualitative research.

_____

Mixed methods studies draw on the researcher's competence to write an appropriate research report. This is challenging since there are not yet that many examples to learn from and the two studies have to be reported simultaneously and within the same timeframe. Different ways of reporting are used in quantitative and qualitative research as well as different ways of convincing the reader that your methods and findings are correct (Sandelowski, 2003). Therefore, in the introduction you should be clear about the rationale for employing two methods in a single study. It should be carefully explained which research questions are answered with which method and what the mix entails. In the methods section, both studies should be described. A visual diagram can be helpful and, in the end, will save words. In the discussion you can reflect on the expectations you had of the perceived surplus value of the mixed methods approach.

Mixed methods designs are popular in policy-oriented research, like evaluation research. Outcomes are employed to change specific social situations by informing people who take decisions about it or deal with the subject in professional practice. These professionals can be policy makers, medical staff, teachers, parents or employers.

The practical use of research findings, whether stemming from a mixed methods research, a stand-alone research or a meta-synthesis, is addressed in the next section.

Practical use

Even when research provides clear indications for policy makers or professionals to change or improve certain social situations or professional practice, the actual application and integration of the findings are not self-evident. We will walk through some of the issues that complicate practical use of research findings. It is beyond dispute that for readers to seriously consider your work for use, they need to be convinced of its quality (see Chapter 9) and be able to judge the quality from the written report (see Chapter 10). When doing well, qualitative researchers can capitalize on the rich and detailed information they are able to provide about the dynamics of social situations. This information is often desperately needed in order to improve certain situations, such as football hooliganism or binge drinking.

In Chapter 2 a distinction was made between fundamental and applied research. In fundamental research the main purpose is to add to the theoretical knowledge about a certain research area. In applied research the principal aim is to yield information in order to change or improve an existing situation. Some research seems to serve both purposes, although one of the two prevails in most cases. For all example studies in Chapter 2, both theoretical and applied purposes can be thought of. We also learned that when your aim is explicitly to alter a situation, then you should formulate a research question that addresses the 'how to' issue; this question forces you to pay attention to the usability of the research findings.

Even if the purpose is explicitly directed at changing a current situation and the findings are clearly stated, it is still uncertain if and how the findings are going to be used. On one hand this is due to the nature of research, and on the other hand it is due to the nature of policy making. Let us first consider the nature of research. Utilization of research is often conceived as its instrumental use. Instrumental use means that policy makers act on the findings – implications and advice – of specific research and adjust policies or interventions accordingly. However, findings seldom offer clear-cut indications or advice on how to implement them in practice. Outcomes almost never demonstrate that we have to do A to change B.

For instance, the issue of football hooliganism was demonstrated to be dependent on many interrelated factors. The phenomenon of football hooliganism has developed over time just as have the policies targeted at the phenomenon. If we consider football hooliganism as a social phenomenon, many factors play a role in its occurrences, its severity and its frequency. Social science research cannot show an obvious one-to-one relationship between new measures and policies, and change. Additionally, newly designed measures often come with an abundance of side-effects that policy makers must first consider. The study of Spaaij (2006) into hooligans is foremost a fundamental research but contains lessons to be learned for practice as well. Some of his most interesting illustrations of research into social policy to decrease hooliganism are listed in Box 8.4.

BOX 8.4   EXAMINING POLICIES TARGETED AT FOOTBALL HOOLIGANISM

As you will remember from Chapter 2, Spaaij was interested in explaining the extent and nature of football hooliganism at different football clubs and in different countries, and variations therein over time. His analysis of policies targeting football hooliganism has led him to formulate three conclusions (Spaaij, 2006: 366):

- Most security measures have secondary consequences reducing their intended effect and transforming the manifestation of football hooliganism.
- A discrepancy between formal and informal policies targeting football hooliganism tends to exist.
- Football fans themselves may be powerful agents in the prevention of football hooliganism and the construction of non-violent fan identities.

One of the policy dilemmas is: Who owns the problem? Who is responsible for tackling football hooliganism? It can be argued that football hooliganism is a societal problem and therefore the responsibility of governments. Considering that hooliganism is not restricted to intergroup fighting and that violent behaviour increasingly takes place outside the football grounds, it has little bearing on the football game itself. There now seems to be an awareness of shared responsibility in which the football club as the organizer of the event is given a central responsibility (Spaaij, 2006).

Over the years hooligan policies have changed in nature. Spaaij outlines six styles: denial/downplaying, exculpation, facilitation, toleration, co-optation and repression. Co-optation for instance is based on the assumption that hooliganism is serious and persistent and that hooligans are committed fans. A dialogue with hooligans is supposed to lead to reduction of violence. The starting point for repression is that the problem is serious and damages the club's public image. The strategy accompanying this starting point is one of banning orders and pervasive controls of offenders. In most countries today there are large numbers of repressive measures designed to curb football hooliganism: the segregation of home and away fans, fencing, closed-circuit television, conversion to seating-only stadia, identity schemes, intelligence-led policing and so forth.

In the local setting all kinds of negotiations take place about the implementation of the formal measures between authorities, the local football club, its fan community and hooligans (Spaaij, 2006: 32). Extensive surveillance and intelligence structures are generally utilized in a less pervasive manner at 'friendly' clubs when compared with clubs with a high level of violent behaviour. Recipients of policy measures anticipate and react to the measures. Identified hooligan strategies are: 'circumvention (e.g. pre-arranged disorder away from the football ground), disregard (e.g. attacking rivals regardless of surveillance and punishment), fraud (e.g. using fake identity cards or forcing access to the football ground without a ticket), and appeal (e.g. formal complaints against the police or appeal against banning orders)' (Spaaij, 2006; 351). All these strategies yield side-effects to the intended results.

Policies encouraging interactions between non-hooligans and hooligans seem to be viable. Spaaij mentions successful attempts in which the violent, masculine identities of football hooligans were challenged by alternative non-violent fan identities.

Evaluation research is a form of applied research in which the effectiveness of existing policy measures or professional interventions, such as medical treatment, psychotherapy, school programmes, nursing interventions and welfare programmes are examined, in order to adjust the original policy or intervention based on the findings. Evaluation studies are often conducted as quantitative experiments and preferably as randomized controlled trials since these designs are considered the best choice for determining causal relationships between intervention and effect. An obstacle for generalizing the outcomes of these experiments is that they are often conducted in highly controlled laboratory settings and that the outcomes cannot automatically be considered evidence for practice in real-life situations, which are much more variable and diverse. This issue underlies the debate about evidence-based practice in, for example, medicine, psychology, nursing and education.

It is acknowledged that qualitative research can help bridge the gap between research and practice (Kazdin, 2008; Roberts, Dixon-Woods, Fitzpatrick, Abrams & Jones, 2002). Its strength lies in its flexibility, enabling researchers to make a detailed examination of specific phenomena in the field with the required instruments to reveal aspects of human experience with treatment, therapy, programmes or intervention. Qualitative research may provide insights into how change may be achieved with a suitable programme or intervention. Mixed methods that enhance quantitative and qualitative research are also considered beneficial for evaluation purposes (Miller & Fredericks, 2006). However, it is not as simple as it seems. A solution for one problem may work in specific situations and not work in others. For research findings to instigate change in professional practice, the research report must be convincing in its description of the outcomes, the intervention and its instructions, the conditions for success, the specific target population and the resource investment (Leeman, Jackson & Sandelowski, 2006).

Sometimes findings do not have an instrumental value per se; instead they serve a conceptual aim, which means that the understanding and insights that they yield might lead to a different view of the social issue that was studied. And in doing so the research might shape policy debates and inspire policy makers to come up with different solutions (Clarke, 2008). For example, underlying the six styles of policy to decrease football hooliganism are different ways of conceptualizing the perpetrators. When hooligans are not conceptualized as a 'problem' but viewed as a useful force that supports the football team, this can encourage, for example, financial and logistical support. However, when hooligans are conceptualized as a serious and damaging problem, this could result in repression of offenders through banning orders and pervasive controls. It is all in the eye of the beholder.

When your research appears to have practical value, the findings should be brought to the attention of those who can effect change. It is important to use a language that is understandable by your intended audience, such as the media, policy makers, practitioners, governmental agencies, politicians and the lay public (Kayser-Jones, 2002). Kayser-Jones has done numerous studies in nursing homes using quantitative and qualitative methods. The outcomes were not always agreeable to the nursing homes and the affiliated industries, yet she is able to continue conducting research in nursing homes. She claims that this is the result of careful building and maintaining trustful field relationships (Kayser-Jones, 2003). In particular, accentuation of shared purposes ('Don't we all want higher standards of care?'), clarity, reciprocity, confidentiality and the dissemination of the outcomes all turn out to be of foremost importance for participating nursing homes. Controversial findings might be of great insight for involved parties and can lead to changes in practice.

Let us turn to policy making once again. Many sources of information are used for making policy decisions, and research outcomes may only be one of them. Policy making is often not a very rational and linear process, but it is brought about by different people, with different interests and views at different moments. Policy making is not a translation of research outcomes into measures or inventions, but it involves judgements and decisions about a certain strived-for direction. Decision making has to do with opinions, values, creativity, evidence (and what is considered as such) and of weighing different side-effects. Our society hosts many complex, social situations that are never black and white. As far as it goes, qualitative research shows us the many-sidedness of most social phenomena.

Readings I learnt much from

Creswell, J.W. (2008). *Research design. Qualitative, quantitative, and mixed methods approaches.* Thousand Oaks, CA: Sage.
Morgan, D. (2007). Paradigms lost and pragmatism regained. Methodological implications of combining qualitative and quantitative methods. *Journal of Mixed Methods Research*, 1(1): 48–76.
Sandelowski, M. & Barroso, J. (2003b). Classifying the findings in qualitative studies. *Qualitative Health Research*, 13(7): 905–923.

Doing your own qualitative research project

Step 8: What are your findings?

1. Now that you are entering the stage of discovering what you have actually found out about your subject. Take a look at the classification of findings in Figure 8.1. Where would you position your findings? Is this what you intended as findings? If not, what transformation of your data is needed to realize the type of findings you were aiming for? Is this still attainable in your project?
2. Are you guilty of one of the mistakes mentioned in Box 8.1 in all or just part of your findings? Think of ways of repairing the findings. If you are not able to, consider writing about it in the discussion section of your report.
3. Reflect on the purposes of your research endeavour: are they mainly fundamental or applied? Clearly describe what your findings can add to a body of knowledge in the scientific field. Try to phrase how your findings can be used in terms of either conceptual or instrumental use by the different parties involved. Do not lose sight of your project's complexity, and be aware of side-effects and interests of different parties.

9
QUALITY OF THE RESEARCH

For readers to use research results, they need to be convinced about its quality and relevance. Different views on the quality of research are valid. Up until now, the quality of research was assessed mostly by using implicit criteria ('I know it when I see it'), but more recently explicit criteria and checklists have materialized. On one hand, checklists can be used by researchers to conduct research according to the criteria on the list. On the other hand, readers use checklists to judge the reporting of the research. The reporting must provide the reader with sufficient information to estimate the value of the research, including the analysis. The report should be concise and honest and at the same time show the unique selling points of the research endeavour. A journalistic approach to writing and rhetoric helps to bring the message across, provided that they are carefully applied.

LEARNING AIMS

By the end of this chapter, you will be able to:

- Argue how reliability and validity relate to the quality concept in qualitative research
- Recognize which view on the quality of the research is used in a particular publication
- Think about the relationship between the researcher and reliability and validity
- Address the challenge of an emerging research design for reliability and validity
- Explain how procedures such as triangulation, member validation, peer debriefing and methodological accountability help to preserve quality
- Plan for procedures to be used in your research to improve the quality
- Apply quality standards to judge the value of social scientific qualitative research
- Elaborate on the difference between statistical and theoretical generalization
- Reflect on the use of rhetoric in a piece of work presented as social science research

Thinking about quality

Judgement of the quality of research implies an assessment of the accuracy of the insights gained as a result of the research. A judgement takes into account whether the findings and conclusions convincingly represent the social phenomenon that was claimed to be examined. To arrive at a judgement, it is necessary to track down how these findings and conclusions were realized, for instance how research questions were formulated that showed relevance to the field, what data collection methods were chosen, how the sample was composed, what instruments were used, how the data were analysed and how the researchers managed their influence on the outcomes.

Why would anyone want to judge the quality of a research? A judgement of the legitimacy of the conclusions is the ultimate criterion by which the findings of a research project may be added to the already existing body of knowledge on a certain social scientific area. Scientific journals send a manuscript that is submitted for publication to reviewers who judge the value of the work. They are therefore referred to as 'peer reviewed' journals (see Chapter 10). When you are writing a research proposal or manuscript, you will assess whether a given piece of research is worth including in the literature review. Or you will consider whether the findings lead to a change in social policy or in professional practice. There are other reasons for assessing research, for instance for supervisors to award a fair grade to an assignment in a research course or for subsidisers to calculate whether they get value for their money. All these activities involve the generation of a judgement of the quality of research.

Quality of research is also referred to as objectivity. It pertains to the correspondence between the social scientist's findings, i.e. the descriptions and explanations of a social phenomenon, and the phenomenon as it is experienced by the people in the field. It also pertains to the controllability of the research process that led to the findings (Kirk & Miller, 1986). 'The making of' the findings (see Chapter 10) needs to be transparent and up to review at all times. All research findings are shaped by the theoretical perspective that was used, irrespective of whether they were generated with qualitative or quantitative methods. Therefore the knowledge gained is thought to be partial and must not be mistaken for actual social reality.

Here the term 'quality of research' is chosen instead of 'objectivity' because the meaning of the word objectivity in qualitative research can be interpreted in many different ways and is therefore surrounded with confusion (Patton, 1999). The various connotations of the word objectivity can apply either to the alleged subjectivity or partiality of the researchers, since they play such a large role in qualitative analysis, or to the subjective knowledge of the participants. Quality of research is a more open term that everyone understands, although it is no less debated. Quality is linked with reliability and validity both in quantitative and in qualitative research (Kirk & Miller, 1986). What both these terms represent is explained in Box 9.1.

BOX 9.1   RELIABILITY AND VALIDITY

Two important indicators for the quality of research are reliability and validity. Usually, reliability is referred to as the consistency of the measures used in social research. When the same phenomenon is repeatedly measured using the same instrument it should lead to the same outcomes, assuming that the phenomenon itself has not changed. The outcome should not be dependent on the timing of the project or on the researcher's choice of instrument (Bryman, 2008). In other words, when reliable methods are being used, repeated observation should lead to comparable outcomes.

Reliability is often determined by calculating internal consistency and stability over time. Cronbach's Alpha coefficient is commonly used to measure internal consistency. The assumption of this procedure is that all items of an instrument together measure the whole construct. Therefore each item must be related to the other items and each item measures part of what the other items measure as well, i.e. partially repeat the measurement. Stability over time is normally measured through a test–retest approach. The researcher distributes the research instrument to the same subjects on two occasions. The underlying assumption of this procedure is that a reliable measurement will yield the same outcomes (provided that the phenomenon to be measured has not changed in the meantime).

The reliability of observations may be increased by standardization of data collection methods, arguing that accidental errors and thus inconsistencies occur less frequently when all procedures are specific. From this viewpoint, a well-trained interviewer with a structured questionnaire is considered a reliable instrument. Additionally, researchers hope that unsystematic errors even out when sufficient observations have been made in a study. Some participants may colour their responses somewhat positively, and other participants downplay their answers. The survey researcher ticks a wrong box, and the researcher misunderstands an answer given. In these cases, the errors are not systematic and the argument is that the errors cancel each other out if the errors are not too common, not too big, and if the sample is large enough.

Validity is being specific about what you set out to assess. This is dependent on the use of the correct measures. If you intend to measure football hooliganism in certain football clubs and you ask for criminal offences you might be on the right track. If you enquired about the favourite food on the terraces, you would be measuring the wrong thing. Relying on answers about favourite food to determine a club's hooliganism is a systematic error: you are just using the wrong measure all the time. Measurement validity or construct validity refers to whether the measure that is formulated for a particular concept really does reflect the concept that it is supposed to measure (Bryman, 2008). For instance, all the questions present on a survey that together intend to measure 'binge drinking' should represent binge drinking.

(Continued)

(Continued)

The most commonly used ways to estimate validity are face validity and content validity (Cutcliffe & McKenna, 2002). Face validity means that others, colleagues for instance, have a look at the way in which a construct is laid out into elements in an attempt to measure the construct itself. Content validity involves a panel of experts who view the instrument and give their approval, often in a few rounds of exchanging opinions and views.

Internal validity means that we can be confident that researchers describe and/or explain what they had set out to describe and explain. When conclusions, in particular when they incorporate relationships between concepts, are correct this is taken as internal validity. Many things can undermine or threaten the internal validity of a study. For example, when a segment of the selected population cannot be reached or does not want to cooperate, this is considered a threat to validity because one part of the 'story' is systematically left out. When the chosen method of data collection does not provide accurate information about the topic of interest, this can bias the result, for instance when participants systematically keep silent about something. When researchers have a particular result that they hope to prove and interpret the data in this desired direction, the validity of a study is also in doubt, even if they do so unintentionally.

Before we move to different contemporary perspectives on quality in qualitative research, we first turn to what it is that qualitative research tries to accomplish. It is deemed logical to calibrate quality judgements on the aims of the entire endeavour. In Chapter 1 we argued that qualitative research is aimed at discovering the meaning that people award to their social worlds and at understanding their actions. In Chapter 2 this aim was expanded with the purposes of qualitative research: exploration, description and explanation.

In this respect it is worth noting what Glaser and Strauss were trying to achieve when they developed their grounded theory approach. They aimed for findings that were grounded in the data collected in a certain field (a substantive field) and which were relevant to the people using the findings. With this in mind they formulated four quality criteria (Glaser & Strauss, 1967: 237):

- *Fitness:* The theory must closely fit the substantive area in which it will be used.
- *Understanding:* The theory must be readily understandable by laymen concerned with this area.
- *Generality:* The theory must be sufficiently general to be applicable to a multitude of diverse daily situations within the substantive area, not to just a specific type of situation.
- *Control:* The theory must allow the user partial control over the structure and process of daily situations as they change through time.

Let us see how these criteria relate to what is considered to determine the quality of qualitative research nowadays.

Perspectives on quality

The awareness about research quality has increased in the past decade (Denzin & Lincoln, 2005). At the start of the twentieth century, also called the traditional period, researchers provided a 'museum-like picture' of the exotic places they had visited. The resulting reports conveyed that the situation was exactly as described. The outcomes were true, because the researchers had been there. No one could check on them or felt the urge to do so. In the following modernist phase, the consideration for the credibility of studies grew, and the awareness of quality increased.

Through the years, perspectives on the quality of qualitative research have changed (Bryman, 2008; Seale, 1999). How you think about the quality of research is related to how you think about the nature of social science research and more specifically your ontological and epistemological ideas (see Chapter 1). When you assume that there is one social reality you will strive for methods that determine this reality as accurately as possible. However, when you believe that people have a say in the construction of their social reality you will employ methods to determine their perspective and their accompanying behaviours. The concept of quality of the research is clearly closely linked to your starting point. The three perspectives that budded from these starting points are discussed briefly below.

In the first perspective of research it is merely a tool to collect empirical data to test the hypotheses deduced from theories about human behaviour. It is thought that social reality exists independently of the researcher, and as a consequence the researcher should be removed as far as possible. All scientific research must strive to arrive at the truth of objective reality and should be neutral, value free, impartial and distanced. In this view on social science research, much value is attached to reliability by the standardization of measurement instruments and by its replication, i.e. repeatability of the measurements. Validity is, among other things, linked to the suitability of the research design for answering the research question as well as to the definition of valid indicators of the concepts to be measured.

Qualitative research is only partially able to meet the demands that this perspective places on the research practice. Standardization interferes with the open-ended character of qualitative research (see Chapters 1 and 2). Any amount of training cannot prevent the need for researchers to make on-the-spot decisions during field work or their idiosyncratic style of field notes. Replication is difficult, although not impossible, as social situations may change and it often remains to be seen whether the field will remain accessible to the researcher. Seale (1999) demonstrates that problems inevitably arise in replication attempts for data collection and interpretation. Researchers holding this first perspective on social reality and social science research usually see qualitative research simply as an explorative research strategy and a useful starting point for a quantitative study.

The second perspective is opposed to the first one and developed in a reaction towards this view. It all started with researchers who wondered whether they could do justice to the people who they had studied in their research reports. This is what came to be known in the literature as the 'crisis of representation' (Denzin & Lincoln, 2005). If there is any doubt on whether researchers can adequately represent the people they investigate, it almost automatically leads one to wonder by what right these researchers exist. In other words, what makes the research activities legitimate? The background to this double crisis lies partly in a postmodernist frame of thinking, that a dominant story is no longer accepted. There is no authoritarian author who knows and understands everything, and there are no accepted criteria for quality formulated by a dominant group of scientists. A study therefore always offers a partial and provisional truth.

Social scientists holding this perspective break with the traditional conceptions of quality being validity and reliability. They formulate other demands for research quality, such as confirmability, dependability, transferability and credibility (Erlandson, Harris, Skipper & Allen, 1993; Lincoln & Guba, 1985). Following from these criteria, the format of the write-up needed to change as well and so experiments took place with different ways of reporting (see Chapter 10). These researchers sometimes added extra criteria which were not purely methodological in nature, but had a more humanistic or political character. Examples of these criteria are: an active participation in the research of all parties involved; an equal treatment of different groups in the field; the usability of the research outcomes; and an active attitude towards empowering the researched (Lincoln & Guba, 1985).

This perspective has received criticism from different angles. By posing alternative demands on qualitative research, it is said to disengage itself from mainstream social science, with all the expected debates on the (non-)existence of a different kind of social science ensuing. A second point of criticism is that the newly formed criteria are, in their nature, derived from the original ones. In other words: it is old wine in new barrels. Confirmability parallels objectivity, dependability resembles reliability, credibility resembles internal validity, and transferability resembles external validity that we come to speak of later on. A third point of criticism is made by those who feel that political or humanistic criteria should not have such a large place in social scientific research.

In the third perspective on quality, the criteria validity and reliability are maintained as worthy aims (Seale, 1999; Kirk & Miller, 1986). Although the terms are retained, the procedures to realize reliability and validity are adjusted to the specific nature of qualitative research. In doing so, qualitative research does not alienate itself from conventional social science, and it does not need to be treated in isolation. Researchers using these procedures should reflect on them by addressing how the research process – the analytical methods, the data collection procedures and the researcher's presence – affects the results. 'It is research that looks at itself' (Alexander, 2008: 355). That way, readers can judge what influence the researchers' presence and research activities may have had on the findings.

Within this perspective on quality in qualitative research, the relationship between reliability and validity is sometimes viewed differently from the way it is viewed in quantitative research. In quantitative research reliability is commonly seen as a necessary (but in itself not sufficient) condition for validity. It is assumed that researchers simply cannot observe what they want to observe (validity) when the measurements are unreliable. In qualitative research, it is difficult to establish reliability by repeating the measurement since it often does not involve measurement with standard instruments. Instead the measures have to be developed specifically for a particular study, and they are often further adapted during use in the field

(Jorgensen, 1989). As a consequence it might be argued that reliability must be doubted when using a human being as a measuring instrument.

At the same time it is accepted within qualitative research, and argued in great length in the previous chapters, that to validly understand human experience there is no alternative but to use a researcher. The question then remains how to deal with the challenges that follow from both these issues. Measures and procedures to assure quality are equal to, to a great extent, the procedures used in the above-mentioned second perspective, and have been fairly well documented in the literature. It is to these procedures that we turn in the next section.

TIP
_____

When reading a research report, find out which perspective on quality the researcher used. This partly determines how the study was conducted and what the researcher considered attainable quality standards.

_____

'Doing' quality

In this section we discuss the measures taken in a specific research endeavour to assure quality. Numerous measures have already been dealt with in previous chapters and together they determine the quality of your research. Think about the formulation of a sound research plan, the thoroughness of the literature review, training and preparation for data collection, the recording and transcription of interviews or field notes, adequate purposeful sampling, and systematic analysis of the data (with the aid of the computer). Below, additional measures are described which can be regarded as more explicitly geared to contributing to the quality of the research: methodological accountability, reflection on the role of the researcher, triangulation, member validation and multiple researchers.

Methodological accountability

Methodological accountability means that researchers accurately document what they have done, how it was done, and why it was done. By including a proper account of all activities, others can judge whether the outcomes can be trusted, and they can repeat the whole investigation if desired (see Chapter 10). Explaining what you have done can give rise to comparative studies with other target groups, in other countries or in additional topics. However, there are several practical problems when replicating social science research, and particularly in qualitative research.

First, the data collection methods are semi-standardized or open. The rationale of using flexible methods was clarified in previous chapters: they allow researchers to observe – hear, see, ask – what seems relevant throughout the research. But the use of flexible methods poses a threat to reliability (Kirk & Miller, 1986). It would be difficult for others to replicate a researcher who improvises on the spot. In interviews, for example, the prompts may be rather unsystematic, and probing is also selective. To retrace what the researcher has actually done, the topic list can be added to a publication as well as an account of the researcher's perspective, i.e. the theoretical starting point and the research questions and purposes. It is expected that these elements will, to a high degree, guide the decisions during data collection.

Second, the analysis is not fully standardized either, despite the many guidelines available. The analysis, as has been argued extensively in this book, does not run in a straight line from data to conclusions. It is quite a task to state clearly how analysis has actually taken place (see Chapter 10). A methodological account helps to make as clear as possible how the data were handled and how transformation has been achieved. An accurate report can be made on the measures that were taken to ensure systematic work efforts such as the way in which software was used and how the collaboration with colleagues was integrated.

Replication of a research remains difficult, even if the steps taken during the research are carefully described in the report. The field could have changed as a result of the research, and natural changes may have occurred in the studied social phenomena as well. This holds not only for qualitative research but also for quantitative research. It might sound contrary to our expectations, but it is actually extremely difficult to create the exact same conditions even in laboratory-style experimental settings. Therefore methodological transparency seems an alternative, because it enables at least virtual replication: it dominantly serves to assess the justification of the researcher's choices and the lines of reasoning, and it facilitates possible replication and comparative studies (Seale, 1999).

Researchers can approach this procedure in various ways. Some keep a log or write extensive methodological memos in which they document facts relevant to the research endeavour (see Chapter 4). Others organize a so-called audit trail, in which an expert, often an outsider, tracks the analytic decisions that were made throughout the study (Cutcliffe & McKenna, 2004). The expert functions as an accountant: their task is to control and check possible inquirer bias. The detailed examination of research procedures will reveal any unethical handling of information.

Reflection on the researcher's role

The degree of the researcher's involvement with the subjects under study depends on the role the researcher has chosen to take on in the field. This role is chosen because it fits best with what the researcher wants to achieve and with the opportunities in the field (see Chapter 4). Involvement is necessary for qualitative researchers to find out what they want to know, i.e. what motivates the individuals under study and what keeps them busy. With the choice of role being the researcher's own decision, the field is influenced in a certain way.

One effect of researcher's involvement is that people have the tendency to change their behaviour when they know they are being studied. A person in charge who occasionally intimidates his employees may choose not to do so when the researcher is present. This phenomenon, called 'reactivity', has a negative influence on validity.

People are believed to get used to the presence of researchers however, when they are in the field for a prolonged period (Patton, 1999). Adaptation takes place on both sides: the researcher will act in a more natural way and participants will most likely fall back into their previous behavioural patterns. In a one-shot interview adaptation is doubtful, and that is why the value of the interview is evaluated as overrated by various critics (Silverman, 1998; Becker & Geer, 1969). The difficulty with reactivity is that it is impossible to find out how and when behaviour or opinions have been changed and what it is supposed to conceal.

When researchers are in the field, it is possible that they too change during the course of the research. When drawn into the world of the investigated individuals, they may become less interested in theory and possibly even in the research itself. This process is sometimes described as 'going native'. This term was taken from anthropology; anthropologists at times become native when they go to work and live in the field and are absorbed into the local culture (Patton, 1999). It is thought that their interpretations become biased as they become part of the community, identify with it, and therefore cannot be expected to reflect theoretically on their area of interest.

How can researchers reflect on their own role and influence in the field? Patton advises to stay sensitive to shifts in one's own perspective by systematically recording it at various times throughout the field work. A good example of how this can be done is given by Hess (2006), who conducted research into the experiences of women who underwent an abortion. It is important for researchers to be aware of their own experiences, opinions, feelings and ideas, and to be able to overcome any possible bias that may be caused by them. Hess already acknowledged her pro-life position in her research proposal and took care to include research articles in the literature review that showed both detrimental and favourable outcomes to abortion. The members of the research committee represented the spectrum of persuasions to keep her scientifically honest. One member was appointed to read the transcribed interviews and to evaluate the way in which the interviewing was done. This member was appointed because she held a pro-choice position on the abortion issue, opposite to the researcher's own position.

TIP

When using software it is useful to reserve one code in your coding system for fragments in the data that pertain to you as a researcher. You can attach memos to these fragments as well.

Some researchers choose to put aspects of their personality in their reports. This would seem useful only in cases where we learn how their personal make-up may have affected the research (Patton, 1999). It is difficult to establish which of the researcher's personal characteristics or beliefs really influence the study; possibilities are age, gender, disposition, economic status and skin colour. Other criteria could be equally relevant for the study and easily play a role. Examples are whether the researcher is divorced, if dementia is prevalent in the family, whether the researcher is married, has children and so on (Reinharz, 1997; Weiss, 1994). There are limits to making known the beliefs, ideas, preferences and wishes of the researcher, if only for the fact that the researcher may not be aware of them.

Reflecting on one's own work during data analysis has received considerably less attention than it has during data collection. Work assessment in qualitative data analysis is underdeveloped, whereas social scientists recognize the importance of being reflective about how data are interpreted, about the role of researchers in the analytic process, and about the pre-conceived ideas and assumptions that are brought to the analysis (Mauthner & Doucet, 2003). The analysis stage is undoubtedly shaped by all kinds of influences and it might be beneficial to identify and articulate them. Researchers cannot be value-free, but they can try to be non-judgmental in favour of the validity of the research and try to reflect on possible influences.

Triangulation

Triangulation refers to the examination of a social phenomenon from different angles. First and foremost, triangulation entails the use of more than one method or source of data in a research endeavour (Bryman, 2008). Researcher triangulation (see below) and theoretical triangulation follow from here. Theoretical triangulation requires that more than one theory is applied to interpret the data. Reasons can include the researchers' intention to explore the explanatory power of different theories or because one theoretical perspective is not enough to explain the phenomenon under study. Spaaij (2006) used a theory on identity construction of young adults and one on the fault lines in different cultures to explain the existence of hooliganism in certain football clubs (see Chapter 2). The use of multiple theories may negate the one-sidedness of a single theory.

Methods triangulation can reveal varied dimensions of a phenomenon leading up to a layered and thick description of a subject under study (see Chapter 10). An example is a study on Latin American children's health (Clark & Zimmer, 2001). Here the researchers used interviews, recorded medical data and photographs (methods triangulation). The photographs of daily situations were taken by mothers at home, by the researchers during home visits, and during an intensive observation in three homes referred to as the 'Day in the life of a toddler' (data source triangulation). The photographic component added to a better understanding and documentation of household behaviours that contributed to children's health outcomes. They learnt most from the day-long period of intense observation that for instance highlighted family relationships (fathers, older children, grandparents), feeding patterns and in particular the extent of bottle use, and the safety and stimulation of home environments. Triangulation enhanced the researcher's ability to observe children's home life and health practices with greater accuracy. Although there is no talk about a complete, all-encompassing image, the use of different methods does achieve a richer view on a complex phenomenon like household health practices.

Recently critical reviews of triangulation have appeared, especially when qualitative and quantitative research are combined (see Chapter 8) (Moran-Ellis et al., 2006). The question is what additional knowledge about a particular phenomenon can be gained from combining the findings from data generated by two or more methods?

Critics point out that these approaches yield different kinds of data, which are not easy to compare. How does different evidence need to be weighed against each other? Patton (1999) argues that a common misunderstanding about triangulation is that the point is to demonstrate that different data sources or research methods yield essentially the same result. In his view the point is really to *test* for such consistency. Somewhat different outcomes need not be seen as disturbing but as challenges to find out more about the relationship between the topic under study and the methods used.

Member validation

Member validation is also known as feedback to participants or member checks. It is assumed that when qualitative research succeeds to provide accurate descriptions and interpretations of human experiences, the people having that experience would immediately recognize them as their own. Therefore, presenting the findings to participants and asking them whether they recognize the findings and judge them as correct can be considered a procedure to verify the research (Cutcliffe & McKenna, 2002). It only seems logical to ask the parties involved if the findings are meaningful and if they will have practical implications. If members of the social world that was studied confirm that the researcher has correctly understood that social world, this adds to the credibility of the results and ultimately to the acceptability to others (Bryman, 2008).

During field research, transcribed interviews and field notes may be presented to participants. The participants may be asked to verify this information. This is a direct test of the reliability of the observation. Any misunderstandings and selections that may have taken place can be removed at this time. Researchers must acknowledge the potential impact of receiving and looking at transcripts (Forbat & Henderson, 2005). Member validation indicates again a need for early dialogue about how confidentiality will be maintained between research participants. An explicit strategy for managing transcript content and sharing transcripts with participants needs to be developed.

Additionally, information on preliminary study results can be discussed with participants at this point. The 'raw' data have undergone a process of analysis, and what the researcher presents to the participant is an aggregate of the individual participants' contributions (Cutcliffe & McKenna, 2002). Participants do not always have to agree with the researcher's interpretations. Researchers probably have access to different information than the participants do and researchers use a theoretical point of view to interpret the data. Furthermore, participants may have interests in the field which are at odds with the outcomes of the study. Of course, in participatory research the findings are produced with active participation of the involved parties and outcomes should be discussed.

Multiple researchers

Using multiple as opposed to singular researchers is often referred to as researcher or analyst triangulation (Patton, 1999). When several researchers collect the data, the potential bias is reduced that comes from a single person doing all the data collection (see the section above on the researcher's role). The comparison of the data provides a means to assess the reliability and validity of the data. With regard to the analysis, teams can foster a higher level of conceptual thinking than can individuals working alone, raising the analysis to a higher level of abstraction (Barry, Britten, Barber, Bradley & Stevenson, 1999). Teams are better in standardizing coding and improving accuracy of the coding process as well as avoiding bias because of incorporating control on each other's interpretations. In particular, researchers from various disciplines or researchers who have different interests in a research project can bring new input into the discussion because of different professional and personal knowledge, experience and baggage.

A well-functioning team in qualitative research is not only beneficial for the tasks involved but also for the social support (Barry et al., 1999). Field workers cooperating in a team learn from each other and can support each other at times of difficulty or stress resulting from field work, which will ultimately benefit the quality of the data (see Chapter 3).

Peer debriefing is thought of as a special type of researcher triangulation, with peers or colleagues that are not part of the research team providing a fresh perspective on the analysis process and exploring explanations the researcher(s) may have overlooked. This helps to minimize bias and prepares for critique. Sometimes peers take on the role of auditors and form a critical panel that is involved in checking the research project in an audit trail (see the previous section on methodological accountability).

Checklists for asserting quality of the analysis

Researchers, reviewers, readers and users of research want clarity with regard to quality and look to guidelines by which they can judge the quality of a study. Research is appraised by means of the report, therefore the required features of a report (see Chapter 10) are inextricably bound with the evaluation criteria for research. In order to find out whether a certain study meets a number of essential criteria, several checklists have been generated, some of which are: *The Critical Review Form – Qualitative Studies* (Letts, Wilkins, Law, Stewart, Bosch & Westmorland, 2007); *A quality framework for assessing research evidence* (Spencer, Ritchie, Lewis & Dillon, 2003); *Reading guide* (Sandelowski & Barroso, 2002b); *Criteria for the evaluation of research papers* (Seale, 1999); and *Desirable features of reports: a checklist* (Lofland & Lofland, 1995). Some journals have developed checklists for reviewing manuscripts as well.

Lofland and Lofland (1995: 218) organized the questions to ask about a field study report in four categories:

1. *Basic organization:* How well is the report presented?
2. *Data and methods:* What is the quality of the data collection, analysis and presentation?
3. *Analysis:* What is the quality of the analytic effort?
4. *Overall evaluation:* What, overall, is the value of this report?

Again it is clear that quality is neither something attached to only one part of the research nor something to be realized by applying procedures such as triangulation and member validation as described in the section above. Quality is something that permeates the whole research undertaking.

Seale (1999) offers a list with criteria for the evaluation of qualitative research papers. The criteria pertaining to the analysis phase of qualitative research are listed in Box 9.2. Comments have been added about the meaning of each topic.

BOX 9.2   TOPICS TAKEN FROM SEALE'S (1999) CHECKLIST WITH REGARD TO QUALITATIVE DATA ANALYSIS

- Is reference made to accepted procedures for analysis?

  This question relates to the application of procedures in the reported study and not to the standardized procedures described in textbooks like this one (see Chapter 10). According to Seale, it also points at the reliability of the analysis and in particular attempts of independent repetition.

- How systematic is the analysis?

  Here, Seale refers to measures to prevent selectivity in the use of data and in the selection of cases for analysis that are fascinating or supporting the researcher's argument. Data should be processed systematically, and no information should have disappeared.

- Is there adequate discussion of how themes, concepts and categories were derived from the data?

  What is important here is the legitimacy of the use of concepts which were already derived from literature and given before data collection (see Chapter 2). The evidence supporting the coding system and the way in which the data are presented are important as well.

- Is there adequate discussion of the evidence both for and against the researcher's arguments?

  The issue is whether the researchers have tried to find so-called negative evidence. In other words, have they tried to find cases which do not support their ideas and interpretations, and have they checked why they do not find them, or when they do find them, why they refute the conclusions?

- Have measures been taken to test the validity of the findings?

  This refers to the quality procedures such as triangulation and member validation as described earlier in this chapter.

- Have any steps been taken to see whether the analysis would be comprehensible to the participants, if this is possible and relevant?

  Seale's primary concern here is the comprehension and use of the findings by the involved parties via member validation. For example, has any effort been made to increase the usability and recognition of the results by the participants so that they may benefit from the research?

The checklists show that quality pertains to each step taken in the research enterprise and to the coherence of all the steps together. It is this kaleidoscopic character of quality in research that makes it so difficult to judge qualitative social scientific research.

External validity or generalizability

External validity or generalizability is one of the most difficult subjects in qualitative research. External validity or generalizability pertains to whether the results of a study can be generalized beyond the specific research context. If research is not externally valid, the findings only apply to the cases examined (participants, organizations, events, places and so on). However, if a research is externally valid, the results are expected to apply to others as well (Bryman, 2008). For research to be externally valid it is of crucial importance how the sample is selected, and it is exactly this that causes doubts about the possibilities of generalizing qualitative findings. Its sampling methods are different from the well-known sampling methods in quantitative research.

The question is, when findings and conclusions are based on the examination of certain cases do they hold for other cases that were not examined? We start from the premise that all researchers who are engaged in a scientific research project ought to think about the external validity of their findings. Some authors proclaim that qualitative research yields findings that only need to be valid for the case(s) under study. Patton (1999) for instance shows reservation towards generalizing when he states that by their nature qualitative findings are highly context- and case-dependent. He states that the focus is often on understanding and illuminating important cases rather than on generalizing from a sample to a population. He continues:

> Findings, then, must be carefully limited, when reported to those situations and cases in the sample. The problem is not one of dealing with a distorted or biased sample, but rather one of clearly delineating the purpose and limitations of the sample studied – and therefore being extremely careful about extrapolating (much less generalizing) the findings to other situations, other time periods, and other people. (Patton, 1999: 1198)

Researchers should think about generalizability: consider the possibilities of external validity and heed Patton's warning to be careful not to over-generalize and to use restraint. For example, in her research on teenage mothers (see Box 1.5), Horowitz (1995) emphasizes the importance of the description of this separate welfare programme to the project and to the parties directly involved. On the other hand, she has managed to create a descriptive interpretation that can be applied to other cases. From a theoretical perspective, Horowitz is able to talk about cooperation between organizations and she formulates recommendations for policy concerning social work, education and reintegration for people who are dependent on welfare. It is our stance that researchers are involved in theorizing and as a consequence are worried about generalizability.

Smaling (2003) distinguishes three types of inductive generalization, namely statistical generalization, theoretical generalization (which he calls theory-carried generalization) and variation-based generalization, that is, generalization based on covering the variation in a certain phenomenon. The first type, statistical generalization, is dominantly used in quantitative research, while the two latter ones are mostly used in qualitative research. Statistical generalization is based on random sampling so that each case has an equal chance of becoming part of the sample. The intention is a statistically representative sample of the population that allows extrapolation of the findings in the sample to the entire population (see Chapter 2).

Theoretical generalization is based on the principle of replication, much as described in Chapter 5 about analytic induction. The researcher theorizes on the basis of a certain sample, then tests the provisional findings and conjectures with new sample cases. Based on the result of this test, the growing theory is adjusted – refined, expanded, corrected – and the process is repeated several times. The theory that is ultimately formulated must then become the vehicle for generalization to other cases that have not been studied, provided that they belong to the scope of the theory (Smaling, 2003). It is evident that the comparison cases need to be chosen purpose-fully in order to subtly test what is still only poorly understood in the preliminary findings, referred to earlier on as theoretical sampling (see Chapter 5).

The third type described by Smaling (2003) is variation-based generalization. This type is applicable when sampling takes place by means of a purposive descriptive form that is non-theory directed. As we saw in Chapter 8, not all research findings are to be called 'theory', some are better referred to as 'thematic survey' or 'conceptual/ thematic description'. The researcher then may attempt at some form of generaliza-tion of the research results by focussing on describing the variations in which a phe-nomenon occurs. The researcher looks intentionally for cases to compare in order to add to the descriptions already documented. New comparison cases from the pop-ulation involved are added to the sample until no new information turns up. At this point, saturation has been reached with regard to the description of the variation. It is believed that the variation in the population has been covered by the variation in the sample.

The research on binge drinking will be used as an example (Engineer et al., 2003). The researchers' goal was to be able to conclude about the entire population of binge drinking youths and not only about the youths included in the sample. Therefore they selected 123 young people on relevant criteria and carefully com-posed 16 focus groups. They involved men and women between 18 and 24 years old, either employed, student or unemployed, living in market towns, large towns, cities and metropolitan areas. They involved a group who became drunk at least once a week or once a month. They created groups of young people who had been involved in offensive or disorderly conduct after drinking as either perpetrator, victim or both, and groups who had behaved in ways that put them 'at risk' after drinking. The researchers clearly attempted to cover the variation within the population of youth engaged in binge drinking

The three types of generalization are based on inductive reasoning in which a gen-eralization is made from research results to a population or to a scope belonging to a theory (Smaling, 2003). Smaling argues that there is a different type of generaliza-tion based on a different type of reasoning, namely on analogy between the cases that are researched and the ones that are not. This so-called analogical generalization can reinforce the other forms of generalization just addressed. 'Analogical generalization' means that the researcher considers the relevant similarities and differences between the cases studied and the cases not studied to argue the possibility that the findings are applicable for the non-researched cases as well. Simply stated, the more similar the cases are thought to be according to sources such as literature, experts and so on, the more likely it is that the findings will hold for these cases.

Remember the study on people with multiple sclerosis and their strategies to deal with this illness in daily life (see Table 7.3). Perhaps you might want to find out whether these strategies are valid for people with other illnesses as well. Analogical generalization would require you to determine the similarities of those experiences with that of the people with other illnesses, since the comparability of the experiences is essential to the argument. The nature of the illness – i.e. the course, the severity of the physical limitations and the presence of curable medication – is crucial for determining the ways in which people experience and come to terms with a disease. In this case you can argue that the findings can more readily be generalized to people with Parkinson's disease (reasonably unpredictable course, severe limitations without curable medication) than it would to patients with diabetes (controllable course through medication, diet and lifestyle, other types of symptoms) or people with AIDS (different illness course, other types of symptoms, available medication). The established correspondence or analogy between the researched and non-researched situations must justify the transferability of the findings and conclusions. Empirical testing of analogical reasoning can contribute to a more stringent formulation of the conditions under which the theory holds and thus of the scope of the theory.

A grounded theory is commonly developed in one area of interest, a substantive field, such as the communication between staff and dying patients on hospital wards. In this specific substantive field the 'awareness context' was developed (see Box 1.4). Do remember that an awareness context in the field of hospital communication represents what the involved parties know about the imminent death. Glaser and Strauss (1967) proposed that the awareness context could be useful in understanding espionage situations, because these situations also deal with who knows what about the other and they can also fit into closed and open contexts as well as contexts based on suspicion or mutual pretending. In this case, they are generalizing on analogy.

The nice thing is that Glaser and Strauss's core concept is so strong that I often come across situations in my professional practice that can be understood within an awareness context. For instance, research into the experience of adoption by the adoptee and the adoptive parents rang a bell: that some of these families meet awareness contexts when finding out and disclosing the adoption. And another example is sex education for children, when children start to wonder where babies come from and parents suspect that their children 'know'. When the theory is further developed because of its application on different substantive fields, it becomes more abstract and addresses a social phenomenon more than a substantive field. In grounded theory such a theory is referred to as a formal theory.

What becomes clear from the example of chronic illness and hospital communication is that they stimulate the reader. A research report may enable the readers to consider what the research results and conclusions mean for specific situations that are of interest to them (Smaling, 2003). Smaling calls this form of generalization communicative generalization. In this case it was me as a reader who saw the resemblance between hospital communication, adoption and sex education. To allow this kind of generalization the original researcher needs to provide the readers with adequate descriptions in order for them to find out whether and how much their situation equals or differentiates from the situation examined in the research. As such, adequate or thick description provides the reader with a database for making judgements about the possible transferability of findings to other settings (Bryman, 2008).

Quality challenges

The issue underlying the quality debate in qualitative research is whether the knowledge gained is accurate and true according to scientific standards. One of the current and future issues that qualitative researchers will have to stay involved in is proving the quality and surplus value of their endeavours. They must demonstrate what they do when they examine a research area, what can be expected of the research findings and to what quality criteria they want to live up to. They must prove the strengths and uses of their research as stand-alone methods as well as in the context of mixed methods (see Chapter 8).

Another challenge is to be clear about what distinguishes social science qualitative research from journalistic work. Qualitative researchers are often compared to journalists, which seems logical since qualitative researchers like journalists are often engaged in field work and writing. Although there are similarities, their professional practices differ in their dealing with theory, sampling, ethical issues like confidentiality, openness about research methods, controllability of procedures used, the role and fame of the researchers/journalists themselves, and the purposes of their work such as the aim of generalizability and entertainment.

A rather dominant divergence that influences the skills needed for journalism and scientific research is that journalists pursue issues that are newsworthy (Silverman, 2001). 'Newsworthy' in this respect is interpreted as disclosing what was previously hidden or concealed. Think about pregnant teenagers who live in a shelter, communication about imminent death, or the perspectives and actions of ufologists who think that space aliens regularly visit earth. Other issues that are thought 'new' in this respect are sharp contrasts, like the intensive emotions that go with technical products like cars, going on with your life despite a chronic debilitating illness, and gender differences in contemporary university education. 'Swiftly passing' is another meaning of new in this context: new is only new once. This hunt for newsworthy items influences the professional culture of editors of journals, magazines and broadcasting media (Keeble, 1998).

The nice thing is that the subjects mentioned above can be of interest to journalists as well as to social science researchers. You may have noticed that all examples are referred to in this book! So then what is the difference? In my opinion, the most important one is the use of theory. It is social theory (the literature review) that determines your research topic and the problem statement. You want to bridge a gap in a specific area of social theory that determines what will be 'new'. It is the common research practice that you will copy in order for your outcomes to be accepted later on as a worthwhile contribution to that same social theory. And it is the theoretical reasoning in the research report that will justify your claim of having delivered a piece of scientific work.

A last challenge for qualitative researchers is to be clear about the use of scientific rhetoric. Social science derives its authority for a large part from its rhetoric in a sense that reasoning, terminology and symbols hold a certain truth claim. How this works is illustrated by Cross (2004) when she makes the case of the study of UFOs, known as 'ufology'. Although ufologists have been officially dismissed by conventional scientific researchers, they have built their own alternative research society. This society builds heavily on the cultural meaning of science to support its endeavours and to make its ideas acceptable to the public (see Box 9.3).

BOX 9.3   SCIENTIFIC RHETORIC IN UFOLOGY

The case of ufology demonstrates that the scientific approach including all rituals, symbols (including the '-ology'), conventions, rhetoric and methods can be key in creating knowledge accepted as scientific. The study of UFOs, known as 'ufology', was rejected by conventional science. However, the research community nowadays models itself after mainstream science. This causes a field of tension because ufology gains legitimacy by claiming to use methods that draw on conventional science, while, at the same time, it must account for its de facto rejection by the mainstream scientific community.

Ufologists assume that UFOs – unidentified flying objects – are real and that extraterrestrials are regularly visiting earth. Space aliens come to lead humans into the cosmic order of the universe, to warn us of coming danger and to harvest human DNA for breeding projects. The methods they use to examine this area of interest are second-hand testimony, hypnosis, skywatches, intuition, and all kinds of scientific procedures such as empirical data and hypothesis testing. The UFO research community claims millions of devotees worldwide.

Cross (2004) asked the following research questions:

- What happens when discredited scientists resurrect themselves outside the conventional jurisdiction of science?
- How do discredited scientists construct their own turf for scientific knowledge-making?
- What influence does conventional science have over the ability of rival groups to spread knowledge – knowledge presented as being scientific – to lay audiences?

To examine these questions, Cross used participant observation at UFO research conferences, museums, research centres and institutes over a two-year period. She also conducted interviews and did extensive archival bibliographic and Internet searches.

Ufologists appear to be constantly concerned about their credibility and they use many rhetorical strategies to establish it. The strategies fall loosely into four categories. The first involves emulating mainstream science, framing the study of UFOs as an ordinary scientific speciality. The second strategy promotes an accessibility of science to non-scientists and focuses on getting the findings of

UFO research – and scientific understanding in general – into the hands of as many people as possible. It also involves amateurs and laypersons in the research process. The third approach presents ufology as an improvement over conventional science both in terms of methods and findings. The fourth approach rejects scientific logic in favour of different, thoroughly unconventional processes of learning that include telepathy, intuition and the use of aliens as informants.

A few examples will make the point. The community has several journals in which the results of their investigations are presented in a scientific way, such as the *UFO Journal, Amateur Ufology News* and the *Journal for UFO Studies* (JUFOS). The UFO community emphasizes 'scientific training' in its activities and discourse. Such training results in titles and credentials that make them sound like professional research positions. An important title is 'Field Investigator'. They organize their own conferences. Accusing science of being elitist, they want to democratize their findings, write popular books and welcome newcomers to share their knowledge and insights. UFO researchers provide practical advice about how audience members can conduct scientific UFO research at home.

As ufologists emulate the practices of conventional science, they frequently critique conventional science. They accuse scientists of hypocrisy, ignorance and closed-mindedness. Some use theories to prove that scientists hold back evidence that exposes their own theories as being wrong. By the use of their strict rules and methods, science is claimed to hamper intellectual and scientific progress. UFO researchers and witnesses feel discriminated in the realm of funding and facilities. They expound that the phenomena they study, like UFOs, extraterrestrials and mystical portals to other time–space locations, need to be examined with additional methods, such as communication with aliens, thought manifestation, revelation, mediation and so on. The common scientific methods fall short of observing these phenomena.

The study illustrates that scientific rhetoric is extremely flexible and can be exported, changed and twisted to lend credibility to even the most unlikely claims of truth. The UFO research community capitalizes upon the ambiguities of what constitutes science. They predominantly use the flags or signifiers of science, rather than the substance of scientific knowledge and its methodologies. The study also demonstrates that language and rhetoric are important for understanding the power of conventional scientific practice.

(Summary based on Cross, 2004)

The ufology example focuses attention on the use of linguistic and rhetorical strategies by social scientists. To distinguish scientific qualitative research from other sources of knowledge, qualitative researchers need to be careful writers (Sandelowski & Barroso, 2002a). These authors suggest that a report of a qualitative study should be clear about what it is exactly that the researcher found out about the topic of concern. Qualitative social researchers can draw from humanities and arts as long as it benefits the scientific product. It is to the reporting of a qualitative piece of work that we will now turn in the last chapter of the book.

Readings I learnt much from

Patton, M.Q. (1999). Enhancing the quality and credibility of qualitative analysis. *Health Services Research*, 34(5): 1189–1208.

Seale, C. (1999). *The quality of qualitative research*. London: Sage.

Smaling, A. (2003). Inductive, analogical, and communicative generalization. *International Journal of Qualitative Methods*, 2(1). Article 5.

Silverman, D. (2001). *Interpreting qualitative data. Methods for analysing talk, text and interaction*. London: Sage.

Doing your own qualitative research project

Step 9: Checking up on quality

1. Which of the three perspectives on the quality of research have you chosen to apply in your research? What are the consequences of this choice for the account-ability of the methods, for relationships with the participants and other parties involved, and for the use of terminology in the report?

2. List the quality procedures that you had planned to use in your research proposal and compare them with the procedures that you have actually used. What have they done to your research project? Do they strengthen your argument? Can you legitimize that you did not use the procedures that you planned for?

3. Spend some time considering what you will share about yourself as a researcher. Think about the following:

    • Why it was you who embarked on this investigation.
    • Your experience in the field of study.
    • Your role and possible influence during data collection, analysis and findings.
    • How you dealt with distance and involvement during field work.
    • How your personal background can have influenced the findings.
    • If any quality procedures were used with respect to the performance of you as a researcher.

4. Find a checklist with quality criteria that suits your purposes. Use it to check on the quality of your own work.

5. Give the generalizability of your research serious thought. How did you think about the sample in your study – did you conceive it in terms of theoretical sampling or in terms of variation-based sampling? Can you think off a different field or subject to which your findings could be transferred when thinking in terms of analogy?

10
WRITING THE RESEARCH REPORT

In the reporting phase, all parts of the research are assigned their definitive places. Traditionally, publications have a predefined format consisting of introduction, methods, results, discussion and conclusion. Qualitative researchers who felt restricted by the traditional format have experimented with writing formats that allowed flexibility in both researchers' and participants' positions. Ways of presenting findings other than written reports, such as photographs, film and drama were employed as well. Qualitative researchers operate in the field of tension between following the mainstream conventions and finding other ways of publishing their findings. The choice depends on what is considered to be the best way to represent your findings and, more strategically, how to publish your work and satisfy the audiences, whether organizations offering grants, hosts, scientists or end-users. This chapter will focus on the written publications.

LEARNING AIMS

By the end of this chapter, you will be able to:

- Weigh different alternatives to communicate your findings, taking the audience into account
- Argue what writing style fits best, taking the positions of the authors and the participants into account
- Deal with participants' concerns with regard to confidentiality
- Outline the elements of a traditional research report
- Write a small-scale qualitative research report
- Account in a clear way how the research was conducted
- Explain 'thick description' in your own words
- Select and edit quotes to the function they serve in the report
- Submit a manuscript that follows the guidelines for authors to a peer reviewed journal

Writing: the last part of the analysis

Writing is often seen as the final phase of the analysis. Frequently, the writing phase involves locating as yet unanswered questions as well as changing the logical order of the plot by adding, re-writing, merging or deleting sections. Decisions related to these issues often interfere with analysis, because it may not yet be certain whether a particular theme needs to be dealt with, and if so, how it fits in with the entire framework of findings. Writing is not all action; a lot of thought needs to be put into this process as well. When you try to articulate the findings in a way that is comprehensible to others, things often become clear for yourself. Alternatives for a written report include photographs, film, poetry, e-publications and drama.

Even so, the resulting report must not be confused with analysis. The proof of the quality of the analysis lies in the findings, that is, the results section of the report (Matthews, 2005). Consider the production of a movie. The movie-going public sees the end product, the movie. But the audience does not see the cameraman shooting scenes, the actor doing several re-takes, the director deciding to make changes and so on. How the film was made is explained in different documentary-style programmes ('the making of . . .') in which actors and directors reflect on such things as stunts, make-up, character interpretations and character development. The same goes for the research process. Processing the data enables researchers to award new, insightful meanings to the data. 'The making of' part of the research ends up in the methods section of the report.

This implies that coding is considered a part of 'the making of'. As such, codes are lost in the story that is told in the results section. Of course some codes are recognizable in the story, otherwise the researcher would not have used them as tags. This especially holds true for the grounded theory approach, in which a researcher gradually unfolds the building blocks – the concepts – and the linkages between them to form an analytical framework. The building blocks are the relevant categories denoted with codes.

Just like the research proposal (see Chapter 2), the final report must be persuasive. Academic readers are mainly interested in the researcher's interpretations and must have faith in the findings. To convince the reader, authors need to demonstrate the appropriateness of the data, the correctness of their interpretations, the robustness of their evidence, and the logic of their line of reasoning. If they succeed, the publication will gain acceptance. The argumentation may weigh somewhat less for practitioners, since they tend to focus predominantly on the applied value of the outcomes for their own practice or situation.

TIP
_____

Search for an article or book that makes sense to you. Have a look at the contents and list the headings that have been used. Doing this will help to familiarize yourself with the inner architecture of a qualitative research report (Creswell, 2006).

Many qualitative researchers derive a lot of pleasure from the writing itself. The writing process is one filled with continually polishing your own work. No one writes a research report in one draft. On one hand, a large benefit of writing a qualitative report is that researchers do not have to start from scratch. They write as they progress, writing memos on conceptual issues and ongoing insights. They also have obtained field notes and quotes from participants. On the other hand, the sheer amount of material is not always experienced as helpful, since authors can feel as if they are drowning in the amount of data they have available to construct 'something logical, something scientific'. At this point we can safely say that when writing is interlinked with data collection and data analysis, it will lower the amount of work when writing the actual report.

TIP

Be sure to keep accurate archives from the beginning (see the section in Chapter 4 on data management), as finding everything you need instantly will make the writing process a lot easier.

The researcher as writer

With the increased demand for quality, qualitative researchers became increasingly aware of the shortcomings of conventional writing to present some of their work. They experimented with presenting their findings in non-traditional ways. Different ways of reporting include theatre, film, poetry and video. But also different writing styles were put to the test, for instance with absent writers and data 'speaking for themselves' and polyvocal texts including a variety of languages, discourses and jargons (Abma, 2002). A choice for a certain way of reporting may be based on philosophical assumptions (see Chapter 1), political considerations, ethics, aesthetics and practicalities. An example of a practical consideration is the Internet, which makes available all kinds of materials, such as interviews and files created during analysis, which would otherwise be difficult to access.

Naivety about the reporting phase cannot be justified. The findings were clearly not yet known and we made it our task to find them. It is therefore up to the researcher to decide what will be included in the written report and what is excluded. Sometimes researchers work in highly political settings in which all contents of the report are negotiated. An example is a project done as a cooperation between Palestinian and Israeli researchers (Chaitin, 2003). The writing stage appeared to be emotionally difficult for both the Palestinian and the Israeli research teams. Due to their strained relationship, correcting each others' statements turned out to be a difficult task. Each of the teams demanded that things were reworded or deleted. Both teams were sensitive, not only to the overall product but to every line, indeed to every word. After a number of e-mail rounds and discussions, they did manage to write a report and publish an article that they all felt reflected their work appropriately (Chaitin, 2003).

There are generally three distinct styles of written reports in qualitative research: the realistic, the confessional and the subtle-realistic styles (Seale, 1999; Weiss, 1994). Recently a fourth style has been detected, which I will call the narrative style.

In the realistic style, the researcher is mostly invisible in the report due to standardization, the use of the passive voice and the instrumental-technical rhetoric. The underlying reasoning seems to be that when no researchers are involved, they cannot possibly have influenced the research. It is self-evident to choose a passive form in which one does not write 'I observed' but 'It was observed'. This provides the report with a scientific authority which suggests that the objective truth is revealed. This, of course, is an illusion. A method section is added in order to describe how the investigation was carried out.

In the confessional style, researchers profile themselves explicitly as the persons having conducted the inquiry. A report in this style is a personal report of the research, including all sorts of side-tracks, errors, personal convictions, experiences and emotions. Though it appears that researchers want to open themselves to criticism, this style of reporting may confirm the authority of the researchers and instead result in a researcher being placed above all criticism (Seale, 1999). Some authors so guiltily confess their activities that it seems as though they are reluctant to take responsibility for what they are writing.

In the subtle-realistic style, the researcher makes clear statements on social reality, while at the same time taking responsibility for them (Seale, 1999). The authors here are not just service hatches of the participants' views, but do not take themselves out of the picture either. Their interpretation is what matters. They reflect on their own work – they are aware of quality issues – and are self-critical. In the report the readers get relevant information about the method to help them judge the value of the research.

In the literature a fourth style is identified, which I will refer to here as the narrative style. Narrative forms of reporting often incorporate postmodern theory and related epistemology, but that is not a requirement. Authors using this style experiment with the plotting, the author's stance, the characters of the participants, voices and rhetoric. The purpose of these alternative writing styles (and performances) is 'to draw the audience in, enabling it to experience the topic from a variety of perspectives and to be touched at an emotional level' (Abma, 2002: 6). The narratives are attempts to reflect the complex nature of research, including the power issues that surround any social research. Although authors in this style are open about their personal backgrounds and engagements and acknowledge their interpretation of the data, they go out of their way to present the participant's stories.

The different writing styles are summarized in Table 10.1. Much of the information that is covered in the rest of this chapter falls within the conventions of subtle-realism because this has been the most frequently used style in recent years.

The position of participants

While writing, researchers (unnoticed) take a position on the participants in the study. They establish a relationship with the participants, either through months of work in

TABLE 10.1   WRITING STYLES IN QUALITATIVE RESEARCH

Invisible author	Visible author
Realistic style – traditional presentation – passive voice – no explicit interpretations – separate methods section	*Confessional style* – detailed description of research process – own up to one's mistakes – relativization of findings
Narrative style – several plots – different sources and texts – author as active interpreter – favours participant's voice – no closure (no summaries, conclusions)	*Subtle-realistic style* – methodical account – reflection on researcher's role – responsibility for choices taken during the research

the field or through a one-off interview. In that relationship, they show respect for the perspective and experiences of the participant. Researchers are wary of offending the participants, or causing harm and damaging the trust they have built up when one day they have to report their findings (Chapter 3). As authors they are afraid to show too much sympathy and benevolence or too much distance and criticism. They fear that their interpretations may discredit the sympathy that they showed during data collection. They sometimes find themselves unintentionally choosing a side when studying multiple involved parties. Inevitably, readers of Horowitz's study on teenage mothers (see Box 1.5) recognized her preference for the mediators instead of the arbiters.

Confidentiality is particularly salient when disseminating results if more than one person is interviewed in the same setting. For example, when spouses are interviewed, additional care must be taken to ensure that details are sufficiently anonymized to prevent both parties from being exposed. If one person of the dyad recognizes his or her own words, it follows that the partner's anonymity is broken (Forbat & Henderson, 2003). This also holds true for data collection in your own organization or in small communities in which everyone knows each other. It is a well-known fact that although anthropologists do their utmost to prevent participants from being recognized, at the end everyone knows who is who and have even made it into a game at birthday parties.

In the narrative style of reporting, authors may deal differently with this issue (see above). Here, it is more common that the participants introduce themselves or are introduced by the authors. They use proper names, although sometimes pseudonyms, to symbolize that the individuals are worthy of being named and respected (see Chapter 3). This presents the participants as real people and helps to overcome indifference and stereotyping (the typical veteran, the typical teenage mother), which is often one of the aims of the narrators (Abma, 2002).

It is important that researchers inform participants about the research and indicate how they plan to use the data in the final report. Based on this, participants can give their approval to this plan in the form of informed consent (Sieber, 1992). It is useful to indicate to participants how the data will be used and interpreted during analysis. By sharing this with them, social scientists show that they take the participants seriously, thereby removing suspicion and lessening potential resistance against unexpected or undesired outcomes. Member validation (see Chapter 9) is an alternative, giving those who have taken part in the study a chance to review and comment.

Finally, it is important that researchers try to refrain from judging and offending the participants (see Chapter 9). Think for instance about a research project that investigates how people come to terms with trauma and hardship. Different coping styles can be described, including the consequences these styles have on the individuals and their families. Some coping methods are considered more beneficial than others. When examining how people come to use the different coping styles, it is important not to make judgements about the individual participants.

Structure of the final report

Many publications, including those on qualitative research, have a standardized structure (Abbott & Sapsford, 1998). Journal reviewers and everyone else who grades or assesses manuscripts know this structure, so researchers can use this to their advantage (Sandelowski & Barroso, 2002b; Zeller & Farmer, 1999). Reviewers get suspicious when they cannot find the standard elements in a manuscript or see aspects discussed in parts where they do not belong. Notice that the quality of your research is judged mainly by the report (Sandelowski & Barroso, 2002b). Usually, a publication consists of four parts: introduction, methods, results and discussion/conclusion. We will turn to these four elements in the next sections.

TIP

Morse and Field (1996) give a recommendation about the order in which parts of the research report may be written:

1. Start when you know what you want to write.
2. Start by writing the results.
3. Construct the reference list.
4. Write the method section (you know what you have done).
5. Re-write the literature study to create fluency between literature and results.
6. Write the discussion to connect results and literature.
7. Write your introduction (you know what you want to introduce).
8. Write the abstract (summary).

Introduction

According to Frank (2004), scientific publications should be more like detective novels in that they should have more exciting plots. Like in a good mystery book, a murder occurs in the beginning and the tension in the rest of the story consists of answering the question of who did it and why. Frank uses this as a metaphor for everything which captivates the reader. In science, this is the 'field of tension' in a research project. For instance, a probable field of tension in a dyslexia study can read as follows: 'How is it possible that someone who is not good at language maintains himself in a work and study environment in which language is of vital importance for communication?' Other examples are: 'Modern governments cannot afford to ignore IS/IT technology, so how do they deal with barriers?' and 'How is it possible that women use tranquillizers and sedatives for years when it has been known since the 1980s that long-term use should be strongly discouraged?' The basis of Frank's article is that readers have limited time and that faced with the gargantuan amount of publications available it is the exciting, readable work that has a bigger chance of being selected.

TIP
_____

The field of tension in a study is closely connected to the problem statement and the literature review. Sometimes it can be discovered by exaggerating the problem. It helps to think about what it is that makes the problem so fascinating for you.

_____

The introduction should provide an overview of the research area. This is mainly realized by providing an integrated inventory of relevant, previous research (approaches, use of theory, findings) resulting in the formulation of research questions, the purpose of the study and the relevance of the present study. The following format can be helpful when structuring the introduction:

- What does the research area entail?
- What are the current issues?
- How have they been dealt with and were alternatives successful?
- How has the area been examined: what methods were used and were they appropriate?
- What aspects have not been sufficiently addressed and/or with less adequate methods?
- What is your research question and what are you going to do to answer it?

The need for a literature review as the preparation for one's own research has been emphasized in Chapter 2. However, after writing the findings of the research, you may discover that there are some worthwhile findings that were not addressed in the introduction section. Any possible available literature may be searched for and added to the introduction. Alternatively, the literature can be mentioned in the discussion section in order to preserve the chronological order of the research process.

In the introduction the authors strategically use the literature to lead the reader to their own problem statement. Therefore, they select what to present and what to leave out, and they do so in a way that ensures the evolvement of a logical and compelling story. A convincing start is not only important for the research proposal, but for the introduction section of the final publication as well. It must be a fascinating story that persuades the readers of the worthiness of the present study. Although in journal articles one has to make the most of one's allotted number of words, in dissertations and theses a chapter may be set aside for the usually extensive literature study.

Methods

The method section is a treatise of how the researcher has executed the research. Based on the description of the procedures used, it should be possible to replicate the study (see Chapter 9). Documentation of the research methods may seem simple, but it is not. The researcher must select, out of all the activities undertaken during the research process, which activities are worth mentioning. The method section has a strategic position in the report. 'Strategic' does not mean that the research activities are to be exaggerated, because this will lead to the disappointment of reviewers and readers as they will either not believe you or assume that you have made disproportionate efforts in relation to the findings (Sandelowski & Barroso, 2002b). 'Strategic' means that this is the place to demonstrate knowledge of the terminology and to show competence for conducting good qualitative research.

The method section provides a researcher with some freedom to write, but a number of things must be dealt with. Always discuss: gaining access to the field, recruitment of participants, researcher role and presentation in the field, data collection, data storage and analytic procedures (Altheide & Johnson, 2005). Ethical procedures are also mainly dealt with in the method section. It is generally a good idea to illustrate procedures with examples from your own research which provide more insight than the textbook version.

The main reason for carefully documenting the analysis method is your scientific responsibility to show how you transformed the data and thus how the findings came into being. In relation to data analysis, the method section needs to give answers to the following questions:

- Was coding used? If so, what types were used, and how was the coding scheme developed?
- If software was used, what was its main purpose?
- How were themes and patterns discerned in the data?
- How were interpretations awarded to the data?
- If working in a team, how was this team put together?
- How (if applicable) were clusters of data integrated to form an explanation of the social phenomenon under study?
- How were conclusions drawn? How were (if relevant) practical recommendations formulated?

All this information is necessary for readers to judge the value of the findings of a study. A well-written chapter on methods contributes to the development of methodological knowledge and the actual application of qualitative methods. The area of qualitative methodology that needs this most is the domain of qualitative analysis. Researchers can report more than they usually do on problems, dilemmas and choices; especially choices that have no standard way of being dealt with and are

TABLE 10.2   DISSECTION OF THE METHOD SECTION IN GOODMAN'S ARTICLE

Section	Contents
Design	• Approach used to data collection and analysis (case-centred comparative approach).
Sample	• Number of participants, criteria for selection, recruitment, composition of the sample, language spoken.
Data collection	• Ethical approval obtained, informed consent, appreciation gift, opportunity to debrief and evaluate. • Further details of access. • Period of interviewing, locations interviews took place, mean duration of interviews. • Nature of interview guide, introduction to interviews, tape-recording. • Additional data collection: interviews with informants, participant observation including activities.
Data analysis	• Data preparation: verbatim transcription of audio-taped interviews, re-transcription, use pseudonyms to protect anonymity. • Data analysis: identifying bounded stories in the narratives, delineating structural elements, use of descriptive narrative techniques, individual analysis and comparative analysis, contribution of native research assistant to check language and interpretation issues, use of additional sources (informant interviews and field notes).

influenced by circumstances in the specific setting. For instance, difficult access to a field of study can lead to a certain phasing of the research. And when software is used, what exactly did it do for this research? Circumstances can pertain to a certain population, a type of subject or the influence of resources, granting organizations and ethical review committees. Reporting difficult choices or even mistakes asks for a large openness in researchers that is seldom displayed.

TIP
_____

When you have really made progress in developing and applying qualitative research methodology, think about the opportunity to report your discovery or reflection in a journal with a clear methodological interest or in the methodological corner that some scientific journals feature.

_____

Let us illustrate what and how to report in the methods section. Table 10.2 analyses the methods section of the article 'Coping with trauma and hardship among unaccompanied refugee youths from Sudan' (Goodman, 2004). The section consists of four subsections: i) Design, in which the overall methodological approach is mentioned, ii) Sample, describing the recruitment and selection of the participants, iii) Data collection, with an elaboration of the main method – interviews – instruments used and ethical issues, and iv) Data analysis, with the preparation of the data and the main analysis techniques.

TIP

When reading a report that appeals to you and that you find scientifically convincing, have a close look at the method section. List the headings and pay attention to the issues raised, problems detected and solutions used. You are never the first one to meet certain difficulties in writing down what you did, so try to learn from others.

Results

The purpose of the results section is to convey to readers what was found in the study. Findings are the outcomes of the researcher's analytical activities (not the activities themselves) and consist of data and everything the researcher makes out of them, whether descriptions, theoretical models or explanations. There is a risk of data and interpretations becoming fouled. In order to enable the readers to distinguish clearly between data (observations) and interpretations (the explanations given by the researcher), it is best to separate them. When researchers draw inferences in the results section – which inevitably and necessarily happens in qualitative research – they should indicate clearly who is talking. Authors cannot and should not limit themselves to the presentation of the data in the results section and withhold their interpretation. Matthews declares that the author's stance must be "'This is what I concluded from the data that were categorized in this way", followed by one or two excerpts to provide supporting evidence' (2005: 806).

Let us have a look at a written part of Goodman's (2004) article on Sudanese youth refugees as an example of how to tackle writing the results section. The aim of the study was to explore how unaccompanied refugee youths from Sudan, who grew up amid violence and loss, coped with trauma and hardship in their lives. Fourteen male unaccompanied refugee youths from Sudan were interviewed. Recently they resettled in the United States. Goodman identified four themes that reflect coping strategies used by the participants: i) collectivity and the communal self, ii) suppression and distraction, iii) making meaning, and iv) emerging from hopelessness to hope. In Box 10.1 one section of the report is analysed in which one coping strategy is expanded on.

BOX 10.1   DECIPHERING OF A SECTION OF GOODMAN'S (2004) RESULTS

Comments	Text from Goodman's article
The paragraph has to have a clear function in the entire plot. The heading is theoretically influenced as well as using the language of the participants.	Collectivity and the communal self: "What is happening is not happening to me alone".
Two types of evidence that collectivity is important: content (what they said) and form (how they said it).	The theme of collectivity, or the communal self, was revealed in the content of the narratives, as well as by the linguistic devices participants used to tell their stories.

Comments	Text from Goodman's article
	Each participant located himself predominantly as part of the group of refugee boys, telling his story with the group voice, mainly using the pronouns *we* and *us*, and only rarely using the personal pronouns *I* or *me*.
There is extra evidence provided by elaborating on the function of operating as a group (survival). Roles (security, food) are identified between the group members (older boys) and others (villagers). It is substantiated by a participant's quote.	A sense of shared experience and collective coping enabled survival. Mayan told about older boys in the group who provided security at night as they travelled, and about villagers, "black like us," who offered corn and grain on their journey. He related his belief that it was only with the help of others that he survived. He stated: If it was me by myself I could not have made it. But people were really friendly and brothers to each other. One of the big kids used to help me a lot. I didn't know him, but he had a lot of compassion towards me.
A second function of the group is described: encouragement, support and advice. The literal statement is repeated and is used as the paragraph's heading. A cultural dimension of social networks is given.	Participants encouraged themselves and each other with the knowledge that, as expressed by one boy, "What is happening is not happening to me alone." Bol stated, "We had to encourage each other, advise each other not to give up, to still struggle for the future life. I encouraged myself and also I listened to other kids. Seeing how they survived made me more encouraged." Participants told of the supportive social networks in their community wherein elders, though very few among the refugees, acted as wise and respected advisors.
In this part of the text the function of the group is further elaborated, as well as an understanding where collectivity stems from. The role of the family is stressed as this is also one of the research questions.	The notion of selfhood in which one has responsibility for others, and even exists for the other, provided the impetus for many of the boys to continue their difficult journey, to not give up, and to plan for their future. Participants expressed a sense of obligation to help other Sudanese refugees in need. Several of the refugee boys expressed feeling obligated to carry on as

(Continued)

(Continued)

Comments	Text from Goodman's article
	representatives of their families. Benedict explained, "If I live, I will be the ambassador of my family. And if God wishes I will be alive and my family will not be lost totally. I will be my family."
The argument is strengthened in pointing at the continuation of collectivity when the refugees arrived in a different country altogether. Goodman uses other sources of data as evidence for the involvement of the refugees with the people who stayed behind in Sudan. The quotes contain cultural expressions about 'suffering in the blood'. Here the author includes short excerpts and weaves back and forth between assertions and evidence.	The participants' sense of a communal identity with their fellow Sudanese refugees continues in the United States, despite separation by great distances. Informal conversations with foster parents and caseworkers recounted numerous phone calls among Sudanese refugees resettled throughout the United States and Canada, as well as phone calls to and from contacts in Africa. Most of the participants expressed great concern and worry for the refugees still remaining in Africa, and a strong connection with the suffering of fellow refugees who were left behind. Ezekiel stated: If you feel comfortable, and the rest of your brothers are suffering, that can give you a lot of trouble in your blood, in your heart inside, how you feel inside. Because your brothers and sisters are suffering a lot. At a later point in the interview, he elaborated: I remember the hunger facing us in Kakuma. I can remember because now in America I'm okay. But my brothers have remained behind and are suffering. In my blood I can feel hunger because my brother is suffering. In my stomach I'm okay, but in my blood I'm still suffering.
The interview excerpt is used to emphasize again the finding dealt with in this paragraph and to draw to an end.	The feelings of concern for those remaining in Africa, even the internalization of these feelings, underscores again the strong sense of community and the idea of the communal self, which is reflected in the narratives.

When writing the results, researchers may benefit tremendously from software designed specifically for qualitative analysis (see Chapter 7). Text fragments which are necessary for writing about the relevant categories can easily be retrieved. This is not to say that all fragments should be literally put into the text (see the next section), but while writing they help to recall what needs to be written about. The memos stored in the software can also be kept close at hand as a prompt. Further on in the research process, all kinds of searches in subsets of documents and of codes can be employed.

There are several books on the market dealing with writing about social science research, for instance Becker (2007), and about qualitative research in particular, such as Holliday (2007) and Woods (2005). Below, a number of issues are addressed that frequently bother qualitative researchers when writing up their results. We deal with the story line, description, data and quotes, cases, using numbers and visual materials.

TIP

When experiencing writer's block, it is advisable to start with writing a relatively easy chapter. This is a chapter in which the researcher feels that the story can easily be related and for which the data are effortlessly retrievable from memory. In doing so, writing is practised and the biggest hurdle is overcome. This is sometimes called 'free writing' and should be employed right at the beginning of a project (Charmaz, 2006; Kleinman & Copp, 1993).

The story line

The key issue of the story line is what has been called 'the architecture of the study' (Creswell, 2006). It is good to get into the habit of thinking early on about the structure of the report and especially about the organization of the results section. In doing so a preliminary table of contents is created, which is then adjusted throughout the writing of the entire report. The reader's interest will be raised when the participant's language is shown in the headings or when a small part of the theoretical model is revealed.

Thinking about the outline is considered to be a heuristic device (see Chapter 7). There are always alternatives to constructing the main story because there is never only one way to organize the findings. They can for instance be structured chronologically or thematically, or according to a theoretical model, the used sources or the perspectives of different groups involved. The main criterion is to convey the message as logical and as persuasive as possible.

TIP

Again, an illustrative study can be very beneficial here. You can use it to get an idea about a possible build-up of your own study. Moreover, you can also learn which structure matches your own ways of thinking and which structures you consider to be inspiring and stimulating.

Description

One of the main purposes of qualitative research is to provide descriptions of what it is like out there. To describe the experience or the phenomenon that you are interested in, your data must contain sufficient, correct information. Matthews (2005) states that it is paramount to ask participants to tell about specific events, situations and experiences. In the course of describing something that happened, informants are likely to include information about how they felt at the time. The reverse is not the case: interviewees do not provide as much detail about what happened while telling about how something made them feel. In this case you might end up with weak data that provide you with feelings but little to draw on to explain those feelings or behaviours. Consider Goodman's (2004) research as an example. For readers to imagine themselves in the youths' coping attempts they have to have a clue about the hardships these youths encountered during their flight, otherwise they will not see the problem and consequently will not understand what it is these youths have to cope with.

The data and the interpretations that are presented need to be woven into the entire story that is being told. Some writers have a tendency to use up too much data at once without properly explaining to readers what the data show, why they are presented, and what their function is in the bigger picture. As a consequence, the reader will feel lost either because of not being able to follow the story or because of not grasping all the different pieces of data and loose ends. Findings will be best represented when both the data and your inferences on them are described properly. So, do tell!

In the literature you will come across the term 'thick description' when it comes to providing adequate descriptions of social events or phenomena. This term, devised by the anthropologist Clifford Geertz, refers to detailed, rich accounts of the places, people and activities in a social setting. Thick description does not mean extensive, trivial descriptions of everything that is encountered during field work. Details are only important when they are significant for the participants and because they provide the context in which the behaviour takes place (Bryman, 2008). Neither is thick description comparable to analytic depth or conceptual density; a researcher can provide adequate descriptions of phenomena without abstraction or theoretical additions.

Data and quotes

Many qualitative research reports feature literal quotes or field observations in the text. This is part of the charm of qualitative research, and makes it easy to recognize when qualitative research is being reported. However, it is not always necessary to include quotes, in some cases summaries or paraphrases will do. A trap for researchers is that they lose track of their own story line as they let themselves be lead by the data and in particular the quotes. Quotes should not be strung together like beads in a necklace. The thoughtless and excessive use of quotes can lead to long, boring publications (Kvale, 2008). It is important for researchers to determine what argument they want to convey, and what story line fits that goal best. Only then can the data be used effectively to support the argument.

Quotes are functional and supportive of the story when they (Weiss, 1994; Sandelowski, 1994):

- provide evidence: The data show that empirical material has been collected in relation to the research questions. Concrete field notes and recorded interviews (see Chapter 4) supply 'low-inference descriptors' (Seale, 1999). These are data which are little interpreted. By providing excerpts, readers are able to check whether the interpretations given by the researcher are appropriate.
- show language and behaviour: In qualitative research, the use of language as a means to convey meaning and action are important. By using literal data, language is heard and action is observed. The reader has the idea of 'being there', another core element of anthropological research coined by Geertz (2004). Especially with the use of in vivo codes, specific expressions or emotions of participants can be utilized.
- make text more vivid: Compelling text may evoke emotions or reactions in the reader. This goes beyond making the text more fun to read just by introducing various speakers or including a number of scenes. Participants sometimes are very gifted in expressing accurately how they make sense of their social world.

A number of additional recommendations about how to deal with quotes have crystallized in research practice. They can be found in Box 10.2.

BOX 10.2 USING QUOTES IN QUALITATIVE REPORTS

- Do not use a quote more than once, even though it may be illustrative of several things you want to say.
- Illustrate a point using no more than one or two quotes. A list of quotes to demonstrate that a lot of people said something does not add much evidence, and makes reading cumbersome. Be critical in your selection and, if necessary, indicate how often people said something (Weiss, 1994).
- Add an indicator to quotes. This is not always done and may not always be necessary, but it gives the reader an indication that not all of the data were taken from one site or one interview worth quoting. An indicator with relevant information, such as gender, age, profession or department, can make placing quotes easier. Participants could also be given a pseudonym, like in Goodman's (2004) article, so that they can be named when quoted. Be careful not to use an indicator that endangers the participant's anonymity if you promised confidentiality.

(Continued)

(Continued)

- Reflect on the length of a quote in relation to comprehensibility. One-liners in which almost nothing is said are generally useless. This is especially the case when the researcher uses practically the same words to introduce the quote. It is hard to give any rules of thumb with concern to the length of a quote. Be sure that it can be understood when read separate from the original document and be clear about what the quote illustrates or what it represents.
- Mark quotes by giving a line space above and below and indenting them.

There are several ways to edit quotes (Weiss, 1994). In editing, it is important that the core of the message is preserved as the speaker intended to put it across. In the preservationist approach, the original message on the recording is displayed as literally as possible. The reason for this is that cleaning up is considered to lead to loss of valuable information, which is needed for interpretation. In the standardized approach, the wording and meaning are preserved, but some editing is done in order to facilitate reading. The 'usual compromise', according to Weiss (1994), is that writers keep the meaning of the answers but leave out their questions, change dialect, merge text from different places in the document and so on.

An example is the research on dyslexia. The authors deliberately left the spelling errors and sentence structure intact for the reader to see. Goodman (2004) did a good deal of editing. She stated that the original transcriptions were carefully re-transcribed, changing only the grammar to make it more readable. Because English was not the participants' primary language, editing in this way made their stories flow more smoothly. Goodman tried to keep intact idiosyncrasies and poetic expression of the narrations. Pauses, false starts and stuttering were not taken into account because they were not deemed essential to analysis.

Up to this point the researcher has done a lot with the collected data; a schematic representation of this is given in Table 10.3.

Presenting cases

There are several reasons why it may be useful to include an extended description of one or more cases in the publication. In a thematic analysis the themes and patterns are dealt with, but at the risk of loosing sight of the bigger picture of the cases involved. One of the reasons for a case description is that it can give the reader a more holistic impression of what a certain experience is like in all its facets. A case description takes all the emerged themes into account and brings them together to provide an overview. Haafkens' (1997) research, for example, provided compelling issues regarding the long-term use of sedatives, such as the first prescription and the role of the social network. After this thematic analysis, seven case descriptions were reported that were thought to be representative of what was found in 50 interviews.

TABLE 10.3   SELECTION AND EDITING OF RAW DATA

Researcher's activities	Selections	Guidelines and indications
Observing	Raw data contain a selection of what to observe and what not, and what to jot down and what not.	Record, train to take concrete field notes (low-inference), keep a diary or log, cooperate with others.
Transcribing	Select what to preserve with regard to sound, intonation, pauses, atmosphere and so on.	Guidelines for transcribing, dependent on kind of analysis.
Interpreting	Selection of data is determined by the theoretical framework, the researcher's perspective and the research questions.	Distinguish data and inferences.
Quoting	Changes as a consequence of editing data, for instance adjustment of slang and removal of false starts. Some changes are needed to guarantee anonymity.	Guidelines for editing, author guidelines in journals, ethical rules.

They provided the participants with a face and an identity (see 'The researcher as writer' in this chapter).

Case descriptions may serve as illustrations of a typology. Types of organizations, activities, individuals or situations demand accurately constructed descriptions of cases based on the criteria which distinguish these types from each other. The construction of a typology was addressed in Chapter 1 and illustrated with a typology of people with multiple sclerosis (Boeije, Duijnstee, Grypdonck & Pool, 2002). In the article case descriptions were offered in the form of short biographies.

Cases can help to bring out the truth from a particular person's perspective. Matthews (2005) emphasizes that authors must make clear that they understand that they are not reporting facts per se but someone's interpretation of them. Interviewees talk about social events all the time and in doing so refer to their relationships with other people and their part in the events. For instance, think about physicians prescribing sedatives to women, group members of youth refugees, peers of binge drinkers, partners of the chronically ill, and colleagues of people with dyslexia. Matthews stresses that it is important to remember that those about whom the participants are speaking might provide different versions. Writing in a way that conveys that the data are someone's perspective is likely to be more convincing than dealing with the informant's assertions as 'the truth'.

Using numbers

Most reports of qualitative research contain words such as 'most', 'several', 'a number', 'many', 'some', 'the majority' and 'a few'. These 'vague quantifiers' are imprecise ways of conveying frequency. Although they are mostly lightly used to facilitate writing, researchers should be aware that they can be interpreted as indications of how often something occurred. Quantitative researchers are interested in variations within and between groups and express this in numbers, proportions and frequencies of people holding certain views or engaging in different types of behaviour (Hardy & Bryman, 2004). From the quantitative researchers' perspective it seems logical to

TABLE 10.4   EXAMPLE OF A TABLE WITH NUMBERS IN A PREDOMINANTLY QUALITATIVE STUDY

Routes towards first prescription		Initial pattern of benzodiazepine use			
Reported previous tranquillizer use	Reported initiator first prescription	as prescribed (N %)	> prescribed (N %)	< prescribed (N %)	N
1. No	Physician	11 (58%)	6 (31%)	2 (11%)	19
2. No	User	2 (75%)	1 (25%)		3
3. Yes	Physician	10 (71%)	4 (29%)		14
4. Yes	User	4 (29%)	8 (57%)	2 (14%)	14
Total		27 (54%)	19 (38%)	4 (8%)	50

Source: Haafkens, 1997

replace the vague indicators with concrete indicators whenever they are known, such as 'six participants', 'everyone' and '50 percent'.

Numbers can be used in qualitative research either to give readers a concrete indication about the prevalence of some phenomena or to facilitate the reporting. However, the objection against the use of concrete indicators is that they are misleading if they were assumed to apply to the wider population (Ziebland & McPherson, 2006). Fifty percent is quite insubstantial when ten to 20 purposefully selected individuals are concerned. In order to avoid the impression that the sample has been drawn randomly and that frequencies apply to the population, qualitative researchers mostly work around the use of numbers.

Still, as was already addressed in Chapter 7, it may be informative for the reader to know in how many cases a researcher's interpretation is grounded (Weiss, 1994). One way of dealing with this is to present tables and cross-tabulations. Tables present a lot of information in a well-organized way. Haafkens' (1997) dissertation features a relatively large amount of tables about the use of tranquillizers by women in her investigation. The first two columns in Table 10.4 feature respectively whether the women had any experience with tranquillizers prior to the first prescription and who took the initiative for the first prescription. Following this, the relationship between these two categories and subsequent use during the next six months was examined. In doing so, a subdivision was made to indicate how many of the participating women followed a specific pattern.

Visual material

If visuals are created to shed light on certain issues, it will certainly strengthen the argument if they are carefully selected, presented and commented on in the report. They can support the verbal data, contribute visual evidence and enrich the text. When images are used to convey a message and make an argument, they are in fact considered 'writing' (O'Reilly, 2005). Since they were created with this purpose, it is legitimate to publish some of them. In Clark-Ibáñez's (2007) research, some pictures that the children had taken were included in the publication and show the interchange between the written and visual material. Parts of video or film can be made available on the Internet for a specified audience.

Pictures are information-rich; they can show many things in one image (and save a lot of words). But because they show so much at one time, they can be ambiguous and lead to multiple interpretations (Alexander, 2008). As with quotes mentioned above, it is the researchers' task to steer the reader to see what is intended in the picture. Images and text are best interwoven, although the dominance of the one over the other might depend on the subject and the style chosen to report the findings.

Conclusion and discussion

For many researchers, writing the conclusion and discussion section is the most difficult part of the final report, because it should be concise, accurate, match the results and be well thought of in terms of consequences for the different parties involved. Sometimes a concluding section as well as a discussion section is written, but writing only a discussion is also common. What are the contents of such a section? The core element is the answer to the main research question. However, it is not necessary to repeat the results; a short summary of the most important outcomes, preferably in different wording, suffices.

What is important is that the researcher evaluates the answers given with respect to the theoretical issues mentioned in the introduction. The link between the results and social theory provides the conclusions with an analytical character, and allows them to rise above concrete examples. Similarities and differences between your results and the work of others (previous research) can confirm your conclusions and clarify why you found what you found. The findings may also be interpreted in terms of the societal relevance or practical purposes which the study attempts to address. And as was noted in Chapter 2, there are a lot of studies which have either an implicit or an explicit applied purpose. Practitioners working in the applied field will therefore be very curious as to what the study can teach them, i.e. what does the researcher recommend they do?

Let's draw again on Goodman's (2004) article on Sudanese refugees. What did she focus on in her discussion and conclusion section? The four themes related to how the participants coped with the trauma and hardship in their lives, which were extensively described in the findings, are interpreted in the discussion and placed into the context of previous studies. The communal identity that she finds to be strong in her participants is explained by Goodman as an aspect of Southern Sudanese culture. She expects that the cultural context of the participants' lives might have played an important role in their coping abilities and in this respect she points at the social support theory. The meaning of the second coping strategy, suppression and distraction, is understood against the background of a three-stage theory about recovery from trauma.

The discussion then switches to highlighting the significance of the research as being one of the few projects to explore how children derive meaning from their traumatic experiences in the context of the cultural dimensions of such meaning-making. The finding that culture influences coping strategies parallels other research in this area. She recommends future research into meaning-giving in other populations of refugees. Here she returns to what she stated in the introduction section, namely that the number of children with serious psychiatric symptoms was extremely low in the resettlement community of young Sudanese boys in the United States. Her explanation, after conducting the research, is that it has to do with their culturally embedded understanding of their experiences. She then asks challenging questions about resilience being part of the social context as much as within the individual. Researchers and practitioners should, in Goodman's eyes, focus on the culturally based strengths of refugees.

The conclusion emphasizes the fact that the chosen method is useful for enhancing insight in the subject area, and the results are summarized in one paragraph. Briefly two limitations of the study are mentioned, relating to the role of the researcher and the one-off nature of the interview. It is remarked that although the group of Sudanese refugees is unique, the findings have implications for the mental health of children worldwide that have experienced war, violence, loss and extreme hardship. Here the author probably indicates the cultural dimension of coping efforts, and she states that her study contributes to the body of literature on stress, coping and resilience. With this reflection on her study Goodman finishes her discussion and conclusion section.

The attractive part of writing a discussion is that it allows researchers some freedom in examining, interpreting and qualifying the results as well as drawing inferences from them (APA, 2005). You can speculate a little, going beyond the strict confines of the data, and you can point to further issues that the research has raised. The researcher can demonstrate which expectations have or have not been met and why, and what makes the issues special or representative in the context in which they were studied. Often the discussion section contains recommendations for further research. Eventually, the importance of the findings is commented on, usually in terms of weaknesses and strengths of the study. A methodological contribution by sharing experiences, especially when they contain innovations or unexpected yields, is usually appreciated by the reader. Do not bring down your own research in this section, but show that you are able to reflect on your own work. Further assessment of the work is up to the reviewers and readers.

TIP
_____

In the discussion, researchers may limit themselves to describe strengths and weaknesses with regard to the methodology which became apparent when the study was conducted. The reader is extensively informed about the research design in the method section. In the discussion section it is advised to focus on elements which have not gone according to plan when the study was executed, but only when they have been relevant to the outcome of the research or if they are beneficial for other researchers to know.

_____

Publishing

In this final section the focus shifts to the reader as judge of the publication. In reading a research report and determining its value, the reader appears to use the following procedure (Abbott & Sapsford, 1998). First, the abstract and introduction are scanned to see what the researcher is trying to convey, and whether this is of interest. Then, the reader reviews the discussion and conclusion section to see what the researcher claims to have found and what this implies. Sometimes, the end of the results section is taken into account as it is often here that integration of the results – the climax – takes place. After this, the quality of the evidence and argumentation are assessed. Finally, the method section is examined to determine whether the choice of methods was appropriate and if their application was adequate. If readers appear to select their sources in this way, this implies that some of the manuscript's parts function as a flagship and appetizer for your potential audience. If these parts are well written, this is pure PR for your study to be read and referred to.

What choices do researchers have for publication? The most important products are papers or assignments, theses and reports (all these do not have ISBNs), contributions to edited volumes, books, dissertations and national and international articles in scientific and/or professional journals. The choice of a certain medium affects your writing: study programmes usually have strict standards for assignments, dissertations are subject to a number of requirements, and journals use guidelines for authors available in the journal and on its website. The American Psychological Association (APA) (2005) offers a manual in which terms and conditions for manuscripts to be published are accurately set out. Journals force the authors to consider how to make the most of the relatively little space they offer. In professional journals, the message and the practical implications should be immediately apparent for an audience with relatively little time for reading.

For most scientists who are employed at universities or research institutes, publishing in a peer-reviewed journal is essential. The procedure is usually as follows. The researcher sends the finished manuscript to the editorial board of the journal. The editor determines whether the topic of the research is suitable for the journal and of importance to its readers. If not, the manuscript is sent back to the author with the message that it does not match the journal's purpose. Sometimes, a recommendation is made for another journal that might be interested. If the editor in chief accepts the article for review, it is forwarded to one or more reviewers. These experts in the field judge the quality of the manuscript. In many cases, this is done by means of a form with a number of predefined categories that reflect the quality criteria of the journal (see Chapter 9), such as the relevance and significance of the submitted article, the use of theory, methodological evaluation, ethical standards, style and structure. The editor gathers the comments from the reviewers and, based on these, writes a final judgement. This is then passed on to the author.

The outcome may be that the article is rejected. In such cases, the comments are usually so serious that further revisions (for that particular journal) are not an option. Communicating this to the author ought to be done in a constructive manner, so that room for improvement of the manuscript remains. However, it still forces the author to start all over again with another journal. The outcome this time may be that the author is sent the reviewers' comments and is asked to make minor or major revisions, after which the paper may be resubmitted. This should be accompanied by a covering letter which details which changes have been made in response to each comment. If the changes are satisfactory for the editor and the reviewers the article is likely to be accepted for publication.

This is the procedure as it should be followed. On some occasions, the manuscript goes back and forth a bit, until everyone has had enough. Sometimes researchers do not agree with the reviewers' comments or think they use the wrong criteria to assess their work altogether. If all goes well, a review procedure is finalized in three to six months, but in some cases it takes years. Researchers open the bottle of champagne at the time the article is accepted, because waiting until the actual publication may take as much as another year. Fortunately, digital processing has speeded up the review procedures enormously, and increasingly the article appears on-line first.

A smart researcher anticipates this procedure when writing. Morse and Field (1996) recommend selecting three journals which match the target audience. In order to do this, the researcher looks at the table of contents, the mission statement of the journal, a few articles, and the editorial board of the journal. The author should never expect the manuscript to be accepted on first submission. Morse and Field (1996) also suggest having four people read the manuscript before making any submissions. For example, an author could ask someone with expertise in the relevant field, someone like the researcher himself, a friend or someone who takes a critical stance towards the research. This should increase the overall quality of the written report and also boost the author's confidence.

Publishing is no sinecure. Researchers need time and proper guidance to learn how to write and to get accepted for publication. Due to increased emphasis on publishing, the number of manuscripts submitted to journals has risen in recent years, leading to a tightening of the requirements for publication. Meeting the quality demands made on analysis in qualitative research and reports was my aim for writing and publishing this book. It is highly likely that this was your reason for reading it, and I hope it has proved satisfactory.

Readings I learnt much from

Becker, H.S. (2007). *Writing for social scientists: how to start and finish your thesis, book, or article* (2nd ed). Chicago, IL: Chicago Press.

Matthews, S.H. (2005). Crafting qualitative research articles on marriages and families. *Journal of Marriage and Family*, 67: 799–808.

Weiss, R.S. (1994). *Learning from strangers. The art and method of qualitative interview studies*. New York: Free Press.

Doing your own qualitative research project

Step 10: Writing the report

1. Now that you know what you want to write about, you can start writing. Think about your role as a writer. How do you see yourself as a writer, and what writing style appeals to you most (see Table 10.1)? Does this style match the position that you

assigned the participants in your research? Does the style fit the audience or are other styles or even other ways of presenting your data better suited to your purposes?

2. Determine the outline of your publication – maybe you have created one already in the analysis stage of your research.

3. Morse and Field (1996) recommended a logical sequence for writing the different parts of your publication. Take a look at it and consider its value for how you like to write. Start writing a results section that you feel comfortable with. When writing with a team of researchers, make sure that tasks are divided accurately so that work is not duplicated and that everyone uses the same style of writing or that the entire report is edited afterwards.

4. A qualitative research report consists of the following elements:

    - Title, authors, and affiliations
    - Abstract
    - Introduction

        - Literature review
        - Research questions and purposes

    - Research methods

        - Choice for certain approach
        - Sample composition
        - Data collection
        - Data analysis
        - Quality procedures

    - Results
    - Discussion

        - Answering research questions
        - Reflection on methodology of the study
        - Theoretical and practical implications

    - Conclusions
    - References
    - Figures and Appendices

    Remember that this structure is not set in stone; if your research demands a different structure or sequence, go ahead and devise something new.

5. In a publication you have to balance the information that is needed to assess the research with the available space to convey your message. First, check if you have provided the readers with enough information to judge your study and to replicate it if they wanted to, then check that you are not guilty of having overdone it.

6. Have your drafts read by others to test whether your report is a good read. Consider the report as a whole and all sections and paragraphs individually. Are all parts needed, and have you written them in a concise and clear style? Are you satisfied with it and confident about it? If so, it is time to publish.

REFERENCES

Abbott, P. & Sapsford, R. (1998). *Research methods for nurses and the caring professions*. (2nd ed.) Buckingham: Open University.

Abma, T.A. (2002). Emerging narrative forms of knowledge representation in the health sciences: two texts in a postmodern context. *Qualitative Health Research*, 12(1): 5–27.

Alexander, V.D. (2008). Analysing visual materials. In: N. Gilbert (Ed.), *Researching social life*. (3rd ed.) Pp. 343–360. London: Sage.

Altheide, D.L. & Johnson, J.M. (2005). Criteria for assessing interpretive validity in qualitative research. In: N.K. Denzin & Y.S. Lincoln (Eds.), *Handbook of qualitative research*. (3rd ed.) Pp. 485–499. Thousand Oaks, CA: Sage.

American Psychological Association (2005). *Publication manual of the American Psychological Association*. (5th ed.) Washington, DC: APA.

Baker, C., Wuest, J. & Noerager Stern, P. (1992). Method slurring. The grounded theory/ phenomenology example. *Journal of Advanced Nursing*, 17: 1355–1360.

Barry, C.A., Britten, N., Barber, N., Bradley, C. & Stevenson, F. (1999). Using reflexivity to optimize teamwork in qualitative research. *Qualitative Health Research*, 9(1): 26–44.

Beatty, P.C. & Willis, G.B. (2007). Research synthesis: the practice of cognitive interviewing. *Public Opinion Quarterly*, 71(2): 287–311.

Becker, H.S. (1982). Becoming a marijuana user. In G. Rose (Ed.), *Deciphering sociological research*. Pp. 170–179. Houndmills: MacMillan.

Becker, H.S. (2007). *Writing for social scientists: how to start and finish your thesis, book, or article*. (2nd ed.) Chicago, IL: Chicago Press.

Becker, H.S. & Geer, B. (1969). Participant observation and interviewing: a comparison. In G.J. McCall & J.L. Simmons (Eds.), *Issues in participant observation: a text and reader*. Pp. 322–331. Reading, MA: Addison-Wesley.

Boeije, H.R. (1994). Kwaliteit van zorg in verpleeghuizen: een onderzoek naar problemen en strategieën van verzorgenden. [Quality of care in nursing homes: a research into problems and strategies of enrolled nurses] PhD-thesis Erasmus University Rotterdam. Utrecht: Tijdstroom.

Boeije, H.R. (2002). A purposeful approach to the constant comparative method in the analysis of qualitative interviews. *Quality & Quantity*, 36: 391–409.

Boeije, H.R., Duijnstee, M.S.H. & Grypdonck, M.H.F. (2003). Continuation of caregiving among partners who give total care to spouses with multiple sclerosis. *Health and Social Care in the Community*, 11(3): 242–252.

Boeije, H.R., Nievaard, A.C. & Casparie, A.F. (1997). Coping strategies of enrolled nurses in nursing homes: shifting between organizational imperatives and residents' needs. *International Journal of Nursing Studies*, 34(5): 358–366.

Boeije, H.R., Duijnstee, M.S.H., Grypdonck, M.H.F. & Pool, A. (2002). Encountering the downward phase: biographical work in people with multiple sclerosis living at home. *Social Science & Medicine*, 55(6): 881–893.

Bogdan, R.C. & Biklen, S.K. (1992). *Qualitative research for education. An introduction to theory and methods*. Boston, MA: Allyn and Bacon.

Bosch, C.F.M. (1996). *Vertrouwheid: verlangen, ervaren en creëren. Een onderzoek naar de werkelijkheidsbeleving van dementerende ouderen verblijvend op psychogeriatrische verpleegafdelingen*. [Trust: longing for, experiencing and creating. A research into the reality of elderly nursing home residents with dementia.] Utrecht: Lemma.

Bruce, C.D. (2007). Questions arising about emergence, data collection, and its interaction with analysis in a grounded theory study. *Journal of Qualitative Methods*, 6(1), Article 4.

Bryman, A. (2008). *Social research methods*. (3rd ed.) Oxford: Oxford University Press.

Bulmer, M. (2008). The ethics of social research. In N. Gilbert (Ed.), *Researching social life*. (3rd ed.) Pp. 45–57. London: Sage.

Campanelli, P.C. (2008). Testing survey questions. In E.D. de Leeuw, J.J. Hox & D.A. Dillman (Eds.), *International handbook of survey methodology*. Pp. 176–200. New York: Taylor & Francis.

Carey, M.A. (1995). Comment: concerns in the analysis of focus group data. *Qualitative Health Research*, 5(4): 487–495.

Carey, M.A. & Smith, M.W. (1994). Capturing the group effect in focus groups: a special concern in analysis. *Qualitative Health Research*, 4(1): 123–127.

Chaitin, J. (2003). "I wish he hadn't told me that": methodological and ethical issues in social trauma and conflict research. *Qualitative Health Research*, 13(8): 1145–1154.

Chapple, A. & Rogers, A. (1999). 'Self-care' and its relevance to developing demand management strategies: a review of qualitative research. *Health and Social Care in the Community*, 7(6): 445–454.

Charmaz, K. (2006). *Constructing grounded theory. A practical guide through qualitative analysis*. London: Sage.

Clark, L. & Zimmer, L. (2001). What we learned from a photographic component in a study of Latino children's health. *Field Methods*, 13(4): 303–328.

Clark-Ibáñez, M. (2007). Framing the social world with photo-elicitation interviews. *American Behavioral Scientist*, 47(12): 1507–1527.

Clarke, A. (2008). Research and the policy-making process. In N. Gilbert (Ed.), *Researching social life*. (3rd ed.) Pp. 28–42. London: Sage.

Collier, M. (2001). Approaches to analysis in visual anthropology. In T. Van Leeuwen & C. Jewitt (Eds.), *Handbook of visual analysis*. Pp. 35–59. London: Sage.

Connelly, L.M. & Yoder, L.H. (2000). Improving qualitative proposals: common problem areas. *Clinical Nurse Specialist*, 14(2): 69–74.

Cook, A.S. & Bosley, G. (1995). The experience of participating in bereavement research: stressful or therapeutic? *Death Studies*, 19(2): 157–170.

Coxon, A.P.M. (1993). Strategies in eliciting sensitive sexual information: the case of gay men. *Sociological Review*, 41(3): 537–556.

Coyne, I.T. (1997). Sampling in qualitative research. Purposeful and theoretical sampling; merging or clear boundaries? *Journal of Advanced Nursing*, 26: 623–630.

Creswell, J.W. (2006). *Qualitative inquiry and research design: choosing among five traditions*. (2nd ed.) Thousand Oaks, CA: Sage.

Creswell, J.W. (2008). *Research design. Qualitative, quantitative, and mixed methods approaches*. (3rd ed.) Thousand Oaks, CA: Sage.

Creswell, J.W., Plano Clark, V.L., Gutmann, M.L. & Hanson, W.E. (2003). Advanced mixed methods research designs. In A. Tashakkori & C. Teddlie (Eds.), *Handbook of mixed methods in social and behavioral research*. Pp. 209–240. Thousand Oaks, CA: Sage.

Cross, A. (2004). The flexibility of scientific rhetoric: a case study of UFO researchers. *Qualitative Sociology*, 27(1): 3–34.

Curtis, S., Gesler, W., Smith, G. & Washburn, S. (2000). Approaches to sampling and case selection in qualitative research: examples in the geography of health. *Social Science & Medicine*, 50: 1001–1014.

Cutcliffe, J.R. & McKenna, H.P. (2002). When do we know that we know? Considering the truth of research findings and the craft of qualitative research. *International Journal of Nursing Studies*, 39: 611–618.

Cutcliffe, J.R. & McKenna, H.P. (2004). Expert qualitative researchers and the use of audit trails. *Journal of Advanced Nursing*, 45(2): 126–135.

Cutcliffe, J.R. & Ramcharan, P. (2002). Levelling the playing field: considering the 'ethics as process' approach for judging qualitative research proposals. *Qualitative Health Research*, 12(7): 1000–1010.

Cutcliffe, J.R., Stevenson, C., Jackson, S. & Smith, P. (2006). A modified grounded theory study of how psychiatric nurses work with suicidal people. *International Journal of Nursing Studies*, 43: 791–802.

Dam, I. van & Rooij, J. van (2002). Gelijke kansen voor dyslectici in werk en onderwijs? Een verkennend onderzoek naar mogelijkheden en beperkingen. [Equal chances for people with dyslexia in employment and education? An explorative research into opportunities and limitations] Assignment Utrecht University.

Delamont, S. (2004). Ethnography and participant observation. In C. Seale, G. Gobo, J.F. Gubrium & D. Silverman (Eds.), *Qualitative research practice*. Pp. 217–229. London: Sage.

Denzin, N.K. & Lincoln, Y.S. (2005). Introduction. Entering the field of qualitative research. In N.K. Denzin & Y.S. Lincoln (Eds.), *Handbook of qualitative research*. (3rd ed.) Pp. 1–17. Thousand Oaks, CA: Sage.

Dey, I. (2004). Grounded theory. In: C. Seale, G. Gobo, J.F. Gubrium, & D. Silverman (Eds.), *Qualitative research practice*. Pp. 80–93. London: Sage.

Dixon-Woods, M., Booth, A. & Sutton, A.J. (2007). Synthesizing qualitative research: a review of published reports. *Qualitative Research*, 7(3): 375–422.

Duggleby, W. (2005). What about focus group interaction data? *Qualitative Health Research*, 15(6): 832–840.

Duijnstee, M.S.H. & Boeije, H.R. (1998). Home care by and for relatives of MS patients. *Journal of Neuroscience Nursing*, 30(6): 2–6.

Eaves, Y.D. (2001). A synthesis technique for grounded theory data analysis. *Journal of Advanced Nursing*, 35(5): 654–663.

Emanuel, E.J., Wendler, D. & Grady, C. (2000). What makes clinical research ethical? *Journal of the American Medical Association*, 283(20): 2701–2711.

Endacott, R. (2004). Clinical research 2: Legal and ethical issues in research. *Intensive and Critical Care Nursing*, 20: 313–315.

Engineer, R., Phillips, A., Thompson, J. & Nicholls, J. (2003). *Drunk and disorderly: a qualitative study of binge drinking among 18- to 24-year-olds*. London: Home Office Research.

Erlandson, D.A., Harris, E.L., Skipper, B.L. & Allen, S.D. (1993). Quality criteria for naturalistic study. In D.A. Erlandson et al. (Eds.), *Doing naturalistic inquiry. A guide to methods*. Pp. 131–162. Newbury Park, CA: Sage.

Erzberger, C. & Kelle, U. (2003). Making inferences in mixed methods: the rules of integration. In A. Tashakkori & C. Teddlie (Eds.), *Handbook of mixed methods in social and behavioral research*. Pp. 457–490. Thousand Oaks, CA: Sage.

Fayard, A. & Weeks, J. (2007). Photocopiers and water-coolers: the affordances of informal interaction. *Organization Studies*, 28: 605–634.

Fielding, N.G. & Lee, R.M. (Eds.) (1991). *Using computers in qualitative research*. London: Sage.

Fink, A. (2004). *Conducting research literature reviews: from the internet to paper*. (2nd ed.) Thousand Oaks, CA: Sage.

Flick, U. (2006). *An introduction to qualitative research*. (3rd ed.) London: Sage.

Forbat, L. & Henderson, J. (2003). "Stuck in the middle with you": The ethics and process of qualitative research with two people in an intimate relationship. *Qualitative Health Research*, 13: 1453–1462.

Forbat, L., & Henderson, J. (2005). Theoretical and practical reflections on sharing transcripts with participants. *Qualitative Health Research*, 15(8), 1114–1128.

Frank, A.W. (2004). After methods, the story: from incongruity to truth in qualitative research. *Qualitative Health Research*, 14(3): 430–440.

Fredericks, M. & Miller, S.I. (1997). Some brief notes on the "unfinished business" of qualitative inquiry. *Quality & Quantity*, 31: 1–13.

Geertz, C. (2004). Being there. In C. Seale (Ed.), *Social research methods: a reader*. Pp. 236–240. London: Routledge.

Gibson, F. (2007). Conducting focus groups with children and young people: strategies for success. *Journal of Research in Nursing*, 12(5): 473–483.

Glaser, B.G. (1978). *Theoretical sensitivity*. Mill Valley, CA: Sociology Press.

Glaser, B.G. & Strauss, A.L. (1965). *Awareness of dying*. Chicago, IL: Aldine.

Glaser, B.G. & Strauss, A.L. (1967). *The discovery of grounded theory: strategies for qualitative research*. Chicago, IL: Aldine.

Goffman, E. (1963). *Stigma: notes on the management of spoiled identity*. Englewood Cliffs, NJ: Prentice-Hall.

Goodman, J.H. (2004). Coping with trauma and hardship among unaccompanied refugee youths from Sudan. *Qualitative Health Research*, 14(9): 1177–1196.

Gorden, R.L. (1980). *Interviewing: strategies, techniques and tactics*. Homewood, IL: Dorsey.

Greckhamer, T. & Koro-Ljungberg, M. (2005). The erosion of a method: examples from grounded theory. *International Journal of Qualitative Studies in Education*, 18(6): 729–750.

Gubrium, J.F. & Holstein, J.A. (Eds.) (2002). *Handbook of interview research. Context and method*. Thousand Oaks, CA: Sage.

Haafkens, J. (1997). *Rituals of silence: long-term tranquillizer use by women in the Netherlands. A social case study*. Amsterdam: Het Spinhuis.

Hammersley, M. & Atkinson, P. (2007). *Ethnography. Principles in practice*. (3rd ed.) London: Routledge.

Hanson, W.E., Creswell, J.W., Plano Clark, V.L., Petska, K.S. & Creswell, J.D. (2005) Mixed methods research designs in counseling psychology. *Journal of Counseling Psychology*, 52(2): 224–235.

Hardy, M. & Bryman, A. (2004). Common threads among techniques in data analysis. In M. Hardy & A. Bryman (Eds.), *Handbook of data analysis*. Pp. 1–13. London: Sage.

Harper, D. (2007). On the authority of the image: visual methods at the crossroads. In Y.K. Denzin & Y.S. Lincoln (Eds.), *Collecting and interpreting qualitative materials*. (3rd ed.) Pp. 130–149. Thousand Oaks, CA: Sage.

Harris, J. & Huntington, A. (2001). Emotions as analytic tools: qualitative research, feelings, and psychotherapeutic insight. In K.R. Gilbert (Ed.), *The emotional nature of qualitative research*. Pp. 129–145. Boca Raton, FL: CRC.

Harry, B., Sturges, K.M. & Klingner, J.K. (2005). Mapping the process: an exemplar of process and challenge in grounded theory analysis. *Educational Researcher*, 34(2): 3–13.

Haverkamp, B.E. (2005). Ethical perspectives on qualitative research in applied psychology. *Journal of Counseling Psychology*, 52(2): 146–155.

Hays, S., Murphy, G. & Sinclair, N. (2003). Gaining ethical approval for research into sensitive topics: 'two strikes and you're out?' *British Journal of Learning Disabilities*, 31: 181–189.

Hess, R.F. (2006). Postabortion research: methodological and ethical issues. *Qualitative Health Research*, 16(4): 580–587.

Hesse-Biber, S.N. & Leavy, P. (2006). *The practice of qualitative research*. London: Sage.

Heuts, P. (2004). Oud-mijnwerkers dalen af in herinnering: Limburgs last. [The men of the mine: retired miners descend into memory] *Bondgenoten Magazine*, 3(5): 18–23.

Holliday, A. (2007). *Doing and writing qualitative research*. (2nd ed.) London: Sage.

Horowitz, R. (1995). *Teen mothers. Citizens or dependents?* Chicago, IL: University of Chicago Press.

Hoskins, M. & Stoltz, J. (2005). Fear of offending: disclosing researcher discomfort when engaging in analysis. *Qualitative Research*, 5(1): 95–111.

Hutchinson, S.A. (2001). The development of qualitative health research: taking stock. *Qualitative Health Research*, 11(4): 505–521.

Hutchinson, S.A., Wilson, M.E. & Skodol Wilson, H.S. (1994). Benefits of participating in research interviews. *Image: Journal of Nursing Scholarship*, 26(2): 161–164.

Imle, M.A. & Atwood, J.R. (1988). Retaining qualitative validity while gaining quantitative reliability and validity. Development of the Transition to Parenthood Concerns Scale. *Advances in Nursing Science*, 11(1): 61–75.

Janesick, V.J. (2004). *"Stretching" exercises for qualitative researchers*. Thousand Oaks, CA: Sage.

Janoff-Bulman, R. (1992). *Shattered assumptions: towards a new psychology of trauma*. New York: Free Press.

Johnson, B. & Macleod Clarke, J. (2003). Collecting sensitive data: the impact on researchers. *Qualitative Health Research*, 13(3): 421–434.

Jorgensen, D.L. (1989). *Participant observation. A methodology for human studies*. Newbury Park, CA: Sage.

Kavanaugh, K. & Ayres, L. (1998). "Not as bad as it could have been": assessing and mitigating harm during research interviews on sensitive topics. *Research in Nursing and Health*, 21: 91–97.

Kayser-Jones, J. (2002). Malnutrition, dehydration, and starvation in the midst of plenty: the political impact of qualitative inquiry. *Qualitative Health Research*, 12(10): 1391–1405.

Kayser-Jones, J. (2003). Continuing to conduct research in nursing homes despite controversial findings: reflections by a research scientist. *Qualitative Health Research*, 13(1):114–128.

Kazdin, A.E. (2008). Evidence-based treatment and practice. New opportunities to bridge clinical research and practice, enhance the knowledge base, and improve patient care. *American Psychologist*, 63(3): 146–159.

Keeble, R. (1998). *The newspapers handbook*. London: Routledge.

Kendrick, K.D. & Costello, J. (2000). 'Healthy viewing?': experiencing life and death through a voyeuristic gaze. *Nursing Ethics*, 7(1): 15–22.

Khanlou, N. & Peter, E. (2005). Participatory action research: considerations for ethical review. *Social Science & Medicine*, 60: 2333–2340.

Kidd, P.S. & Parshall, M.B. (2000). Getting the focus and the group: enhancing analytical rigor in focus group research. *Qualitative Health Research*, 10(3): 293–308.

Kirk, J. & Miller, M.L. (1986). *Reliability and validity in qualitative research*. Beverly Hills, CA: Sage.

Kitzinger, J. (1994). The methodology of focus groups. The importance of interaction between research participants. *Sociology of Health and Illness*, 16(1): 103–121.

Kleinman, S. & Copp, M. (1993). *Emotions and fieldwork*. London: Sage.

Knoblauch, H., Flick, U. & Maeder, C. (2005). Qualitative methods in Europe: the variety of social research. *Forum: Qualitative Social Research*, 6(3). www.qualitative-research. net/fqs/

Koenig, B.A., Back, A.L. & Crawley, M.L. (2003). Qualitative methods in end-of-life research: recommendations to enhance the protection of human subjects. *Journal of Pain and Symptom Management*, 25(4): 43–52.

Kuijer, R.G., Buunk, B.P. & Ybema, J.F. (2001). Justice of give-and-take in the intimate relationship: when one partner of a couple is diagnosed with cancer. *Personal Relationships*, 8: 75–92.

Kvale, S. (2008). *Interviews. Learning the craft of qualitative research interviewing*. (2nd ed.) Thousand Oaks, CA: Sage.

Lee, R.M. (1993). *Doing research on sensitive topics*. London: Sage.

Lee, R.M. & Fielding, N.G. (2004). Tools for qualitative data analysis. In M. Hardy & A. Bryman (Eds.), *Handbook of data analysis*. Pp. 529–546. London: Sage.

Lee, J. & Kim, J. (2007). Grounded theory analysis of e-government initiatives: exploring perceptions of government authorities. *Government Information Quarterly*, 24(1): 135–147.

Leeman, J., Jackson, B. & Sandelowski, M. (2006). An evaluation of how well research reports facilitate the use of findings in practice. *Journal of Nursing Scholarship*, 38(2): 171–177.

Lempp, H. & Seale, C. (2006). Medical students' perceptions in relation to ethnicity and gender: a qualitative study. *BMC Medical Education*, 6(19): 1–7.

Letts, L., Wilkins, S., Law, M., Stewart, D., Bosch, J., & Westmorland, M. (2007). Critical Review Form – Qualitative Studies (Version 2.0). McMaster University. http://www. canchild.ca/Portals/0/outcomes/pdf/qualform.pdf

Lewins, A. & Silver, C. (2007). *Using software in qualitative research: a step-by-step guide*. London: Sage.

Lincoln, Y.S. & Guba, E.G. (1985). *Naturalistic inquiry*. Newbury Park, CA: Sage.

Lofland, J. & Lofland, L.H. (1995). *Analysing social settings. A guide to qualitative observation and analysis*. Belmont, CA: Wadsworth.

Lukkarinen, H. (2005). Methodological triangulation showed the poorest quality of life in the youngest people following treatment of coronary artery disease: a longitudinal study. *International Journal of Nursing Studies*, 42: 619–627.

Maso, I. (1987). *Kwalitatief onderzoek*. [Qualitative research.] Amsterdam: Boom.

Maso, I. & Smaling, A. (1998). *Kwalitatief onderzoek. Theorie en praktijk*. [Qualitative research: theory and practice] Amsterdam: Boom.

Mason, J. (2002). *Qualitative researching*. (2nd ed.) London: Sage.

Master, M. (2007). Drives. *TopGear*, 174: 71–86. London: BBC Magazines.

Matthews, S.H. (2005). Crafting qualitative research articles on marriages and families. *Journal of Marriage and Family,* 67: 799–808.

Mauthner, N.S. & Doucet, A. (2003). Reflexive accounts and accounts of reflexivity in qualitative data analysis. *Sociology,* 37(3): 413–431.

Maxwell, J.A. (2004). *Qualitative research design. An interactive approach.* (2nd ed.) Thousand Oaks, CA: Sage.

Mays, N. & Pope, C. (1995). Observational methods in health care settings. *British Medical Journal,* 311: 182–184.

McCracken, G. (1988). *The long interview.* London: Sage.

McLellan, E., MacQueen, K.M. & Neidig, J.L. (2003). Beyond the qualitative interview: Data preparation and transcription. *Field Methods,* 15(1): 63–84.

Merkle Sorrell, J., & Redmond, G.M. (1995). Interviews in qualitative nursing research: differing approaches for ethnographic and phenomenological studies. *Journal of Advanced Nursing,* 21: 1117–1122.

Merriam, S.B. (1998). *Qualitative research and case study applications in education.* San Francisco, CA: Jossey-Bass.

Miles, M.B. & Huberman, A.M. (1994). *Qualitative data analysis. An expanded sourcebook.* (2nd ed.) Thousand Oaks, CA: Sage.

Miller, S.I. & Fredericks, M. (2006). Mixed-methods and evaluation research: trends and issues. *Qualitative Health Research,* 16(4): 567–579.

Moffatt, S., White, M., Mackintosh, J. & Howel, D. (2006). Using quantitative and qualitative data in health services research – what happens when mixed method findings conflict? *BMC Health Services Research,* 6: 28.

Moran-Ellis, J., Alexander, V.D., Cronin, A., Dickinson, M., Fielding, J., Sleney, J. & Thomas, H. (2006). Triangulation and integration: processes, claims and implications. *Qualitative Research,* 6(1): 45–59.

Morgan, D.L. (1997). *Focus groups as qualitative research.* Thousand Oaks, CA: Sage.

Morgan, D. (2007). *Paradigms lost and pragmatism regained.* Methodological implications of combining qualitative and quantitative methods. *Journal of Mixed Methods Research,* 1(1): 48–76.

Morrison-Beedy, D., Côté-Arsenault, D. & Fischbeck Feinstein, N. (2001) Maximizing results with focus groups: moderator and analysis issues. *Applied Nursing Research,* 14(1), 2001: 48–53.

Morse, J.M. (1999). Qualitative methods: the state of the art. *Qualitative Health Research,* 9(3): 393–406.

Morse, J.M. & Field, P.A. (1996). *Nursing research. The application of qualitative approaches.* Cheltenham: Stanley Thornes.

Morse, J. (2003). A review committee's guide for evaluating qualitative proposals. *Qualitative Health Research,* 13(6): 833–851.

Morse, J. (2005). Ethical issues in institutional research. *Qualitative Health Research,* 15(4): 435–437.

Morse, J.M. (2006). Diagramming qualitative theories. *Qualitative Health Research,* 16(9): 1163–1164.

O'Reilly, K. (2005). *Ethnographic methods.* London: Routledge.

Pasman, H.R., The, B.A., Onwuteaka-Philipsen, B.D., Wal, G. Van der, & Ribbe, M.W. (2003). Feeding nursing home patients with severe dementia: a qualitative study. *Journal of Advanced Nursing,* 42(3): 304–311.

Patton, M.Q. (1999). Enhancing the quality and credibility of qualitative analysis. *Health Services Research,* 34(5): 1189–1208.

Polkinghorne, D.E. (2005). Language and meaning: data collection in qualitative research. *Journal of Counseling Psychology,* 52(2): 137–145.

Punch, K.F. (2005). *Introduction to social research. Quantitative and qualitative approaches.* (2nd ed.) London: Sage.

Radley, A. & Taylor, D. (2003). Images of recovery: a photo-elicitation study on the hospital ward. *Qualitative Health Research,* 13(1): 77–99.

Reinharz, S. (1997). Who am I? The need for a variety of selves in the field. In R. Hertz (Ed.), *Reflexivity and voice.* Pp. 3–20. Thousand Oaks, CA: Sage.

Richards, L. (2005). *Handling qualitative data. A practical guide.* London: Sage.

Ritchie, J. & Lewis, J. (2003). *Qualitative research practice. A guide for social science students and researchers.* London: Sage.

Roberts, K.A., Dixon-Woods, M., Fitzpatrick, R. Abrams, K.R. & Jones, D.R. (2002). Factors affecting uptake of childhood immunisation: a Bayesian synthesis of qualitative and quantitative evidence. *The Lancet*, 360(16): 1596–1599.

Rowling, J.K. (2008). *Harry Potter and the deathly hallows.* London: Bloomsbury.

Rubin, H.J. & Rubin, I.S. (2004). *Qualitative interviewing. The art of hearing data.* (2nd ed.) Thousand Oaks, CA: Sage.

Sandelowski, M. (1994). The use of quotes in qualitative research. *Research in Nursing & Health*, 17: 479–482.

Sandelowski, M. (1995). Qualitative analysis: what it is and how to begin. *Research in Nursing & Health*, 18: 371–375.

Sandelowski, M. (2003). Tables or tableux? The challenges of writing and reading mixed methods studies. In A. Tashakkori & C. Teddlie (Eds.), *Handbook of mixed methods in social and behavioral research.* Pp. 297–319. Thousand Oaks, CA: Sage.

Sandelowski, M., & Barroso, J. (2002a). Finding the findings in qualitative studies. *Journal of Nursing Scholarship*, 34(3): 213–219.

Sandelowski, M. & Barroso, J. (2002b). Reading qualitative studies. *International Journal of Qualitative Methods*, 1(1): article 5. (Checklist included).

Sandelowski, M. & Barroso, J. (2003a). Writing the proposal for a qualitative research methodology project. *Qualitative Health Research*, 13(6): 781–820.

Sandelowski, M., & Barroso, J. (2003b). Classifying the findings in qualitative studies. *Qualitative Health Research*, 13(7): 905–923.

Schatzman, L. & Strauss, A.L. (1973). *Field research: Strategies for a natural sociology.* Englewood Cliffs, NJ: Prentice-Hall.

Schwartz, D. (1989). Visual ethnography: using photography in qualitative research. *Qualitative sociology*, 12(2): 119–153.

Seale, C. (1999). *The quality of qualitative research.* London: Sage.

Seale, C., Charteris-Black, J., Dumelow, C., Locock, L. & Ziebland, S. (2008). The effect of joint interviewing on the performance of gender. *Field Methods*, 20: 107–128.

Seidel, J.V. (1991). Method and madness in the application of computer technology to qualitative data analysis. In N.G. Fielding & R.M. Lee (Eds.), *Using computers in qualitative research.* Pp. 107–116. Newbury Park, CA: Sage.

Seidman, I. (2006). *Interviewing as qualitative research. A guide for researchers in education and the social sciences.* (3rd ed.) New York: Teachers College.

Sheller, M. (2004). Automotive emotions: feeling the car. *Theory, Culture & Society*, 21(4/5): 221–242.

Sieber, J.E. (1992). *Planning ethically responsible research. A guide for students and internal review boards.* Newbury Park, CA: Sage.

Sieber, J.E. (2008). Planning ethically responsible research. In L. Bickman & D.J. Rog (Eds.), *Handbook of applied social research methods.* (2nd ed.) Pp. 127–156. Thousand Oaks, CA: Sage.

Silverman, D. (1998). The quality of qualitative health research: the open-ended interview and its alternatives. *Social Sciences in Health*, 4(2): 104–118.

Silverman, D. (2001). *Interpreting qualitative data. Methods for analysing talk, text and interaction.* London: Sage.

Sim, J. (1998). Collecting and analyzing qualitative data: issues raised by the focus group. *Journal of Advanced Nursing*, 28: 345–352.

Smaling, A. (2000). What kind of dialogue should paradigm-dialogues be? *Quality & Quantity*, 34: 51–63.

Smaling, A. (2002). The argumentative quality of the qualitative research report. *International Journal of Qualitative Methods*, 1(3), Article 4. Retrieved 26 June 2008 from http://www.ualberta.ca/~ijqm.

Smaling, A. (2003). Inductive, analogical, and communicative generalization. *International Journal of Qualitative Methods*, 2(1). Article 5. Retrieved 22 Apr 2009 from http://www.ualberta.ca/~iiqm/backissues/2_1/html/smaling.html.

Snow, D.A. (1980). The disengagement process: a neglected problem in participant observation research. *Qualitative Sociology*, 3(2): 100–122.

Spaaij, R. (2006). *Understanding football hooliganism. A comparison of six Western European football clubs.* Amsterdam: Vossiuspers Amsterdam University.

Spencer, L., Ritchie, J., Lewis, J. & Dillon, L. (2003). *Quality in qualitative evaluation: a framework for assessing research evidence. A quality framework.* Government Chief Social Researcher's Office. London: Cabinet Office.

Spradley, J.P. (1980). *Participant observation.* New York: Holt, Rinehart and Winston.

Sque, M. (2000). Researching the bereaved: an investigator's experience. *Nursing Ethics,* 7(1): 23–34.

St John, W. & Johnson, P. (2000). The pros and cons of data analysis software for qualitative analysis. *Journal of Nursing Scholarship,* 32(4): 393–397.

Stinson Kidd, P. (1993). Self-protection: trauma patients' perspectives of their motor vehicle crashes. *Qualitative Health Research,* 3(3): 320–340.

Strauss, A.L. (1987). *Qualitative analysis for social scientists.* Cambridge: Cambridge University Press.

Strauss, A.L. & Corbin, J. (2005). Grounded theory methodology. An overview. In N.K. Denzin & Y.S. Lincoln (Eds.), *Handbook of qualitative research.* (3rd ed.) Pp. 273–285. London: Sage.

Strauss, A.L. & Corbin, J. (2007). *Basics of qualitative research. Techniques and procedures for developing grounded theory.* (3rd ed.) Thousand Oaks, CA: Sage.

Tashakkori, A. & Creswell, J.W. (2007). The new era of mixed methods. *Journal of Mixed Methods,* 1(1): 2–8.

Taylor, S.E. (1983). Adjustment to threatening events. A theory of cognitive adaptation. *American Psychologist,* November: 1161–1173.

Tesch, R. (1991). *Qualitative research. Analysis types and software tools.* New York: Falmer.

Thorne, S., Paterson, B., Acorn, S., Canam, C., Joachim, G. & Jillings, C. (2002). Chronic illness experience: insights from a metastudy. *Qualitative Health Research,* 12(4): 437–452.

Vicsek, L. (2007). A scheme for analyzing the results of focus groups. *International Journal of Qualitative Methods,* 6(4): 22–34.

Walker, D., & Myrick, F. (2006). Grounded theory: an exploration of process and procedure. *Qualitative Health Research,* 16(4): 547–559.

Weiss, R.S. (1994). *Learning from strangers. The art and method of qualitative interview studies.* New York: Free Press.

Wester, F. (1995). *Strategieën voor kwalitatief onderzoek.* [Strategies for qualitative research] Muiderberg: Coutinho.

Wester, F. & Peters, V. (2004). *Kwalitatieve analyse. Uitgangspunten en procedures.* [Qualitative analysis. Backgrounds and procedures] Bussum: Coutinho.

Wilson, H. & Hutchinson, S.A. (1996). Methodologic mistakes in grounded theory. *Nursing Research,* 45(2): 122–124.

Woods, P. (2005). *Successful writing for qualitative researchers.* (2nd ed.) London: Routledge.

Zee, H. van der (1983). *Tussen vraag en antwoord. Beginselen van sociaal-wetenschappelijk onderzoek.* [Between question and answer: principles of social scientific research.] Amsterdam: Boom.

Zeller, N. & Farmer, F.M. (1999). "Catchy, clever titles are not acceptable": Style, APA, and qualitative reporting. *Qualitative Studies in Education,* 12(1): 3–19.

Ziebland, S. & McPherson, A. (2006). Making sense of qualitative data analysis: an introduction with illustrations from DIPEx (personal experiences of health and illness). *Medical Education,* 40: 405–414.

INDEX

Research Methods Books from SAGE

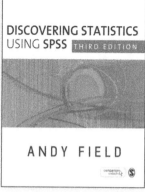
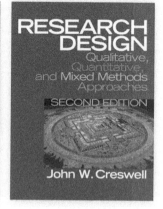

The Qualitative Research Kit

Edited by Uwe Flick

Read sample chapters online now!

www.sagepub.co.uk

Supporting researchers for more than forty years

Research methods have always been at the core of SAGE's publishing. Sara Miller McCune founded SAGE in 1965 and soon after she published SAGE's first methods book, *Public Policy Evaluation*. A few years later, she launched the Quantitative Applications in the Social Sciences series – affectionately known as the 'little green books'.

Always at the forefront of developing and supporting new approaches in methods, SAGE published early groundbreaking texts and journals in the fields of qualitative methods and evaluation.

Today, more than forty years and two million little green books later, SAGE continues to push the boundaries with a growing list of more than 1,200 research methods books, journals, and reference works across the social, behavioural, and health sciences.

From qualitative, quantitative and mixed methods to evaluation, SAGE is the essential resource for academics and practitioners looking for the latest in methods by leading scholars.

www.sagepublications.com